D0467097

Maximum Performance Management

How to Manage and Compensate People to Meet World Competition

MAXIMUM PERFORMANCE MANAGEMENT

How to Manage and Compensate
People to Meet World Competition

Joseph H. Boyett, Ph.D.

and

Henry P. Conn

Foreword By

Fran Tarkenton

Glenbridge Publishing Ltd.
1988

Second Printing 1989

Copyright© 1988 by Glenbridge Publishing Ltd.

All rights reserved. Except for brief quotations in critical articles or reviews, this book, or parts thereof, must not be reproduced in any form without permission in writing from the publisher. For further information contact Glenbridge Publishing Ltd., Macomb, Illinois 61455.

Library of Congress Catalog Card Number: 88-81707

International Standard Book Number: 0-944435-03-3

Dedication

This book is dedicated to Paul Fulton, President of the Sara Lee Corporation, who truly believes in managing for maximum performance. Paul has been a powerful champion of the innovative management and compensation practices described in this book and has moved aggressively to install these practices within his own company. He is a true leader in America's drive to once again become a *World Class* performer.

This book is also dedicated to Robert Lee Boyett, James Harvey Towns, and Barney Murrell—three leaders who managed for performance.

Contents

Contents

Contents

Contents

Contents

Foreword

If there is any single most important lesson I have learned from my years in professional football and as a business owner and manager, it is this: People working together in a spirit of partnership make it happen. To me, that is what *Maximum Performance Management* is all about—creating the spirit of partnership.

The ability of American managers to create a sense of partnership with employees has never been more important than it is today. I am convinced teamwork is the only way America can remain competitive. Whether we like to admit it or not, we are in a real danger of losing the worldwide competitive struggle. The game is almost over. Time is running out. If we are to win, we must get maximum performance from every person in the organization—from every player on our team. To do that, we need a new gameplan, since obviously what we have been doing isn't working.

The co-authors of this book, Hank Conn and Joe Boyett, are my friends and associates in Tarkenton Conn & Company, a consulting firm I started over nineteen years ago. They are uniquely qualified to write the gameplan for a new American competitive strategy. Throughout the nineteen years our consulting firm has been in business, we have worked with 500 companies and over 500,000 managers, supervisors, and employees to implement management and compensation practices that have enabled these companies to build a partnership with their employees and to become more competitive. Joe, Hank, and our consulting team have worked hand and hand with line managers to accomplish the changes others only describe. The *hands-on* experiences are the basis for the practical advice and specific guidance provided in this book.

Unlike other popular management books, *Maximum Performance Management* does not just describe what we have to do in American business to compete in a world marketplace. This book goes beyond description to provide step-by-step instructions for implementing new management and compensation practices that will enable all American companies to compete. *Maximum Performance Management* is a comprehensive, specific, and workable gameplan to help all of us respond to the global competitive challenge and to win.

FRAN TARKENTON

Acknowledgments

This book would not have been possible without the advice and input of numerous individuals. In particular, we would like to thank Paul Fulton, to whom this book is dedicated, and the many managers, supervisors and employees of the Sara Lee Corporation who have worked with us to make *Maximum Performance Management* a reality. They shared our belief in the power of the management and compensation practices described in this book, and taught us much about the process of implementing these ideas.

We would also like to to express our gratitude to the following individuals whose advice, counsel and willingness to share experiences has been invaluable in shaping the ideas presented in this book. They are: Rube Mettler, Chairman of the Board and CEO, TRW; Joe Gorman, President and COO, TRW; Stan Pace, Chairman of the Board and CEO, General Dynamics; Bill Reynolds, Chairman of the Board and CEO, GenCorp; Nev Curtis, Chairman of the Board and CEO, Delmarva Power & Light Company; Jim Edwards, President, Spencer Plastic Products Corporation; Stephen Leahey, Assistant Vice President of Operations Planning, Bell Canada; Bill Werther, The Samuel N. Friedland Professor of Executive Management, University of Miami; Leon Skan, Executive Director, American Productivity Management Association; Carl Thor and Jack Grayson, President and Chairman of the Board respectively, The American Productivity and Quality Center; and Bob Meyer, Executive Director, Work In Northeast Ohio Council.

Also, we would like to thank our colleagues at Tarkenton Conn & Company for their advice and support. In particular, Jane Porter, Dot Mohr, Shirl Handly and Alice Barger played an important role in shaping the content of this book. They traveled hundreds of thousands of miles and devoted countless hours to implementing the practices we describe in this book. They know in detail how to make change happen. Without their in depth, practical knowledge of what works and doesn't work, the implementation guides found in this book would not have been possible. For administrative support we owe a huge debt to Theresa Bowker and Leigh Ann Conn for their dependability and professionalism in meeting the day-to-day requirements of our business while simultaneously taking on the additional burden of preparing the manuscript of this book. Leigh Ann, in particular, deserves credit for typing, copying, mailing, editing and a thousand other details associated with making this book a reality. For his moral and financial support for our project we owe a great deal to our boss, Fran Tarkenton. His boundless energy and enthusiasm for the principles represented in this book kept us on track.

Finally, we express our appreciation to our wives—Jimmie and Becky—and children—Lisa, Christa, Phillip and Leigh Ann—for their faith, support and willingness to endure our constant travel, late arrivals and preoccupation with the subject matter of this book.

All of the above deserve credit for what is right about this book. Any errors or mistakes are ours alone.

Introduction

This book is about managing and compensating people in organizations. It is written for the chief executive officer, the executive vice president, the division manager, the department manager, and the third shift supervisor. It is written to managers and supervisors in manufacturing and service industries. It is written for everyone who goes to work every day with the primary task of getting the maximum performance from the people who report to them. We assume that you are one of these people and that you have chosen this book looking for answers. How do you make it happen for yourself and for your people? Our purpose in this book is to give you the answers. Our intention is to give you a prescription for action. We intend to tell you things you can do—starting today—to get nothing less from your people than their maximum performance. We call this book *Maximum Performance Management* because the techniques described here will result in maximum performance.

The ideas we present in this book are not new. There has been no recent revelation concerning management. Researchers of management and human behavior in organizations have already discovered much about how to get maximum performance from employees. Yet, these techniques are not widely known. Too many books and articles reach too narrow an audience. Popular books on management describe the ideal without providing a prescription—specific things you must do—to get there. You are left with a vision of what can be but no practical steps you can take to make that vision a reality. This book is thus intended to give you a step-by-step guide to getting the best from your people.

Each year we spend thousands of hours and fly thousands of miles to advise major corporations on performance management practices. We work with a firm that has implemented these practices in Fortune 1000 companies for over nineteen years. Together we have spent nearly fifty years in hands-on management, doing the things you do every day. We've made the same mistakes you have made. We've learned the hard lessons you have learned. But we have had one advantage. Our work requires that we read the significant books and articles on management to keep up-to-date. By necessity and choice, we are members of the major national productivity organizations. We attend their meetings, and we listen. In our travels, we talk with managers in every type of business; and we listen. We hear what works and what doesn't work. We hear from the academicians, but most importantly, we hear from the line managers. We hear from the managers and the supervisors in the offices and plants and factories of America. What is in this book is not ours. It is owned by the people who study management and who manage. The collective wisdom is enormous, and we are attempting to summarize it here. But there is a catch.

Management is as much an art as a science. It requires enormous patience and persistence. You can learn the techniques, but you have to apply the techniques for them to work for you. And you have to apply these techniques with honesty and integrity. The essence of management is getting people to do what they might not otherwise do. As a manager, you have an enormous responsibility to yourself and to your people. You can use the techniques we describe in this book in your own, in your employees', and in your company's best interest, or you can use them in your interest without regard for your company's or employees' welfare. The latter strategy might even succeed for a while, but not for long. We have great faith in the American worker and in his/her capacity not to be fooled—not by much and not for long. But if you have a genuine interest in helping others achieve their maximum potential to everyone's benefit, read on. You will find a prescription for success; but, don't think the task will be easy.

The techniques we describe in this book are neither instant nor easy. Even when you faithfully apply these techniques, you might not see results for weeks or months. Don't expect to turn your people on instantly. And, you will have to do the right things right over and over again—forever. This is not a one-time, instant cure. Perhaps most frustrating for us in our travels is dealing with the desire of managers at every level for instant, magical answers. But there aren't any. Results come from perseverance and patience, from the right things done over and over again.

What kind of results should you expect? If you apply these techniques faithfully, there is every reason to expect that the performance level of people reporting to you will increase by 20 to 50 percent, or even more. We did not create these numbers; they are the results of research. But even if no research supported these techniques (and a vast body of research does), we think they would still make sense—common sense. And as you are reading what follows, you will probably be saying to yourself "of course, I knew that," and so on, for there isn't anything really new here. We are just putting it together in a new way. Here is, then, a systematic way of using management techniques for maximum performance.

PART 1

Maximum Performance Management and you

Chapter 1

The Basis for Maximum
Performance Management

As an executive, manager, or business owner, you will probably agree
that the business climate in the 1980s presents some of the most difficult
management challenges ever faced. Today, no business or part of a
business is safe from competition. No job is secure. Survival of your
business, your division, your department, and even your job depends
upon your organization's ability to do many things well. Exactly what
you have to do depends on your company's unique needs and the
competition it faces. However, it is more than likely that you are
seeking some of the following:

- Not just better, but the best quality

- Not just better, but the best customer service

- Not just better, but the best response to changing market and
  customer demands

- Not just some, but total flexibility

1

- Not just occasional, but continuous innovation

- Not just some, but a distinctive difference

In short, regardless of how you define success, just an "okay" performance is unacceptable. You must have excellent performance from all of your employees.

The consequences of failure to achieve and sustain excellence are clear. Your business could lose significant market share; the plant you manage might close; the division or department you manage might be significantly reduced in size or even abolished; jobs could be eliminated. These things have happened and are happening right now, and they will continue to happen to us unless we manage in a totally new way. What's wrong with the way we manage now? Plenty.

In spite of all the rhetoric on "new management styles," employees in most organizations are still managed as they were thirty or forty years ago when the world was willing to buy whatever we could produce, regardless of quality. Although we should know better, we still treat most of our employees as "workers" and not as "partners." We are still controlling problem behavior rather than rewarding positive behavior. Many of us took the advice of popular management books and defined our companies' values and strategies, but we did a poor job of communicating those values and strategies to employees. We talk about involving employees in decision making and problem solving, but our quality circles and other involvement programs reach only a fraction of our employees. We talk about the need to reward performance, encourage teamwork, and focus employees on quality and customer service; yet, our organizational structures and compensation systems encourage turf building, destructive competition, and little concern for quality or customer needs. It is time we did things differently.

We need a comprehensive approach to a style of management that enables every employee to aspire to excellence. Now only a few employees are excellent. Most employees are performing well below their capacity, and our piecemeal efforts to improve performance aren't working. But many of our employees can be excellent, and most employees can contribute much more than they now do. In this book, we show you how to design and install management practices that will get maximum performance from your people.

But this book is about more than that. We aren't just going to describe managing in the right way; we are going to show you exactly what to do to change the way people are managed in your organization. This is a "How To" book—how to define values and strategies, how to communicate values and strategies to employees, how to reorganize for performance, how to measure performance, how to develop an effective management information system, how to set goals, how to use positive consequences to encourage good performance, how to compensate people to encourage performance, and how to design and install an employee involvement system.

In this chapter, we explain this approach to management and discuss your best options for improving performance. We look at the typical workforce and examine why only a few employees are excellent. We explain why selection and training are not usually effective in securing an excellent workforce. Finally, we explain how, as a manager, you can alter the environment in which your people work to make significant performance gains. We start by looking at the typical workforce.

The Typical Workforce

You know who your excellent performers are. You count on them to get the job done. This small percentage of real achievers produce a high volume of quality work on time and with an acceptable cost. Most importantly, your excellent employees are easy to manage. They require only minimum direction, genuinely enjoy the work they do, and possess mental and physical talents ideally suited to the work they are asked to perform. If your workforce consisted entirely of excellent performers, management would be simple and you would not need this book. However, all of your employees are not excellent. There are at least two other worker types (see figure 1).

You probably have a small percentage of problem employees. In this category are employees with drug, alcohol, and emotional problems. Employees who lack the basic talent or skills to do the tasks they are asked to perform also fall in this category. These few problem employees consume a disproportionate share of your time and attention.

Most of your employees fall somewhere between these two extremes. They are neither excellent nor problems. Though their performance varies from day to day, week to week, and month to month, it typically varies within a relatively narrow range. The performance of these employees is fairly consistent and average. It is also well below capacity. Unlike excellent performers who might be at or near their peak, your typical employees have a considerable margin for improvement.

THE TYPICAL WORKFORCE

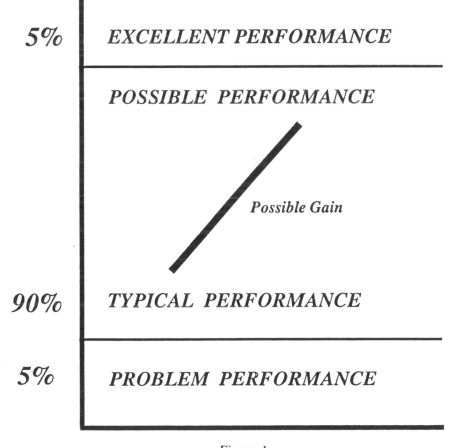

Figure 1

Given these three types of employees, your problem is threefold: (1) how to keep the excellent performers excellent; (2) what to do about the problem employees; and (3) how to raise the average performance of the "typical" employees. This book concentrates on how to raise the average performance of your typical employees, because the same techniques that raise the performance of typical employees create an environment in which excellent performers flourish. Also, these techniques have a positive effect on problem employees, or can create fair and reasonable conditions under which problem employees can be disciplined or terminated. By focusing on your typical employee, you impact a large segment of your workforce, and you have the best chance of raising the average performance of the group. If your excellent performers remain excellent and your typical performers more closely approximate excellence, significant performance gains have been made.

Why Only a Few Employees Are Excellent

Why are only a few of your employees excellent? What makes them excellent? How can typical employees more closely approximate excellence?

A considerable body of research on human behavior in organizations has focused on just these questions. Generally, this research has taken two approaches. One approach attempts to explain excellence by examining the internal or personality characteristics of those employees who achieve excellence (what they bring to the job). The other approach attempts to uncover the external or environmental factors that allow excellence to emerge (how these individuals are managed).

It is far beyond the scope of this book to examine the various theories and research studies that have been conducted on the internal and external influences on human behavior in organizations. We are more interested here in suggesting practical applications of this research. Yet, *Maximum Performance Management* (MPM) is based upon a model or way of organizing thinking about the factors that influence performance, and that model should be presented here.

We start with the internal characteristics employees bring to the job. How do your excellent employees differ from your typical employees? There are many differences between excellent and average employees, but there are three *primary* differences (see figure 2).

Knowledge and Skills

Excellent employees bring to the workplace the knowledge and skills necessary to perform the tasks they are expected to perform, or they acquire the necessary knowledge and skills quickly with little, if any, formal assistance. They can be given a minimum amount of direction and left to their own devices. They have both technical skill and knowledge of what is critical for business success. A manager does not have to explain his or her expectations to these employees in elaborate detail. Excellent employees initiate necessary work without any cue from management; they already know what needs to be done and how to do it.

INTERNAL FACTORS CONTRIBUTING TO EXCELLENT PERFORMANCE

Knowledge & Skills	Technical Ability Understanding of Business Requirements Education Training
Motives	Values Beliefs Drives Needs Intrinsic Motivation
Abilities	Mental Physical

Figure 2

Internal Motivation

A second difference between excellent and average employees is that excellent employees obtain great personal satisfaction from their work. These employees arrive early, stay late, and even perform the work without compensation on their own time if allowed to do so. The motivation of excellent employees comes from their own inner drives and needs, which are met by performance of the work itself. By accident or design, excellent employees are those who perform work that has meaning and significance to them above and beyond any financial, social, or other rewards. They want to do what needs to be done because the work matters to them.

Mental and Physical Ability

Finally, excellent employees bring to the job unique mental and physical talents that give them a decided advantage. For example, if the work requires hand and eye coordination, excellent employees have such coordination to a greater extent than do other employees. If the work requires a facility with numbers and the ability to recognize and recall sequences of numbers, excellent employees have that ability. What is important is not the particular mental or physical ability, but the unique match between the ability required by the job and the natural ability of the excellent performer. They have exceptional ability to perform the required tasks of their job.

Knowledge and skills, internal motivation, and natural ability create a powerful synergism for excellence. If we were able to match each job with a person ideally qualified for that job in respect to knowledge, skills, motives, and abilities, the task of management would be exceedingly simple. Once hired, and provided we did not change the nature of the job, such employees would perform at exceptional levels forever. We could simply give them the keys to the plant or office and leave them alone.

Why We Cannot Create Excellence by Matching People to Jobs

Unfortunately, we are seldom able to make ideal matches. Usually, we cannot even identify all the necessary prerequisites for a perfect match between the employee and the job. Even if we could, most organizations are dynamic. Over time, the nature of the work and the content of jobs change to meet the changing needs of the organization. Rarely does a job remain exactly the same for very long. Also, we are limited in our ability to select the people who work for us. Most employees were selected by someone else, perhaps many years earlier, for a job that no longer exists or that they no longer perform. Even when we can select an employee for a job, the pool of available talent is limited. We do not select from all possible talent; we are limited to those persons available at the time we have a vacancy and to those who have applied. Our choice is always a compromise — we select the best available rather than the best. Selection is an important but limited means for securing excellence.

Since selection is a limited option, what other steps can we take as managers to provide a better match between people and jobs? We have few options for changing people to match jobs. For example, we cannot improve employees' basic mental or physical capacity to perform the job. Employees are either born with these traits or develop them early in life. Nor are we likely to change our employees' internal drives and needs (motives). These basic personality characteristics are also formed early in life, and we are not likely to alter these traits very much at a later age. Even if we could do so, most managers lack the necessary knowledge to try and would have severe moral and ethical objections about doing so even if they knew how.

Why We Cannot Train People to Be Excellent

With respect to the internal characteristics of employees, the one area where we have a reasonable chance for direct influence is in enhancing knowledge and skills, particularly job content skills through training. Perhaps we intuitively recognize this potential, for enormous sums are spent on training each year. Unfortunately, little, if any, of this training results in significant improvements in performance. Most training is wasted. Why?

First, poor performance is rarely caused by a skill deficiency correctable by training. Most employees can pass the ultimate test for appropriateness of training suggested by Robert F. Mager and Peter Pipe many years ago: "They could perform the task if their life depended upon it." In short, they already know how to do the job, so training will not help.

Even when a skill deficiency does exist and training is provided, usually there is no follow-up to training. Employees are not required to apply their new skills immediately after training and are not provided with on-the-job coaching for applying these skills. In the absence of such follow-up, only a small portion of new skills are ever applied.

Finally, most training is designed for the "average person," but since there is no "average" person, the pace, method of instruction, instructional aides, and so on are wrong for many people. All of us learn under different conditions. Some of us learn best primarily through words, others need pictures, sounds, and symbols. Some of us can adjust to the pace of learning in a group, others need to proceed at their own pace—faster or slower than the group. Some of us learn best by listening to a knowledgeable lecturer, others have to be involved in and experience what is being taught. Because of these individual differences, most training exercises are less than optimum for most people.

The ability of managers to create excellence directly by matching people to jobs or by enhancing knowledge and skills through training is limited then. If training and selection were the only two ways to influence performance, we can expect to attain excellent performance in only a few instances. In fact, that is exactly what we do see: A few employees are excellent, most employees fall far short of excellence, and a few have serious performance problems.

We continue in an endless cycle when we rely solely upon selection and training in our search for excellent performers. We rotate people through jobs hoping to find the right match. We try to swap our problem or average employees for those we have heard about or seen who are excellent. We add new positions to create vacancies in an attempt to select excellence we can't seem to create. We rely heavily upon those few employees we have who are excellent, and we fear losing them to other managers or other companies. If we can, we try to guarantee retention of these few excellent employees by providing compensation far beyond what we think our competition can or will match—the so called "Golden Handcuffs."

Most managers ignore the very tasks of management that are most likely to lead to excellent performance. We focus upon matching people to jobs, and we almost never focus upon the working environment. Yet the environment is the one area wherein we have the most control.

How We Can Create Excellence

Excellence is a function of the knowledge and skills, motives, and abilities of employees. Since we cannot directly change them, we are stuck with the internal traits and characteristics our employees bring to the job. We can, however, adjust the work environment to compensate for weaknesses in knowledge and skills, motives, and/or abilities. Fortunately, as managers we have three leverages for doing this. They are the following (figure 3):

EXTERNAL FACTORS CONTRIBUTING TO EXCELLENT PERFORMANCE

Information	Shared Values and Business Strategies Linked Missions and Goals Measures and Feedback Identification of Critical Behaviors

Consequences	Social Reinforcement Contingent Awards Pay-For-Performance (Variable Portion Up to 40% of Total Compensation)

Involvement	Non-Voluntary Management Directed Teams Cross-Functional Task Forces

Figure 3

1. Information to overcome limitations in knowledge and skills.

2. Consequences to overcome deficiencies in natural drive and motivation.

3. Involvement of employees to overcome weaknesses in natural ability.

These methods provide managers with the greatest leverage for improving the typical employee's performance. Let's look at each of them.

Information

Excellent employees enjoy greater knowledge and skills than typical employees have. Knowledge and skills represent nothing more than information. Being knowledgeable is being better informed. Possessing a skill is possessing the information about how something works or how something is done and about how to apply that skill constructively. Excellent employees already have or can easily acquire the information they need. To improve the knowledge and skills of typical employees, we need to make information more readily available. What type of information?

1. We should start with training, education, and awareness programs to share basic information about what is valued and required for the business to be successful. Typically, employees have only limited knowledge about business values, strategies, and direction. We need to ensure that every employee understands the corporate strategic direction and what is critical for success. On what basis will the company compete—on quality, cost, service? Employees and managers must share a common sense of purpose and mission.

2. In addition to knowing overall company direction and strategy, employees need to know how they fit into that strategy. They need to know the mission and critical performance objectives for their own areas. Although excellent employees have often set their own performance goals and can relate those goals to what is

important for the company as a whole, the typical employee might see little relationship between his or her day-to-day activities and any larger purpose. We need to ensure that operational goals and objectives are established at every level of the organization, that they are tied back to some overall corporate strategy, and that they are widely communicated.

3. Just having goals is not enough. Excellent employees not only know critical goals and objectives, but they know how they are performing in these areas. These employees arrange their own feedback on performance. As a result, they have more knowledge about where they stand and are able to make minor corrections in their performance before it gets out of control. Typical employees frequently have no idea whether their level of performance is good or bad. They need more feedback than just once or twice a year in a performance review. These employees need directive and specific feedback. There must be frequent, data-based feedback at every level, so there must be performance measures, goals, and performance reporting at every level. For this feedback to be understandable, we need to make ample use of graphs and charts to make it visible.

4. Finally, employees need specific information concerning how their day-to-day behavior affects critical performance measurements. Behaviors—what people do or say—are the only things people can change. Frequently, the typical employee is not performing well because he or she does not know the required behaviors for performance. In contrast, the excellent employee is more adept at making the connection between what is measured and what is done. We need to ensure that employees have information on the correct behaviors. Particularly in areas of problem performance, we need to identify the repertoire of behaviors that lead to success. We need to observe and analyze the behaviors of those who are performing at high levels, and we need to use training, job aids, and so on to get this information to all employees. This is the one area in which training can help.

Consequences

It would be nice if information alone would be sufficient, but it rarely is. Even when the typical employee knows what needs to be done and has the necessary skills, there is no guarantee that he or she will perform. Repeatedly in our interviews with employees, they tell us that good performance doesn't matter. In the typical employee's view, there are few, if any, incentives, and usually a number of disincentives to increasing productivity. Increase production, and management will change rates. Increase production, and there will be layoffs. Increase production, and the resultant financial gains go to managers or owners, not to employees. Whether you produce a lot or produce a little—so they tell us—you get paid the same. Don't expect a "thank you" or word of praise from managers or supervisors for extra effort. It won't happen.

Good performance must matter for the typical employee. We might not be able to change internal drives and motives, but we can arrange consequences in the work environment to encourage performance. The positive incentives for good performance must outweigh any counterincentives for poor performance. Praise, recognition, and social reinforcement for good performance should be used frequently. Awards, trophies, tokens, gifts must be contingent upon performance, not just "give away" programs. Raises, promotions, retentions during layoffs must be contingent upon performance, not upon years of employment. Finally, a significant portion of each person's pay must be variable and tied to objective measurements of team performance in critical areas. This variable portion should be as much as 40 percent of total compensation if we expect significant gains.

How do we ensure that consequences are tied to performance? First, we need top management commitment to making consequences contingent upon performance. There must be no doubt that the company is committed from the highest level to retaining and rewarding those who perform in a meaningful way. We therefore have to ensure that every manager and supervisor has been trained and coached in the use of positive and negative consequences to manage performance. Finally, we have to review existing compensation systems to ensure that we are paying for performance. Is there a portion of each person's pay that is variable—goes up or down based strictly upon performance controllable by that person? Is the variable portion of pay a significant portion—large enough (15 to 40%) to make a difference to the person? Is this incentive portion tied directly to objective measurements and not to someone's subjective judgment? Does the incentive encourage teamwork, cooperation, *and* maximum individual effort, as opposed to encouraging employees to maximize their individual performance at the expense of the company or their work group?

Involvement

Given adequate information and meaningful consequences for performance, our work environment will be conducive to high performance from all employees. But information and consequences are not enough. Excellent and typical employees are different in their basic mental and physical capacities. To lessen the difference in ability between average employees and the more naturally gifted, we need methods, tools, techniques, procedures, and so on. We need ways for the typical employee to work smarter with less demand for innate capacity or ability. But what are these ways?

Traditionally, we have designed and then imposed new methods and new technology on employees. All too often our efforts are met with resistance. Sometimes this resistance is totally unjustified, the stubborn refusal of employees to adapt to changes clearly in their own best interest. Occasionally, we find to our dismay that the resistance is totally justifiable. In fact, employees do know more about what will and will not work in the real world. As a result, we make expensive mistakes or the implementation of good ideas are delayed.

Gradually, most of us have come to the realization that employees must be involved in arranging their own work environment. Not only do the people performing the work have the best ideas about how it should be performed, but we now realize that people don't resist their own ideas. We are much more likely to develop a solution to a problem and implement that solution if we get employee input. Yet, many of us have become disenchanted with quality circles and other employee involvement efforts. That poor experience, however, shouldn't mean that we abandon employee involvement. What it does mean is that we should have learned from our mistakes.

What should we have learned? First, we should now know that voluntary involvement programs don't work. Too few employees participate. Employee involvement has to be mandatory. We need every employee's ideas, not just those from a chosen few. Second, we should have learned that involvement systems require management direction. Providing more information to employees will help, but we still need to guide and direct employees in their problem-solving efforts. We must shift the focus of employee problem solving from "where to place the water cooler" to "how to improve quality or on-time delivery of goods or services." Third, we need to make employee problem solving a structured part of the way we run the business, not just a program. Employee problem solving should be a regular part of management and supervisory team meetings at every level. Fourth, if we expect employees to become involved in business problem solving, then we must provide all employees with training and coaching in problem-solving skills. Although employees have much to offer in respect to developing creative solutions, they are often frustrated in their efforts simply because they lack the necessary skills in problem identification, causal analysis, and development of creative solutions. A few employees might have acquired some of these skills through participation in voluntary involvement programs, but most employees do not have and have no way of acquiring such skills without our help. Finally, for those problems that cross organizational and functional lines, we need to create problem-solving task forces to deal with plantwide, departmentwide, and divisionwide problems.

The Synergism of Information, Consequences, and Involvement

The power of information, consequences, and involvement to improve the performance of average employees comes not from each component individually, but from the synergistic effect of all three. Earlier we noted that excellent employees are excellent because of their advantages over average employees in knowledge and skills, motives, and abilities. Yet not one of these factors alone gives excellent employees their advantage. An employee with outstanding knowledge and skills but no internal drive to perform well is not an excellent performer. Likewise, an employee with a strong drive for performance but who lacks the necessary knowledge and skills cannot be excellent. Similarly, when an employee has knowledge, skills, and internal motivation, excellence might not be achieved if he or she lacks the mental or physical capacity for excellence. This is not to say that outstanding knowledge and skills cannot make up for diminished mental or physical capacity. There are many examples of people with mental or physical handicaps that achieve excellence. However, they do so because they have the internal motivation to develop their knowledge and skills to a level sufficient to overcome any diminished abilities. Excellence, then, results from the combined impact of knowledge and skills, motives, and abilities, and not from any single one of these.

Similarly, in the external work environment, improvement in average performance is not a function of information, consequences, or involvement alone. Rather, improvement results from the combined impact of these three. This synergistic effect defines one of the major differences between MPM and other performance improvement strategies. Many management techniques fail because they are limited in scope, either in theory or application. For example, Management By Objectives (MBO) programs have failed because they focused on information while neglecting consequences and involvement. Quality circles failed when they focused upon involvement with inadequate attention to information and consequences. Behavior modification and compensation programs failed when they focused on consequences to the exclusion of information and involvement.

Why does such a synergism result from information, consequences, and involvement? First, information, consequences, and involvement are dependent upon each other. For example, the provision of balanced consequences within an organization depends on the existence of adequate information. Consequences must be contingent upon performance, but this contingency cannot exist unless business values, strategies, required accomplishments, behaviors, goals, and so on are known. Without this information, there is no basis for judging performance and providing consequences. The effectiveness of consequences is similarly dependent upon employee involvement. Unless employees can engage in decision making and problem solving, they cannot influence performance. If employees have no ability to alter performance, consequences become random, uncontrollable, and noncontingent. Similarly, employee involvement is dependent upon both information and consequences for effect. Without information, employees have no basis for problem identification or problem solving. Without consequences, employees have no incentive to become involved. Finally, information is dependent upon both consequences and employee involvement. Without the involvement of employees, reliable information systems cannot exist since employees are usually the source of operating information. Also, the meaningfulness of goals and performance measures is dependent upon their acceptance by employees. Without involvement and participation, employees will refuse to accept measures and goals as legitimate.

Information, consequences, and involvement also support each other. Feedback on performance (information) is a positive consequence to most people. By providing information, management simultaneously provides consequences. The provision of information also supports employee involvement since it provides guidance and direction to problem-solving efforts. Employee involvement supports both consequences and information. When employees are involved, peer recognition and peer pressure provide important social consequences for performance. When employees are involved in building and maintaining information systems, the resulting information is usually more accurate and complete. Finally, consequences support both information and involvement. When adequate consequences exist, usually there is more concern about the quality of both information and problem-solving efforts.

Summary—What This Book Enables You to Do

Maximum Performance Management is a comprehensive and systematic approach to managing human performance in organizations. It is based upon the assumption that significant performance gains are possible if management arranges the work environment so that the vast majority of employees performing below their potential can improve. MPM accepts that not all employees can be excellent. But all employees can approach excellence if given the opportunity to do so. Providing that opportunity is management's task.

We suggested that management has three leverages available for helping average employees approach excellence: information, consequences, and involvement. The remainder of this book is a guide to using these leverages. As you work through these chapters—and we mean "work through" and not just read them—here are some of the things you will be learning and doing:

1. *Defining and communicating values and strategies.* In chapter 3, we examine values and strategies—what they are, how they

are set, and how they are communicated to employees. We show you how to determine what makes your organization unique and in what areas you will compete. Most importantly, we show you how to effectively communicate your values and strategies to the only people who can make them a reality—your employees.

2. *Creating an organization that will implement values and strategies.* Having clearly identified values and strategies is not enough. Many organizations have developed a Statement of Values, and many have a Strategic Plan. Most, however, have difficulty implementing those values and strategies. In chapter 4, we explain why a gap exists between values/strategies and what people do. We show you how to reorganize your business and bridge that gap, and we show you how to align the organization with your strategic objectives so that every employee focuses on what is critical for success.

3. *Measuring performance.* An axiom of management is, "What gets measured gets done." Yet most of us have poor measurement systems. In chapter 5, we show you how to develop measures of performance, even for hard-to-measure white collar/knowledge worker groups. We demonstrate why traditional measurement systems don't work, and we show you how to develop measures for every organizational level that are tied directly to key business objectives.

4. *Creating an effective performance feedback system.* Research has repeatedly shown that feedback is one of the most powerful tools for improving performance, yet reliable, accurate, and timely information on performance is sadly lacking in most companies. In chapters 6 and 7, we show you how to create a management information system that provides regular feedback to managers, supervisors, and employees on current performance against specific goals and objectives. We show you how to create a reporting system that ensures that everyone knows exactly what is expected of them and how they are doing compared to these expectations.

5. *Providing social consequences for performance.* We said that a key leverage for improving performance is providing consequences—make good performance matter. In chapters 8 and 9, we show you how to use social consequences (praise, recognition, etc.) to encourage good performance.

6. *Tying employee compensation to performance.* In chapter 10, we explain why many existing compensation systems—including the one you might be currently using—discourage good performance. We describe what many companies are doing to correct this problem and what these changes mean to you as a manager and employee. In chapters 11 and 12, we describe how you can design and install nontraditional compensation systems that will hold down base wage increases, connect as much as 40 percent of employee compensation to performance gains, and encourage employees to be more flexible in the jobs they will perform.

7. *Involving employees in a continuous effort to improve performance.* Employee involvement is management's third leverage for significant performance gains. In chapter 13, we demonstrate how to design and implement an employee involvement system that encourages every employee in your company to look constantly for ways to increase performance. In chapter 14, we show you how to move toward an ultimate system where your organization is flat (few layers of management), supervision is minimal, and employees are self-directed, self-controlling, and self-managed.

In the chapters that follow, we cover a lot of ground. Along the way, we ask you to complete exercises, conduct meetings, and assemble task forces to carry out specific steps. At each point, we explain what you should do. This book is intended to be a real working manual. But, we can't do the work for you. You have to do what we suggest. And the first thing we suggest is that you ensure that MPM is right for you. You can do that by taking the self-assessment we present in the next chapter.

Chapter 2

How to Determine if
Maximum Performance Management
Is Right for You

In the last chapter, we outlined the basis for *Maximum Performance Management*. In this chapter, we examine the conditions that must exist for MPM to be successful. MPM is not right for everyone all of the time, and it might not be right for you, at least not right now. In this chapter, we provide an up-front self-assessment—a series of questions you should ask yourself before launching into MPM. Your answers to these questions will help you determine whether you are ready for MPM and, if you are not ready, what you have to do to get ready.

Question #1: Do You Accept Responsibility for Employee Performance?

There are many factors that influence employee performance, but to use MPM, you must accept the proposition that your behavior has a substantial impact. This placement of responsibility for performance with you as the manager is more philosophical than scientific. We cannot prove to you scientifically that 10, 50 or 90 percent of performance is directly related to your management practice and style. Yet, we ask you to accept this responsibility. Why? The reason is similar to why we must accept responsibility for your understanding of the principles of MPM outlined in this book. There could be many reasons why, after reading this book, you do not grasp MPM or have the knowledge to put it into practice. We could say you didn't understand because you did not read our book with sufficient care. We could say you failed to understand MPM because you lacked the background, education, and experience to appreciate its finer points. We could give many excuses for why you failed to grasp our ideas. On the other hand, we could accept responsibility for your knowledge of MPM and assume that, if you fail to understand what we are presenting, that the blame rests with us and not with you. Perhaps the difficulty lies with MPM itself or with the way we have explained it. The importance of our accepting responsibility (and we do) is this: If we believe we are responsible, then we will devote more care and attention to MPM and the way it is presented. Similarly, if you accept responsibility for the performance of your people, you will devote more care and attention to managing their performance; and managing human performance in organizations requires all the care and attention you are capable of giving.

Question #2: Do You Have Confidence in Your Employees?

To use MPM effectively, you must expect that your employees have the desire to perform at superior levels and are genuinely capable of doing so if given the right work environment. Your expectations are important because of what is called the "self-fulfilling prophecy." Established first in research conducted in the late 1960s and confirmed in a number of studies conducted throughout the 1970s, the "self-fulfilling prophecy" is that people will live up or down to others' expectations. The classic demonstration of this principle was in a school where teachers were told that some of their students were brighter than others. In fact, there was no real difference in intelligence between the students since the "bright" students were picked at random, yet the students whom the teachers thought were "bright" actually performed better. In a similar study with adults reported by Tom Peters in *In Search of Excellence* (Harper & Row, 1982, pp. 58-59), two groups were given identical sets of ten puzzles to work. When the groups were finished, they were told that their solutions to the puzzles would be scored and that they would be given the results. In fact, the solutions were not scored and the "results" the groups were given had been decided in advance. One group was told it got seven out of ten puzzles right. The other group was told it got seven out of ten puzzles wrong. Then a second set of ten puzzles was given to the two groups. This time, the solutions were actually scored. The group that thought it had gotten seven of the ten puzzles right on the first set actually did better on the second set. The point is that expectations people hold about themselves and expectations authority figures hold about them do actually affect their performance. If you have confidence in your employees and high expectations for their performance, your employees are more likely to perform at a high level. On the other hand, if you have little confidence in your employees and expect little from them, they are much more likely to perform poorly. The old adage that "Winners Win" appears to be very true. If you treat your people as though they are winners and you create an MPM environment for them, chances are they will develop the confidence to be winners.

Question #3: Is This the Right Time for MPM?

MPM is a long-term strategy for improving human performance and effectiveness. Results from full application of MPM principles can take weeks or months. Our experience with MPM suggests that the shortest period of time for results to become evident is probably three months, with the longest time being as much as one year. This range is largely a function of how closely the old management practices approximated the MPM model. As a consequence, MPM is not a strategy to undertake if you are facing a short-term emergency situation.

If significant improvement in productivity, quality, or profitability within a relatively short period is critical to your business, we suggest you adopt a more directive and authoritarian style of management than that called for by MPM. An emergency business situation is analogous to a fire in a crowded theater. Faced with a life-threatening situation, people need calm, knowledgeable, and authoritative direction specifically about what must be done for survival. Once survival is assured, then a different style of leadership is not only appropriate but in our opinion necessary to avoid future emergency situations.

One of the best examples of such an emergency situation occurred with one of our clients. At the time this particular client first sought our help, it had lost significant market share and competitiveness due to poor quality. Major customers were demanding substantial improvement in quality over the short term upon threat of terminating their contracts. Under such circumstances, our client wisely chose to pursue aggressively short-term quality improvement rather than to focus on an MPM-type strategy. This client brought in a new management team composed of individuals extremely knowledgeable in the quality aspects of that particular manufacturing process. Using their technical knowledge and tight manufacturing controls, this team was able to secure the immediate quality gains necessary for survival. Once the emergency was past, management was then able to turn to an MPM approach to gain future competitive advantage.

Question #4: Can Significant Performance Problems Be Solved by Employees?

MPM will enhance human performance within your organization; thus, if poor organizational performance is a result of human behavior, then MPM is a viable strategy. However, MPM is not a viable strategy if the opportunity does not exist for significant performance gains through changes in human behavior. For example, if the major cause of poor productivity is that you are overstaffed, MPM strategies to increase productivity not only will fail to solve the productivity problem but will make it worse. Similarly, if the primary cause of your performance deficiency is that your people are working with antiquated equipment, then an MPM strategy is only likely to frustrate your people, since they cannot make the equipment do what it is incapable of doing. Likewise, if you have the wrong product, the wrong business strategy, the wrong distribution channels for your product or services, and so on, MPM will not help. MPM results in people doing things better, faster, and with greater ease. But doing the wrong thing better, faster, and with greater ease will not lead to success.

Two examples from our experience illustrate this point. In one, a client was aggressively acquiring office automation technology to improve performance of functions that were unnecessary. In the second example, a client was operating two plants when customer orders and market conditions could only support one. Since it was unlikely that the market share could be increased in the immediate future, MPM was not a viable strategy. This client first closed one of the two plants to bring production capacity in line with demand. MPM was then used in the remaining plant to improve performance. Though closing plants and/or eliminating functions are never pleasant, it is important to take such steps as quickly as possible when necessary.

Question #5: Do You Have a Genuine Need to Improve?

MPM works very well when there is a genuine need and desire to improve performance. It does not work well if undertaken for a manager's personal aggrandizement or because it is the newest thing to do. We like to talk with clients about what compelling business reason justifies an MPM strategy. If no such compelling reason exists, then MPM will be more difficult to accomplish. MPM requires changes in the behavior of managers, supervisors, and employees, and typically people resist change unless they see a legitimate reason to behave differently and see advantages to themselves and for the organization. However, when people understand the need for change, resistance is significantly less and change is more likely to be successful. Before undertaking MPM, then, you need to identify a legitimate business reason for doing so. Too often we encounter managers who want to implement MPM but have not yet established a compelling business reason for such an effort. Usually these people have heard or read about a particular strategy or technique and want to try it out because it is the newest, most popular thing to do. Unless such efforts are undertaken for a sound reason, however, they will fail. Before you undertake MPM or any other such strategy that requires your people to change, you should be able to state clearly and concisely why improvement in performance is necessary.

Question #6: Are You Willing to Manage as a Coach and Facilitator?

Over the last two decades, there has been a significant change in the type of person most of us manage. Among other things, the new work force is better educated than at any time in the past. Employees today have been trained to ask questions and are not reluctant to do so. Our employees are not meek, and they expect to be heard. Most importantly, today's employee is self-interested. He or she wants to know, "What's in it for me?" and there had better be something in it for them. The old days of undying loyalty to the company and/or subservient dependence upon the company, if they ever existed, exist no more. Michael LeBoeuf in his book *The Productivity Challenge: How to Make It Work for America and You* (McGraw Hill, 1982, pp. 100-101), made this comparison between the worker of the 1950s and that of the 1980s and beyond:

- The typical worker of the fifties was a man who worked and had a wife who stayed home and cared for children. Today, only about 15 percent of workers are of this kind and the typical worker of the eighties is almost as likely to be a woman as a man. In the majority of today's households there are no children or the wife works.

- The typical fifties worker believed that working hard to be a good provider was his most important role as a man. Today's younger worker probably has a working spouse (although many are single) and sees the role of breadwinner as a burden to be shared.

- The worker of the fifties had experienced the Great Depression and World War II. He believed that sacrifice, hard work and self-denial were the keys to security and economic well being. Contrast this to today's new workers, who grew up in times of prosperity, Vietnam, and Watergate. Not surprisingly, they are less likely to believe that hard work pays off, that self-sacrifice is necessary, or that authority can be trusted. Today's younger worker is much less likely to be the organization man who sacrifices himself for the good of the company.

- Fifties workers believed in discipline, organization, and following orders without questioning, but today's new workers are better educated. And education makes questioners out of people. The new breed wants to know why it's done that way and why they have to do it.

- Finally, the traditional worker believed in a fair day's work for a fair day's pay. And that's where the problems begin. The new breed demands much more than a fair day's pay. As labor relations analyst John R. Browning put it, "They want nothing less than eight hours of meaningful, skillfully guided, personally satisfying work for eight hours" pay. And, that's not easy for most companies to provide."

Not only are the employees we manage different, but the type of work performed by these employees has changed. The mid-1960s represented a kind of watershed in the American workforce. At that point, employment in white-collar and service areas surpassed that in blue collar areas for the first time in our history. Increasingly, today's workforce is composed not only of white-collar workers, but "knowledge workers"—professionals who have a loyalty to their profession that may be more important to them than their loyalty to a particular company. These "knowledge workers" are more expensive than any group of employees in the past, and many cannot be easily replaced. In manufacturing, jobs are increasingly automated and require teamwork and cooperation. Lead times and inventories are shrinking. Quality, service, and the ability to rapidly adjust to changing customer demands have become critical. Competition is international.

The tremendous changes in the workforce and the workplace force a new way of managing upon us. Traditionally, the role of management has been to make decisions and solve problems. The attractiveness of management was often in the power associated with title and position. To be in control, to make the decisions, to command—these have been the aspirations of junior and middle-level managers. Yet these very prerogatives of title and position, if used with today's workforce, can be disastrous for human performance. To understand why such an approach to management is disastrous today, we need to examine the workforce itself—educated, vocal, self-interested, demanding meaning and significance from work. But we also need to look at the work that must now be performed, for it requires more and more creativity, judgment, innovation, flexibility, teamwork, and commitment to quality and customer service. Given our needs and our employees' needs, a new style of management is required.

What is the new style of management? Tom Peters and Nancy Austin in *A Passion For Excellence* (Warner Books, 1986, p. 324) describe the new managers as "people who find and nurture champions, dramatize company goals and direction, build skills and teams, spread irresistible enthusiasm. They are cheerleaders, coaches, storytellers and wanderers. They encourage, excite, teach, listen, facilitate." John Naisbett and Patricia Aburdene in *Re-Inventing the Corporation* (Warner Books, 1985, p. 60) have said, "In the re-invented corporation, we are shifting from manager as order-giver to manager as facilitator. We used to think that the manager's job was to know all the answers. But in the 1980s, the new manager ought . . . to know the questions, to be concerned about them and involve others in finding answers. Today's manager needs to be more of a facilitator—someone skilled in eliciting answers from others, perhaps from people who do not even know that they know." Peter Drucker in *Management: Tasks, Responsibilities, Practices* (Harper & Row, 1974, p. 281) said it this way: "The proper role of the supervisor is not supervision. It is knowledge, information, placing, training, teaching, standard-setting and guiding. . . . As the resource to the achieving worker and his work group, the supervisor . . . can serve . . . both the objective needs of the enterprise for performance and the personal needs of workers for achievement."

Successful application of MPM requires this new style of management. Under MPM, your role must be as a leader, coach, teacher, and facilitator. This does not mean that you give up authority to make the final decision, nor does it mean that you abandon responsibility for problem resolution. What it does mean is that your role as a manager is to encourage decision making and problem resolution at the lowest possible level. To use MPM effectively, you must be prepared to accept this new role.

Summary

In this chapter we have outlined six conditions for implementing MPM:

1. You must be willing to accept responsibility for the performance of your people.

2. You must have confidence in your employees as well as high expectations for their performance.

3. The timing for MPM must be right—there cannot be an emergency business situation that would rob you of the time you need to implement MPM and to see results.

4. There must be significant performance problems that can be solved through changes in the behavior of your people.

5. There must be a genuine need to improve performance.

6. You must be willing to manage as a coach and facilitator, rather than decision maker and problem solver.

The existence of these conditions does not guarantee that MPM will work for you. Yet, our experience has been that if these conditions exist, you have the right environment, and that given the right environment, MPM has a high probability of success. If any of these conditions don't exist (you answered "no" to one or more questions), then we suggest you review that portion of this chapter and ask yourself, "What can I do to change the situation?"

Assuming you have the prerequisites in hand, turn to the next chapter and start installing MPM.

PART 2

Information

Chapter 3

How to Define and Communicate Values and Business Strategies

Excellent employees know what needs to be done. The typical employee is unsure. For all employees to aspire to excellence, you must provide clear direction about what is important. Your values and strategies must be clearly defined, and most importantly, you must communicate these values and strategies to all employees. Defining and communicating values and business strategies are usually regarded as top management functions. But they are not only top management functions. Every manager and every supervisor must perform these duties. Setting and communicating values and strategies are basic to leadership, and leadership is required of managers regardless of level. Thus, this chapter is for the chief executive officer (CEO) or for the first-level supervisor.

In this chapter, we examine values and strategies—what they are, how they are set, and how they are communicated to employees. We start with values since they have a constraining influence on the type of business strategies that can be adopted. Also, values establish the basic tone of any business or any component of a business. Values define "who we are," "what makes us different," and "what we will or will not do." In effect, values are the cement that holds strategies and people together.

What Are Values?

Values are the small set of normative prescriptions for what constitutes acceptable behavior in the organization. They are the few imperatives that everyone who wishes to remain part of the organization must follow. James MacGregor Burns in his work *Leadership* (Harper & Row, 1978, p. 75) has said, "Values indicate desirable or preferred end-states, or collective goals or explicit purposes, and values are standards in terms of which specific criteria may be established and choices made among alternatives. . . . Values are also defined as modes of conduct, such as prudence, honor, courage, civility, honesty, fairness. . . . Some values are both ends in themselves . . . and the means of achieving further end-states, . . . such as in the case of the young man who goes to college to get a job but values the education for its own sake."

Once set, values are rarely changed. When they are, the change is usually caused by unbearable pressure. A change in values usually causes great trauma for an organization. Values establish the fundamental character of the business. People who share an organization's values are attracted to it. Those who don't are repelled. When clearly defined and communicated, values provide a common rallying point for employees and provide a purpose for day-to-day activities. When values are vague or poorly communicated, employees are likely to feel adrift, disconnected, seeing little meaning or purpose in the work they do. Worse, in the absence of clearly articulated values there can be extreme conflict. Operating from fundamentally different assumptions about what is critical and acceptable, employees pursue different and often conflicting objectives.

The clear definition and communication of values is so important that this task of leadership might be the most important of all. For example, in their book *In Search of Excellence*, Tom Peters and Bob Waterman have said about values (1982, p. 279), "Let us suppose that we were asked for one all-purpose bit of advice for management, one truth that we were able to distill from the excellent companies research. We might be tempted to reply, 'Figure out your value system'. Decide what your company stands for. What does your enterprise do that gives everyone the most pride? Put yourself out ten or twenty years in the future: what would you look back on with greatest satisfaction?''

What are some typical values? Peters and Waterman suggested seven dominant values characteristic of the excellent companies they found (p. 285):

1. A belief in being the "best."

2. A belief in the importance of the details of execution, the nuts and bolts of doing the job well.

3. A belief in the importance of people as individuals.

4. A belief in superior quality and service.

5. A belief that most members of the organization should be innovators, and its corollary, the willingness to support failure.

6. A belief in the importance of informality to enhance communication.

7. Explicit belief in and recognition of the importance of economic growth and profits.

A number of the prerequisite conditions for MPM that we discussed in chapter 2 of this book were, in fact, statements of values—our values, but also values we believe all managers who use MPM must hold. We talked about:

• Managers accepting responsibility for performance

• Belief in employees and high expectations for performance

• A genuine desire to see employees succeed

• Belief in coaching and facilitating as the proper role of managers

Sometimes values encompass areas that could just as well be strategies. A commitment to quality, customer satisfaction, or innovation could be a competitive strategy or a fundamental belief.

Whether such a commitment is a value or a strategy often depends upon the depth of the commitment, whether there is a willingness to give it up and adopt an opposing commitment. Strategies change—in fact, they are expected to change—not so with values. Values are expected to endure, and as we suggested earlier, are only changed with great reluctance. For example, if the commitment to quality is so strong we would rather go out of business than sacrifice quality, then quality is most likely a value. However, if we are committed to quality as a leverage against competition and we are prepared to forego that commitment should another method—for example, being the low cost provider—become more desirable, then the commitment is most likely a strategy and not a value. Perhaps the best way to tell a true value from a strategy is that failure to achieve the former engenders guilt within us while the failure to achieve a strategy occasions only temporary disappointment.

How to Determine Your Organization's Values

How are an organization's values determined, and who is responsible for setting values? In effect, the answers to these two questions are intertwined. Values flow from the leadership of the organization and are determined by the most deeply held beliefs of that leadership. Thus, the values of the organization or unit you lead must be set by you as a basic responsibility of leadership. The determination of basic values is one task of management so important that it cannot be delegated. But how do you go about clarifying basic values? Where do you start? Here are some exercises that might help.

Value Exercise #1: Being the "Best"

Earlier, we noted that one of the dominant values of excellent companies as reported by Peters and Waterman was "a belief in being the best." Yet "being the best" can mean many different things. Your own personal definition of what it means to "be the best" is a clue to what you value.

Here is an exercise to use in deciding what "being the best" means to you: Take a blank sheet of paper and draw a line down the center of the page, dividing the paper into two columns. At the top of the left column write: "To me 'being the best' means always doing these things." At the top of the right column write: "To me 'being the best' means never doing these things." Down each column list the things you would "always do" or "never do" if you were the "best." As you write, try to be as specific as you can.

Once you have made your list, review what you have written and do the following:

1. For the "always do" column, for each item ask yourself, "If it was impossible for us to do this, would I still want to be in this business?" If your answer is "no," circle this item as a possible value.

2. For the "never do" column, for each item ask yourself, "If we did this, would I feel not just disappointed but really guilty about having done it?" If you would feel guilty, circle this item as a possible value.

Value Exercise #2: Imitating the Best

Often the best way to sort out what we value is to reflect upon the qualities we admire in others. Therefore, as an exercise, pick a company, division, or department you have worked for or done business with in the past. What was it about this company that you most admired? What seemed to be most important to the people who worked for this company that showed in the way they did business and that made you think, "That's the kind of company I would like to work for or do business with?" Try to be specific about the things you admired. When you have finished your list, ask yourself, "Which of these qualities should we emulate?"

Value Exercise #3: Avoiding the Worst

Our third exercise is the reverse of exercise number 2. In this case, think of a company, division, or department you have worked for or with that you really disliked. What was it about this company that you disliked so much? What did the people who worked for this company do (or fail to do) that made you not want to do business with them? Make a list of these things. Be as specific as you can. When you have finished this list, review it for clues about what you value.

Value Exercise #4: Sources of Pride

Most of us love talking about what we do. In the thousands of interviews we have conducted with managers, supervisors, and employees, we have never had a problem getting an answer when we ask the person to tell us about the work he or she does. The opportunity to talk with pride about our work—even to shade the truth a little to make our work seem somehow more important and interesting—is an opportunity few of us turn down. Showing genuine interest in a person's work is not only a compliment, but a "sure fire" conversation starter.

In this exercise, assume you have been paid such a compliment. A relative, good friend, or casual acquaintance has shown genuine interest in your work. What do you enjoy most about it? What makes it so attractive to you? What are you most proud of? What is unique about your company, your division, your department that sets your group apart from the rest? Jot down what you would say.

Another way to do this exercise is to assume that you have been asked to speak to the local high school about your work, your profession, or your company. What key points would you make in such a speech?

When you have made your notes, review them. Ask yourself which of these points are enduring. Which would you like to be able to repeat with the same confidence in the same speech or conversation ten or twenty years from now?

Reality Checking

After working through the above exercises, you should have arrived at some personal value statements. Now it is important to do some reality checking. Review each of the values you have defined and ask yourself the following:

1. How consistent is this value with what is (or has been) rewarded in this organization?

2. How committed am I personally to this value? Is this value something I am really prepared to live by?

Your answers to these questions are a check on the reasonableness of these values for the organization you are a part of and for yourself at this time. Remember, if the values you have identified are significantly different from those that are (or have been) rewarded (with money, position, recognition, etc.) by the organization, then changing the values of the organization will be time consuming and difficult. Don't expect revolutionary changes, and expect to pay a considerable price, perhaps a considerable personal price, for your advocacy of such changes. As we said earlier, values change slowly and the process is usually traumatic for the organization. Typically, there are numerous vested interests in the existing value system of the organization that will vehemently resist any change and anyone advocating change.

Whether or not the values you outlined above are consistent with the existing values in your organization, advocacy of these values will require your total commitment. If you are not truly committed to these values, you will not be able to survive the trauma associated with their furtherance. More importantly, if you are not truly committed, your behavior will not be consistent with these values, and as a result, these values will never be accepted by your employees. For this reason, we recommend that you review the value statements you have listed. Ask yourself, "If it were impossible to operate the business consistent with these values for whatever reason, would I be prepared to terminate my association with the organization or the business and accept the financial, social, and personal sacrifice disassociation might entail?" If your answer is "no," then you are not sufficiently committed to this set of values, and you should continue to revise these value statements until you have stated them in such a way that you are prepared to make this sacrifice. Concerning values, there can be no equivocation.

How to Communicate Values to Employees

We now assume you have worked through the exercises on values and have done some reality checking. At this point, you have a set of values to which you feel fully committed, to the point of being willing to make the necessary personal sacrifices in support of them. How do you communicate these values to the people who work for you? There are three methods for accomplishing this task.

1. *Written Communication.* First, we recommend that you prepare a one- or two-page written statement outlining these values. Although a written document is the least effective means of communicating anything, especially values, by putting your value statement in writing you make the statement official and provide a document that can be referred to in the future. Be sure you carefully review and revise this document until you are confident that it accurately reflects the values you wish to convey. When you are satisfied, make sufficient copies and distribute them to all who report to you.

2. *Formal Verbal Communication.* In addition to a written statement, you need to incorporate value statements into formal presentations to make to your people. Many individuals simply will not read the written document. Even those who do will not give it the attention it deserves unless they hear these statements of basic beliefs directly from you. For this reason, we recommend that you incorporate a discussion of these values into your presentation at formal meetings with your employees. At a minimum, this review of basic values should be part of your initial distribution of the written statement, of your orientation meetings or training sessions for new employees, and of your special meetings (perhaps in conjunction with a holiday or special event) held at least once or twice each year.

3. *Informal Verbal Communication and Demonstration.* Written communication and formal presentations represent the starting point for communicating values. However, they are rarely successful by themselves, for values, by their very nature, are generalizations and therefore subject to a range of interpretation. If values are to be a driving and unifying force within your organization, then the range of possible interpretation must be narrowed. That narrowing is accomplished not through written documents or formal presentations, but through application of the values to day-to-day events and through myths and stories

told about those applications. The use of myths and stories to make what are sometimes abstract concepts real has been a favorite technique for communicating values for thousands of years. Practically every great religious, political, social, and business leader has been adept at making abstract concepts concrete through the use of myths, stories, and demonstrations that apply these concepts to everyday life. How can you use these same techniques to make these concepts real to your people? In two ways. First, while identifying the values themselves, you drew upon incidents and experiences you had in the past. Use these examples to illustrate values in discussions with your employees. Second, pay scrupulous attention to your own day-to-day behavior, for that behavior will inspire future myths and stories. For example, if you promote customer service and satisfaction as a value, your personal response to a customer with a problem will be watched closely as a clue to not only your commitment to the value but to how that value should be interpreted in daily events. If you preach a commitment to customer service but your behavior is inconsistent with that commitment, your employees will do the same.

How to Develop Your Business Strategy

The values you have identified represent fundamental prescriptions for behavior within the organization. As we said earlier, these values constrain your choice of strategies. Any business strategy that is inconsistent with basic values cannot be pursued, or if pursued will undermine the foundation of the organization and lead to a redefinition of basic values to align them with strategies. In short, values and strategies can influence each other, but true values by definition limit choices of business strategies. If a strategy is pursued that is inconsistent with a stated value, then for employees the stated value ceases to be real since it is no longer supported by management behavior. In the case of extreme conflict between stated values and chosen strategies, we could expect the same, but often worse, disarray and conflict that exist in the absence of clearly articulated values.

Values partially define the organization. Strategies flesh out that definition and provide more specific direction to employees concerning the objectives of daily activities. Good strategies are not only consistent with values but provide a focus for activities, without covering every operational detail. With a good strategy, employees should know the critical objectives of the organization as a whole but should retain considerable flexibility in determining how these objectives will be attained.

As with the identification of values, the development of business strategies is typically viewed as a top management exercise. Although we agree that business strategies should flow from the top to the rest of the organization, we feel strategic thinking is needed at every level. Upper management is constrained in the strategies it can pursue only by corporatewide values. Each lower level is constrained, however, not only by those same values but also by the strategies of each level above it, as well as by the strategies of other units at the same level. We will later discuss the process of communicating strategies and linking strategies within and between levels. For now, we will turn to a definition of what we mean by strategic thinking and to the process that should be followed at each level.

Too often in the past, strategic planning has been a financial/numbers/forecasting exercise. Though we don't reject the importance of the quantitative aspects of strategic planning, we think quantitative exercises represent only one part (and perhaps not the most important part) of the planning process. What, then, is strategic planning? We think it is a continuous process of examining the business—what it is now, what it has to be in the future, and how it can become what it has to be. Admittedly, finding these answers is difficult. What is needed is some process, some way of organizing thinking about these issues. Such a process was suggested by Benjamin Tregoe and John Zimmerman in their book, *Top Management Strategies* (Simon & Schuster, 1980). While Tregoe and Zimmerman aimed their book and the process they described at senior level managers, we feel the process, with some modification, can be applied at all levels. For that reason, we used the Tregoe and Zimmerman approach as a basis for developing strategies. Note, however, that MPM is primarily concerned with techniques for managing human performance, so our discussion of the strategic planning process will be limited. You will not learn all about strategic planning from our discussion. Our purpose here only is to discuss some of the strategic issues that should be examined by every manager at every level as a preliminary event to communicating strategies to employees.

Of the various ideas suggested by Tregoe and Zimmerman in their book, we think the concept of a "driving force" for the corporation and its operating units important to the stratagem of MPM managers, regardless of level. The major advantage of starting strategic thinking with this "driving force" concept is that it gives structure to the development of strategies. In effect, the driving force, once identified, places limits on possible strategic choices, just as values constrain these choices. Thus, given a certain set of values and a driving force, the range of choices about such important strategic issues as the type of products or services we will offer, the markets or customers we will serve, the key capabilities we must have, and our expectations concerning growth, profitability, and so on are limited. As a result, we need not consider all possible choices, only those consistent with decisions that have already been made.

Tregoe and Zimmerman (p. 40) define "driving force" as "the primary determiner of the scope of future products and markets." Essentially, the driving force is the ultimate answer to the question, "What is our business?" Practically every business enterprise is defined by how it answers two fundamental questions: (1) What types of products or services will we offer our customers? and (2) What types of markets or customers will we try to serve? Since no business can hope to offer all possible products or services to all possible markets or customers, the answers to these questions are critical since they define the area of business we have chosen. The importance of the driving force is that, once selected, it suggests answers to these two fundamental questions.

Selecting a driving force essentially means deciding what primary criterion we will use to select among possible products, services, markets, and customers. But how do we find our driving force? Some possible procedures, and therefore some possible driving forces, were suggested by Tregoe and Zimmerman and are listed below. As you review these, notice how each driving force suggests different answers to the two fundamental questions; What products/services should we provide? and, What markets/customers should we serve? Also keep in mind that there can be one and only one driving force.

1. *Products Offered Driving Force.* Here the primary answer to the question, "What is our business?" is that we provide a certain

type of product or service. Since we define our business in this way, other choices we must make are simplified. For example, we would not consider offering a new product or service unless it was very similar to that we already offer. We focus on doing business with customers or groups of customers who have a need for that particular type of product or service.

2. *Market or Customer Needs Driving Force.* Here our primary focus is on meeting the needs of a specific group of customers. We might consider a range of products or services that are unrelated except in that they are desired by a particular type of customer. In short, when market or customer needs are our driving force, we focus on meeting as many needs as possible for a clearly defined type of customer. Any new markets or customers we add will be very much like the customers we already have.

3. *Technology or Body of Knowledge as a Driving Force.* Our primary business here is acquiring and using a particular technology or body of knowledge. Whatever products or services we offer involve the application of that technology or body of knowledge. The customers we have and any new customers all have a need for this product or service. In short, unrelated products/services or customers that don't need our technology or body of knowledge are not legitimate for our type of business.

4. *Production or Delivery Capability as a Driving Force.* Here our primary business is having the knowledge, skills, systems, procedures, tools, and so on to produce things or deliver services in a certain way. We will consider any type of product or service that requires the production or service delivery capabilities we possess, even if these products or services are quite different except for their method of production or delivery. Additionally, we will pursue any market or group of customers as long as they have a need for our particular production or delivery systems. In respect to technology, we will use anything that will enhance our production/delivery capability.

5. *Method of Sale as a Driving Force.* We are here primarily involved

with using a particular method to sell products and services. Any product or service that can be reasonably sold using our method can become one of our products or services. Likewise, we focus on customers likely to respond to our method of sale, regardless of their other characteristics. As a result of this primary driving force, we have different types of customers and different products or services, all unrelated except that they are appropriate for our particular method of sale. An example of this type of company would be a mail order or catalog sales business.

6. *Method of Distribution as a Driving Force.* This business utilizes a distribution channel to get products or services to a customer. The distribution channel may be used to distribute many different types of products or services to many different types of customers, as long as the products or services can be distributed through these channels. Cable systems, telephone companies, and delivery companies are examples of companies that might adopt method of distribution as their driving force. In each case, their primary objective is making maximum use of their distribution system for as many different types of products/services and customers as possible.

7. *Natural Resources as a Driving Force.* Here our primary business is the use, conservation, and control of a resource produced by nature. We seek products and services where this natural resource can be applied. Our customers have in common only the need for this natural resource. Examples of such companies include oil and gas companies, mining companies, or forest products companies.

We believe it is important for you to identify your organization's driving force, whether you are at the level of senior management or lower, for two reasons. First, as we mentioned earlier, once selected the driving force will make other strategic decisions easier. Such decisions include the following:

1. Given our driving force, what kinds of products/services should we offer, and what kinds of markets/customers should we serve? Your answers to these questions essentially define your business—

what it is and what you would like it to be.

2. Given our driving force, our products/services, and our markets/customers, who are or could be our major competitors and on what basis do we wish to compete? Since every business has competition or potential competition, success will depend upon your ability to compete, to offer something your competitor does not or cannot offer. Though there might be many ways to compete, we feel most businesses compete in one or more of the following twelve areas:

   1. Capacity—The volume or range of products/services offered.

   2. Rate—Efficiency, performance, or capacity per hour, day, week, or other time period.

   3. Accuracy/fitness for use—Perceived quality of products/services offered as compared to some absolute model or standard.

   4. Comparative quality—When no absolute model or standard exists, perceived quality of the product or service versus a previous or competing product or service.

   5. Uniqueness/novelty—Perceived quality due to some unique or novel characteristics not available elsewhere.

   6. Timeliness—Ability to provide the product/service by a promised, scheduled, or target date.

   7. Throughput time—Elapsed time for delivery of products/services upon demand/request.

   8. Availability—Ability to have the product/service available on demand and as needed.

   9. Planned cost—Ability to provide the product/service within estimated or planned cost.

10. Relative cost—Ability to provide the product/service at a cost less than that of a comparable product/service.

11. Benefit/value—Ability to provide a product/service with high perceived value irrespective of relative cost.

12. Customer service—Customer's perception of care, attention, responsiveness, friendliness, concern, and so on with which products/services are provided.

3. Given our driving force, our products/services, our markets/customers, and our competitive strategy, what key capabilities must we have to outperform our competition? Key capabilities include the technology/knowledge we must possess, the production capacity we must maintain, the marketing/sales abilities we require, our distribution capability, and the resources we must have at our disposal, such as raw materials, human resources, financial/capital resources, information, and so on.

4. Given our driving force, our products/services, our markets/customers, our competitive strategy, and our capabilities, what expectations should we have for future size, growth, and profits?

The second reason a clear driving force is important is that it will make the task of communicating strategies to your employees easier, for there is one simple common theme to communicate. But how do you decide upon your organization's driving force? When you read through the seven possible driving forces identified by Tregoe and Zimmerman, you might have found several possible candidates for your particular driving force. Possibly none seemed right. Don't be too surprised if you are uncertain about your current and future driving force at this point. Most managers are. What you need is help.

In our discussion of values and how they are determined, we placed the responsibility of setting values entirely with you, for we view the setting of values as a basic responsibility of leadership. In contrast to value setting, selecting a driving force and developing related strategies is a responsibility of the management team. To develop strategies, you need the assistance of your team because they offer different perspectives on the nature of the business. Your role in setting strategies is to guide and facilitate discussion and to make the final decision in case of protracted disagreement.

When assembling your team on strategy development, we suggest you first consider for participation those who work directly for you. In addition, you should consider any other individuals, who because of their special knowledge, experience, or insight, could add value to the discussion. We recommend the team be composed of not less than five and no more than nine people. This size provides a variety of viewpoints while remaining sufficiently small so that decisions are made within a reasonable time. If you feel you need more than nine members, consider bringing in the additional people only for those segments of the process where their particular expertise is most valuable.

Once the management team for developing and/or refining your basic business strategies is identified, this group should meet on a regular basis to discuss strategies. We suggest you plan to facilitate at least five meetings with this team initially and that you hold follow-up discussions on strategies with it at least once or twice each year. The result of these meetings should be a strategic plan for your business. We outline the topics for each of these meetings below.

(Note for nonprofit organizations and managers of functional units within a company: The outline of the five meetings as presented below is appropriate for setting organization-wide strategies for companies or organizations seeking profits. Nonprofit organizations and managers of functional units within organizations can employ the process with the following modifications: (1) Functional unit managers should be familiar with the organization-wide driving force and strategy. The driving force of a functional unit, the products/services of the unit, markets/customers, and so on do not have to be the same for functional units as for the organization as a whole, but they must not be in conflict with organization-wide strategies. If you are setting strategies at a lower level, ask at each step whether by implementing your strategies you will contribute to the implementation of organization-wide strategies. If you are not sure, reconsider the strategies you are pursuing at your level. If you are not sure about organization-wide strategies, you must obtain that information or, at least, make assumptions about that strategy based upon the knowledge you can obtain. In addition, you must consider the impact of pursuing the strategies you develop on other functional units within your

organization. (2) The return/profit issues we discuss in respect to the fifth meeting will not apply to you. You should rather be concerned with the impact of the strategies you select on your operating expenses and budget.)

First Meeting: Introduction and Planning Session

- Review and discuss basic values.

- Review the purpose of strategies and their relationship to values based upon information in this chapter.

- Review the concept of driving forces as discussed in this chapter.

- Discuss the objective of the management team in developing strategies. Essentially, this team is responsible for answering questions such as:

  1. What is our business?

  2. What is our driving force?

  3. Given our driving force, what products/services should we provide, and what markets or customers should we serve?

  4. What competition do we have and what are our strengths and weaknesses compared to that competition?

  5. Given our strengths, weaknesses, and competitors, what *opportunities* do we have, or what *needs* should we satisfy?

  6. What capabilities should we develop/maintain to provide these products/services and serve these markets/customers? Capabilities include such things as technology, a body of knowledge, production capacity, marketing/sales, distribution channels, and resources (financial, human, information, raw materials, etc.).

  7. Based upon the answers to questions 1 through 5, what can

we expect in size, growth, and financial performance over the next five years or longer? Are we satisfied with this size, growth, and level of financial performance, or must we rethink our driving force, products/services, customers, or capabilities?

- Discuss how the team will answer these questions. What process will the team follow? We recommend following the agendas for the five meetings outlined here.

- Discuss the topic for the next meeting: reaching agreement on the organization's driving force. (You could ask all members of the team to read the portions of this chapter on driving forces, or they could read Benjamin Tregoe and John Zimmerman's book, *Top Management Strategy*.)

Second Meeting: Identifying the Driving Force

- Review the seven basic driving forces suggested by Tregoe and Zimmerman.

- Discuss which of these seven represents your particular organization's driving force.

- Continue this discussion until there is consensus on a single driving force. (If there is disagreement, this discussion can extend over several sessions.)

Third Meeting: Identification of Products/Services and Markets/Customers

- In light of the driving force that has been identified, review each product/service you currently provide and each market/customer you currently serve. Ask your team: In light of what we now know about our driving force, would we be involved with this product/service or serve this market/customer if we were not already doing so? If your answer is no, discuss how to exit this product/service line or to terminate service to this market/customer. Your purpose here is to accomplish what Peter

Drucker, in his book *Management*, has referred to as "sloughing off yesterday." Drucker points out that an often overlooked aspect of planning "is getting rid of the no-longer-productive, the obsolescent, the obsolete" (Drucker, *Management*, p. 126). By asking these questions, your team will be testing current assumptions about the nature of the business against the concept of a driving force. Your team should develop an "exit plan" for quickly getting out of any business that does not fit or is obsolete.

- Once you have eliminated obsolete products/services and decided how to terminate services to markets/customers that do not fit your driving force, you are now prepared to review what remains. Ask your team: Given the products/services and markets/customers that we have decided to retain, are there new products/services or markets/customers we should develop that are consistent with our driving force?

- Your objective in this meeting should be to develop with your team one of the following two types of lists: (1) a list of all of the products or services you plan to offer with the markets/customers identified for each product/service on your list; or (2) a list of all of the markets or types of customers you plan to serve with the products/services you will offer to each of them. You can produce a list associating products/services with markets/customers (as in the first type) or markets/customers with products/services (as in the second type), but be sure you can associate each product/service with one or more markets/customers and each market/customer with one or more products/services. The point of this exercise is to identify all the products/services you will provide and markets/customers you want to serve. Additionally, by matching these two, you have ensured that each product/service you will offer has an identified market/customer and that for each market/customer you have a product/service to offer.

- Continue this meeting—through several sessions if necessary—until you have consensus on the products/services and markets/customers that are consistent with your driving force.

Fourth Meeting: Identifying the Competitive Requirements

For any given product/service you wish to provide and for any given market/customer you wish to serve, there are other organizations that already provide or could provide these same products/services to these same markets/customers. Therefore, you *always* have competition or the potential for competition. Even when you have a monopoly— your industry is protected and regulated or you run an in-house functional unit that other areas of your company are required to use— you always run the risk of losing the monopoly or protection from competition. Even if you currently don't have competition, never assume that condition will continue, particularly if you are now successful. You must therefore ask your team to undertake some competitive analysis.

- Ask them: Given the products and services we wish to provide and the markets/customers we wish to serve, who else now provides or could provide these same types of products/services to these same markets/customers? Have your team develop a list of at least one actual or potential competitor for each type of product/service and/or market/customer.

- Once you have developed a list of competitors for each product/service you plan to offer, have your team compare your organization to each competitor in respect to each of the twelve competitive areas we defined earlier:

  1. Capacity

  2. Rate

  3. Accuracy/fitness for use

  4. Comparative quality

  5. Uniqueness/novelty

  6. Timeliness

7. Throughput time

8. Availability

9. Planned cost

10. Relative cost

11. Benefit/value

12. Customer service

For each competitor and each competitive area make two lists:

1. Your strengths compared to that competitor

2. Your weaknesses compared to that competitor

- Once you have a complete list of your strengths and weaknesses in each of these twelve competitive areas, have your team identify the areas in which you intend to compete. Usually you will find that you can compete in only a few of these twelve areas. The objectives of high performance in those areas in which you wish to compete become your Competitive Requirements. For example, if you decided to compete in the areas of customer service, benefit/value, and comparative quality, your competitive requirements will be to:

1. provide a high level of customer service;

2. provide high perceived value in the product/service;

3. provide quality equal to or better than your competitor can provide (best or joint-best quality).

- You should continue with this competitive analysis until you have reached consensus on your major competition, your strengths and weaknesses versus your competitions', and your specific competitive requirements given your strengths and weaknesses.

Fifth Meeting: Identification of Key Capabilities

In the previous three meetings, you reached consensus on a driving force, the products/services you wish to offer, the markets/customers you wish to serve, your major competitors, and your competitive requirements. In this meeting, you should turn the team's attention to those capabilities your organization must possess to provide these products/services and to meet the needs of these markets/customers. Think of capabilities as assets you can employ to meet your competitive requirements.

- Capabilities/assets you might need could include:

  1. A particular technology

  2. A body of knowledge or a skill

  3. A production capacity or capability

  4. Marketing capability

  5. Sales

  6. Distribution channels

  7. Raw materials

  8. Financial resources

  9. Human resources

  10. Information or information systems

- For each of these capabilities/assets, ask your team to determine:

  1. Based upon our driving force, the products/services we want to provide, the markets/customers we want to serve, and the competitive requirements we have identified, what level of capability do we require in each of these areas?

2. What capability do we currently possess in each of these areas?

3. How do we reallocate and/or acquire the additional capabilities that are necessary?

- As with the previous meetings, this meeting might extend over several days or sessions. Also, you might find that the team needs to assemble additional facts, financial data, and so on in order to answer these questions. Additional people can be consulted or brought in to meet with the team to discuss specific points. The team should complete its discussions on capabilities only when it has reached consensus on the answers to these questions and has prepared a document outlining its findings.

Sixth Meeting: Assessing Size/Growth and Return/Profit Implications

Based upon decisions the team has made concerning driving force, products/services, markets/customers, competitive requirements, and required capabilities, during the sixth meeting the team should assess the implications of these decisions for the organization's potential size, growth, return on investment, and profitability. In short, the team has set its strategy in meetings 1 through 5. Meeting 6 is devoted to the implications of this strategy. If, in the course of this review, the team determines that the strategy it has selected will not yield the type of growth, profits, and so on that are deemed minimally acceptable given financial or other goals, then the entire strategy must be reexamined.

How to Communicate Your Business Strategy to Employees

By working through the six meetings we outlined above (or by completing a similar planning process) with your management team, you clarified your basic strategies. To implement these strategies, you must communicate them to your employees. This communication is important and too often neglected. Frequently senior management does an excellent job of developing strategies but stops with the publication of a strategic plan. Too often this plan is never circulated, much less effectively communicated, to employees at every level. As a result, basic behaviors that must change for the plan to be accomplished never change. The plan becomes a paper exercise that never effects the company.

The actual process of communicating strategies is similar to that of communicating values. A written summary should be prepared and circulated to employees outlining the strategy. Discussion of strategies should be a part of formal meetings with employees. Most importantly, your informal contacts and personal behavior (what you pay attention to, reward, emphasize, etc.) must be consistent with the strategy.

Although most managers agree with the importance of communicating strategies, often there is a reluctance to do so. Unlike values, strategies might contain sensitive information. How, then, do we decide how much detail can be shared? Our recommendation is that you share as much detail as you can without divulging information that would give a competitor an advantage should it be improperly disclosed. Rarely do we feel that information should be withheld from employees because it is too complex for employees to understand. Our experience has been that employees are capable of understanding much more detail about strategies than is normally assumed. We also feel that the potential damages from the improper disclosure of strategic information to a competitor are often more imagined than real. Once strategies are developed, they are difficult to keep entirely secret from a competitor who truly desires to uncover them. Also, once acted upon, strategies are relatively easy for a competitor to deduce. In the final analysis, we feel that much more damage results from withholding information from employees, for employees cannot support and implement a strategy they do not understand.

Sometimes strategic information is not shared with employees because the strategy, when implemented, will have a negative impact on employees. For example, the strategy could call for the elimination of jobs, product lines, or services. Again, we feel the danger of negative effects from revealing such information is exaggerated. First, such strategies are difficult to keep secret. Most employees know about these proposed actions before they are implemented. Second, when such actions are taken, management is probably in a stronger position with employees if it has prepared employees for the action and explained the strategic necessity in advance.

Summary

In this chapter, we examined the development and communication of values and business strategies. We suggested that the identification of basic values is a leadership task and one of the major responsibilities of each MPM manager. Some typical values were discussed, and exercises for arriving at a statement of values were provided. We also outlined a process for developing strategies that begins with identifying the driving force of your organization. To communicate values and strategies, we suggested methods that ranged from written documents, to formal presentations, to informal communication. We emphasized that values and strategies are communicated primarily through day-to-day contact and through behavior by managers that is consistent with stated values and strategies. In the next chapter, we will discuss how these values and strategies are broken down to the level of operating units and how the accomplishments of individual units are linked together to provide an overall framework for supporting corporate performance.

Chapter 4

How to Reorganize for Performance

In chapter 3, we discussed methods for defining and communicating values and business strategies. Clearly defined and widely communicated values and strategies give employees a common rallying point and purpose for day-to-day activities. Yet, even when management does define and communicate values and strategies well, employees are frequently uncertain about the specific day-to-day performance required to achieve the results desired. In this chapter, we will explore the gap between values/strategies and employee behavior and how that gap can be bridged. In addition, we will discuss how to create an organizational structure that will link employee behavior to the strategies of the organization.

The Gap between Values/Strategies and What People Do

If you have completed the tasks outlined in the preceding chapter, you have devoted considerable effort to identifying what your organization must achieve to be successful now and in the future. You have a clearly defined strategy for competing in the real world that is founded upon some fundamental values or beliefs. Isn't that enough? If you do a good job of communicating the values and strategies to your people, can't they take it from there? Some can, but they are the excellent employees we spoke about in chapter 1. Chances are these excellent employees shared the values and intuitively understood the strategic realities of the business even before you formalized them. For most of your people, the values and strategies you developed and communicated will help provide general direction, but they are far from sufficient. Values and strategies are just too far removed from what people do day-to-day.

There is a very wide gap between values and strategies and day-to-day behavior of employees. This gap often prevents good business strategies from ever being implemented. To understand this gap and to discover what can be done about it, we need to define some terms and review some of what we know about values and strategies.

In the preceding chapter, we said that values are a small set of normative prescriptions for what constitutes acceptable behavior in the organization. Values partially define the organization, and strategies flesh out that definition by specifying critical objectives for the organization as a focus for day-to-day activities. Neither values nor strategies deal with the specifics however. In most cases, values, and to a lesser extent strategies, deal with broad prescriptions for behavior such as, "Be the best," "Treat people as individuals," "Take care of the details," "Be the low cost provider of service," or "Be the highest quality provider."

For values and strategies to be implemented, they must be translated into much more specific terms. Only through such translation are we likely to get consistent performance. In short, we must come as close as possible to specifying behaviors. We use the term "behaviors" here in a specific sense:

- Behaviors are things people say or do.

- A behavior can be observed (heard or seen) while it is occurring.

- Examples of work behaviors would include a person typing a letter, a person using a tool to accomplish a work task, a person making a telephone call, a person reading a report, a person completing a form, or a person waiting on a customer.

Notice that these examples are very specific and that each one can be broken down into more discrete behaviors. For example, "using a tool" could be broken down into moving, grasping, lifting, holding, and so on. All of these more discrete actions are themselves behaviors.

Why so much concern about behaviors? Well, behaviors are the only thing employees can really change. For example, employees cannot directly make the company the "highest quality provider." What employees can do, however, is check their own work to ensure that it is in compliance with quality standards. Making such quality checks and perhaps keeping a quality control graph is a behavior—it can be observed while it is occurring and is controllable by the employee.

To understand the gap between values/strategies and behaviors, visualize a pyramid with a small number of values/strategies at the top and thousands (perhaps millions) of behaviors at the bottom (see figure 4).

The Gap between Values/Strategies and Behaviors

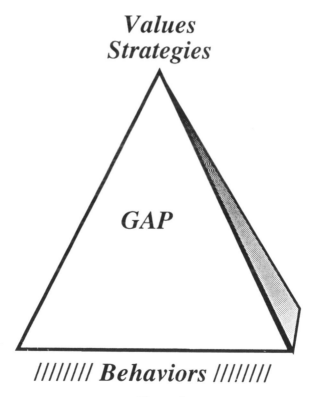

Figure 4

To operate a business in accordance with basic values and to achieve objectives, you have to ensure that employees change their behavior so that it is consistent with the company's values and strategies. But how do you manage employee behavior when there are millions of behaviors and this gap between strategies and behavior?

One approach to this problem has been essentially to ignore the gap between strategies and behaviors and to focus on changing only a few, clearly definable and measurable behaviors. In application, if not necessarily in theory, much of the behavior modification or behavior management approach to human performance improvement has dealt in this way with the strategy/behavior gap and the problem of multiple behaviors. As a result, numerous studies have been done on accomplishing behavioral changes such as increasing the frequency of hand washing among kitchen workers or increasing the frequency of smiling by front-line employees in a fast food restaurant. Such interventions, using feedback, training, praise, recognition, and so on, have been highly effective in obtaining the desired behavior. For example, for the hand washing and smiling interventions, increases in the desired behavior were 58 and 203 percent respectively. Yet, there are some practical problems with widespread use of this technique. First, as important as hand washing is to the performance of cafeteria workers and smiling is to front-line fast food employees, in neither case are hand washing and smiling sufficient to achieve the objectives of the organization. Although customers of food service establishments are most likely interested in the cleanliness and friendliness of employees, they are also interested in the quality of the food, the cost, the speed of service, and other things. Thus, when we focus on improving individual behaviors, we ignore other behaviors or results of behaviors that are of equal or more strategic importance. In short, since the ultimate goal of the organization should be to achieve its strategic objectives, we cannot ignore the gap between strategies and behaviors. How, then, do we bridge this gap?

The Importance of Missions and Accomplishments

In our work with hundreds of organizations and thousands of managers, we inevitably found the strategic objectives too broad and the behaviors too narrow to base management on. An intermediate level was needed—something more concrete and meaningful to employees than strategic objectives yet more expansive than discrete behaviors. We call that intermediate level "missions and accomplishments." It is through missions and accomplishments that day-to-day behavior can be managed and made consistent with strategic objectives.

What are missions and accomplishments? We view missions as subsets or component parts of strategies. Every strategy has one or more associated missions. Accomplishments are the results of specific behaviors and lead to the achievement of missions. To visualize this relationship and to illustrate how missions and accomplishments bridge the gap between strategies and behavior, we can return to our pyramid.

As we do so, notice first that values, strategies, missions, accomplishments, and behaviors progressively represent more and more specific prescriptions for what constitutes desirable performance. Second, notice that an achievement at one level leads to success at the next higher level. Thus, if the required behaviors are performed as they should be, accomplishments will be achieved. The achievement of accomplishments leads to the fulfillment of missions, and when missions are achieved, strategies are implemented. Finally, notice that our pyramid now begins to take on the appearance of an organizational chart (table 1). In fact, the strategy, mission, accomplishment, and behavior pyramid should be the structure of the organization.

Why Traditional Organizational Structures Hinder Performance

In our work with companies, we are constantly amazed at the poor rationale or lack of rationale for organizational structure. Too often, we find structures that are outmoded given the current strategic direction or structures that are chaotic because of repeated reorganizations without regard to strategies, missions, and critical accomplishments. Such poorly structured organizations find it extremely difficult to implement strategies because responsibility is fragmented among competing units and unit managers. Not infrequently, poor structure perpetuates functions that not only lack strategic significance but can in fact be detrimental to the current strategy. To create an MPM performance organization, it is important that the structure of the organization be reviewed and that any necessary reorganization be accomplished to ensure that the structure supports successful implementation of current strategies, missions, and critical accomplishments.

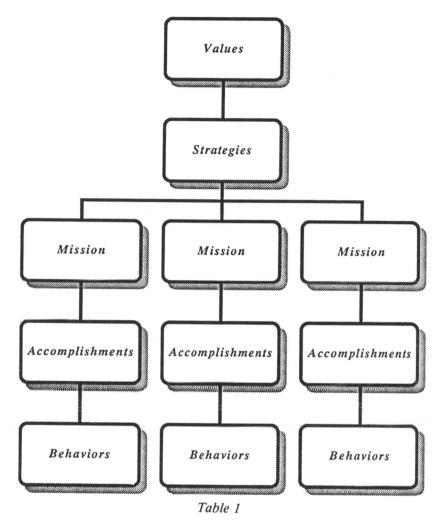

Table 1

We believe that the chief reason organizational structures fail to support organizational strategies lies in the approach most managers take when designing or redesigning organizations. Most of us create a functional structure, where similar or related specialities are grouped together. For example, our departments or divisions might include Personnel, Manufacturing, Marketing/Sales, Research and Development, Accounting, or Legal Services. A functional approach to organization seems to make sense. After all, aren't these the things a company has to do? Also, doesn't it make sense for people who do the same kind of work to be grouped together? Yes and No.

The Problems with a "Functional" Structure

Functional organizations have "made sense" for a long time. Practically every company is or has been organized along functional lines. In addition, the functional approach to organization seems to feed on itself. As the organization grows, we divide up major functional groups into smaller groups, again, along functional lines. Thus, if the manufacturing division becomes too large for a single manager, we divide it into smaller departments such as Production, Engineering, Maintenance, and so on. Each of these departments has its own specialized function to perform.

Our devotion to functional organization structures is not totally unreasonable. By organizing in this way, we can justify bringing into the organization specialists in a particular kind of work. These specialists prefer working with people who have the same technical knowledge. In addition, by specializing we create opportunities for these specialists to advance in their own discipline. Beyond specialization, a functional organization can provide economy of operation since we avoid duplication and ensure full utilization of specialized tools and equipment. Finally, through functional organization we gain control over policies and procedures. Since all work of a particular type is performed or approved by a single group who is responsible for that particular job, we can ensure consistency. For all these reasons, a functional approach to organizing work makes sense. But does it really?

For all of the advantages of a functional organization, there are a number of severe disadvantages. First, the more we subdivide work into specialized functions, the less accountability there is for performance. Functional groups focus on their specialty, yet rarely is the performance of their specialty what the organization is really trying to accomplish. Organizations are not solely in the business of manufacturing, maintenance, or research. Most organizations are in the business of providing a product or service to meet the needs of its customers. Manufacturing, maintenance, research, and so on are functions that must be performed, but performing these functions is not the ultimate objective of the business. Providing the product or service and meeting the needs of the customer are the strategic objectives of the business. Yet with a functional organization, no one is clearly accountable for these critical end results, except at the very top of the organization. When the product or service is not provided, when the needs of the customer are not met, only *one* person (the general manager or president) can be held totally responsible. After all, manufacturing just makes it, sales just sells it, research just develops it. No one else is responsible, and no one else can be held responsible. How many times have we heard that research develops what manufacturing can't make at a reasonable cost; that manufacturing can't make what can be sold in time and at a reasonable cost; and that salesmen promise the customer anything to get the sale, regardless of whether or not we know how to make what the customer wants or have the capability to make it even if we knew how?

With a functional structure comes control and consistency, but at what price? Functional groups become isolated and are slow to respond. Decisions about changes potentially affect all areas of the company, therefore decisions have to be made with care and at the proper level. Problem resolution in a functional structure gets pushed up higher and higher within the organization. Because of the danger of making a bad decision that could have significant consequences for the company as a whole, managers resist making any decisions at all. No one is responsible, and no one can be held accountable except the top manager.

Along with the functional organization comes the highly trained specialist who wants to work in his or her specialty and no other. The more specialized the company becomes, the more difficult it is to change direction and to be flexible. When taken to the extreme, work becomes so specialized that employees refuse to help each other. How often have we heard, "That's not my job"? Some specialized groups sit idle while others are swamped with work. Backlogs grow. The product or service isn't provided. The customer's need isn't met. Why? Because everyone is responsible only for their narrowly defined job. Only one person is thus responsible and can be held accountable for the only job worth doing—providing the product or service and meeting the customer's need.

The Problems with a "Divisional" Structure

As a response to the failure of the functionally structured organization, some companies have turned to a divisional approach.

With a divisional approach, the large company is broken up into smaller divisions that are like small companies themselves. There could be product divisions or geographic divisions. Each division is responsible for its own product or service and/or for meeting the needs of its own customers. Good, as far as it goes. But what happens within the division? In all probability, each division is organized internally along functional lines. We thus have the same functional problems, the same failures to meet customer needs, only on a smaller scale.

If both functional and divisional structures ultimately fail, how should the performance organization—the MPM organization—be structured? We agree with Peter Drucker who said over ten years ago, "How the structure is to be built depends on what results are needed. Organization has to start with the desired results" (Drucker, *Management*, p. 530). Thus, to design the structure of the performance organization, we return to our strategy, mission, accomplishment, and behavior pyramid (table 1).

We never fully explained when we presented this pyramid the meaning of missions and accomplishments. We indicated that missions and accomplishments were related and that they bridged the gap between behaviors and strategies; we said missions were subsets or components of strategies; and we said that accomplishments were the results of specific behaviors. We also mentioned that achievement of behaviors leads to achievement of accomplishments, which leads to achievement of missions, which leads to implementation of strategies. We described interconnected achievement from top to bottom, bottom to top, linking individual employee behavior with top level corporate strategies. But how does this pyramid relate to the performance organization structure? Read on.

How to Design a Performance Organization

In the previous chapter, we developed strategies by identifying our "driving force." Once identified, our driving force suggested choices about the products/services we would provide and the markets/customers we would serve. Our remaining efforts at developing strategies centered around identifying our competitive requirements (how to capitalize on our strengths and overcome our weaknesses compared to our competition) and around the key capabilities we needed to achieve our competitive requirements. We can now return to this strategic analysis as a basis for our structure *and* as a basis for understanding the meaning of missions and accomplishments.

Recalling our strategy, we know that our primary objective for the business (the results we want) is to provide certain, identified products/services to meet the needs of certain, identified markets/customers. Taking our clue from Drucker, we should organize in a way most likely to get us those results. Simultaneous with designing such a structure, we will be clarifying both missions and accomplishments.

To design our performance organization, we start with the results we want (products/services to meet market/customer needs). We have two choices regarding organization: (1) we can organize along product/service lines; or (2) we can organize along market/customer lines.

Product/Service Line Organization

If we organize along product/service lines, we will create organizational units (divisions, departments, sections, etc.) whose primary *mission* is the following:

- To provide identified products/services to meet the needs of certain markets/customers so that existing customers are retained and new customers for these products/services are obtained while achieving or exceeding projected levels of profitability.

The critical *accomplishments* for a product/service line component are to achieve the *competitive requirements* for this particular product/service line and its markets/customers.

The critical *behaviors* for a product/service line component are the demonstration of *key capabilities* for achieving these competitive requirements.

A company organized along product/service lines might look like table 2.

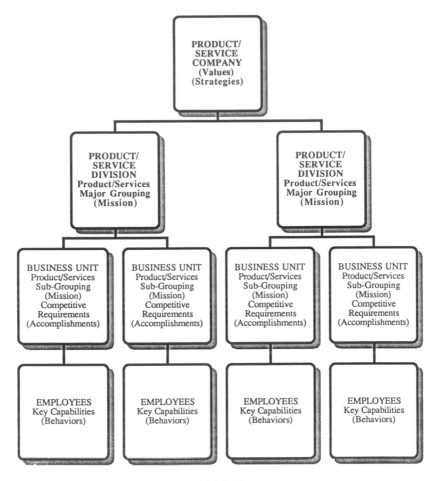

Table 2

Market/Customer Line Organization

If we organize along market/customer lines, we will create organizational units (divisions, departments, sections, etc.) whose primary *mission* is the following:

- To meet the needs of certain markets/customers by providing and developing a range of products/services they desire so that existing customers are retained and new customers of this type are obtained while achieving or exceeding projected levels of profitability.

The critical *accomplishments* for a market/customer line component are to achieve the *competitive requirements* for these particular markets/customers and the products/services provided to them.

The critical *behaviors* for a product/service line component are the demonstration of the *key capabilities* for achieving these competitive requirements.

A company organized along market/customer lines might look like table 3.

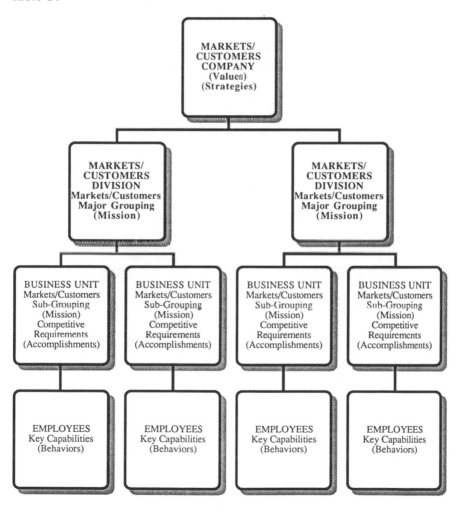

Table 3

Differences between the Divisional Approach and the Performance Approach

In reviewing the two sample organization charts we just presented, you were probably struck with the similarity between this type of approach and the divisional approach. In fact, the two approaches are very similar. In both approaches, we start by breaking the company into divisions responsible for specific product/service or market/customer (in the divisional approach, geographic) lines. The differences between the two approaches become evident, though, at the next level of organization (what we call departments). Here, the performance approach, instead of creating departments according to function, creates departments according to a subgrouping of products/services or markets/customers. With the performance approach, we then continue to subdivide the company to the extent possible along product/service or market/customer lines so that every organizational component is responsible for providing products/services or meeting the needs of specific markets/customers.

You probably have already thought of a number of problems with the approach to organizational structure we are advocating. What about work that by its very nature requires a functional approach to organization? For example, what about work that requires highly trained specialists? What about the economies of operation that comes from full utilization of equipment and avoidance of duplication with the functional approach? What about regulatory or security requirements that can only be met through the concentration and control that comes from a functional structure? Let's examine each of these problems.

First, what about the specialist capabilities dictated by competitive requirements? These capabilities have to be provided in some way. True. But let's look at what we really need. We need special capabilities, not specialists, and we need these capabilities to meet specific competitive requirements that might (and most likely will) change when our strategy changes. To provide this capability, we could choose to hire a specialist(s), or we could contract for this capability with an outside supplier. If the work is highly specialized and a change in strategy could make performance of the work unnecessary, then we should contract for the work with an outside supplier. Such work should be contracted out even if in the short term it will be more expensive than hiring specialists to work internally. In the long run, contracting out will be less expensive, and the work product will be more objective and potentially of higher quality. Too often we have seen highly specialized functions originally created to meet a short-term, but strategically important, need that no longer is required. Such groups continue to perpetuate their existence by looking for something to do. Typically, even when there is general recognition that the group no longer performs a useful purpose, managers are reluctant to abolish the group and fire the specialists. After all, they made an important contribution at one time, and they are trying to stay busy. We are not saying that specialized functions should never be created. What we are saying is that, because of the self-perpetuating nature of organizations, specialized groups should be established with caution. If specialists must be hired, ideally they are hired into a product/service or market/customer department as part of that department's staff. Then the opportunity exists to broaden their specialty so that it can serve a number of different functions. Seldom should specialists be isolated in a separate component.

In respect to functional grouping to ensure economy of operation and full utilization of expensive equipment, we feel such structure sometimes (but not always) makes sense. But before you jump to the conclusion that such a grouping in fact does make sense, consider several points. The purpose of the business is to produce a product, provide a service, and meet a customer's need. Obviously, it is important that this be done with the greatest economy and efficiency possible. But what do we gain from economy and efficiency if we fail in the ultimate purpose? Too frequently, the concentration of resources results in long ques and growing backlogs as work piles up waiting to pass through one central point. In spite of projections and promises, we know from bitter experience that projections are more likely to be optimistic than pessimistic and that well-intended promises too often are not kept. Thus, all proposals for centralization should be examined with the utmost caution. After all, it is often better to have a hundred less efficient and unsophisticated operations than one highly efficient and sophisticated operation delayed and hopelessly backlogged.

Finally, we get to the issue of regulatory requirements and security. In respect to regulatory requirements, there is little we can say. If you have to, you have to. Often well-intended regulations are detrimental to performance. We can only hope that the loss in performance is more than made up for by the higher purposes served by the regulations themselves. All we can say about regulations is never accept a single interpretation of what the requirements really are. Often, even the regulators don't fully understand the regulations they enforce. So, ask and ask again.

In respect to the security issue, our advice again is to ask and question. Many poor ideas for unnecessary concentration have been sold based upon the promise of increased security. Also, many legitimate proposals for changes to improve performance have been dismissed without a fair hearing simply because of security concerns. Before accepting any argument that functional concentration is necessary for security reasons, ask yourself if concentration really heightens security. For example, does the concentration of information or some other valuable resource really make it more secure, or does it merely give those who would breach your security just one place to look? Perhaps the disaster that could destroy your resource now has only one place where it has to occur? Sometimes the best security is obtained through distribution of what is valuable, not by its concentration. Then, at least, there are more places to breach for information, and disasters must occur simultaneously in many places.

We leave these decisions about required functional structures and concentration up to you, for they are largely matters of judgment. We do argue, however, for a substantially (if not wholly) performance and strategically driven approach to organizational structure. Even when you must create a functional structure, we encourage you to identify missions and accomplishments for such groups, just as you did for the rest of the organization. To do so, treat specialized or functionally centralized groups and any groups with no external markets/customers of their own as staff or service groups. Rather than having external markets or customers, these groups differ only in that they provide products or services to other groups within the company. These other groups within the company are the customers of the staff or service groups. Such an understanding will allow you to develop missions and accomplishments even for these staff or service groups. Be sure every group has a clearly defined mission and associated accomplishments since, as you will see in the next chapter, missions and accomplishments are necessary for the development of measures.

Achieving "Employment Security," Not Job Security

In the preceding discussion, we indicated that one major difference between the performance approach to organizational structure and more traditional approaches was in our attempt to carry product/service or market/customer line responsibility to lower levels of the organization. When it is impossible to organize a division along product/service or market/customer lines, we advocated a functional approach with centralized functions servicing other internal components as their primary customer. Each organizational component in the performance organization then has a clearly identified mission to provide products/services to identified markets/customers (either internal or external). The unit exists solely for the strategic purpose of accomplishing that mission. Should a future strategy no longer call for the particular products/services or markets/customers serviced by a component, this component is then no longer required. A functional unit serving internal needs could become obsolete if the products/services it offers are no longer needed by the organization or could be provided more economically by an external supplier. In short, in the performance organization, all organizational units are by definition *impermanent*.

The impermanent nature of the organizational structure we are advocating here has important implications for the company. For example, since organizational units under such a structure are impermanent, positions within these organizational units are impermanent. In such an organization, there is no *job security* per se, only *employment security*. The performance organization makes every effort to guarantee continued employment, but not necessarily in a specific job or job specialty. Long-term employment requires that the company commit itself to employee development (preparing the employee to assume more than one role) and that the employee be willing to be flexible in job assignments. It is exactly because of this impermanence that the performance organization discourages overspecialization (to be too specialized is to run the risk of loss of employment should company strategies change significantly) but encourages cooperation and teamwork (being able and willing to help out in a number of different capacities and being rewarded with retention during periodic changes in structure).

A Guide to Redesigning Your Organization to Support Performance

In the previous chapter, you selected a management team to work with you in developing strategies for your organization. You will now work with this same team to redesign the organization and to identify the missions and key accomplishments of components in your new structure. As in the case of developing strategies, you accomplish this task through a series of meetings.

Organization Meeting #1: Introduction and Planning Session

- Review with your management team the decisions you have made so far concerning values, strategies, products/services, markets/customers, competitive requirements, and key capabilities.

- Review the material in this chapter concerning:

  1. The gap between behaviors and strategies

  2. The importance of missions and accomplishments to bridge that gap

  3. The performance approach to organizational structure

  4. The product/service line organization and its mission

  5. The market/customer line organization and its mission

  6. The relationship of competitive requirements to key accomplishments

  7. The arguments for and against a functional organization

  8. Issues on specialization, economy of operation, regulations, and security

- Discuss the objectives of this series of meetings:

  1. To redesign the organization along a product/service line or market/customer line

  2. To clarify missions and key accomplishments for each component in the redesigned organization

- Discuss the issue of *employment security* versus *job security*:

  1. Is employment security consistent with the values you have outlined?

  2. Are there any policy, regulatory, and/or contractual (i.e., union) restrictions on your ability to adopt an employment security versus job security orientation? What are these restrictions? Can they be overcome?

  3. How are employees likely to react to a change from job security to employment security? What are the potential advantages and disadvantages of an employment security orientation from the employees' perspective?

- Discuss the objective of the next meeting:

  1. To review the existing organizational structure

  2. To redesign the organization as closely as possible along a product/service or market/customer line.

Organization Meeting #2: Review and Redesign of the Organization

- Review the existing organizational structure and assess how closely the existing organization matches a product/service or market/customer line structure.

- Determine whether a product/service or market/customer structure is most appropriate for your type of business. Some factors to consider in reaching this decision include:

1. The similarities/differences between markets/customers—If the various markets/customers you service are significantly different and have unique needs, you may want to organize along market/customer lines to ensure that you develop an appreciation for and can respond to the specific needs for each market/customer.

2. The similarities/differences between products/services—If the various products/services you plan to offer are significantly different and, as a result, require specialization in development, production, distribution, marketing/sales, etc., then you may want to organize along a product/service line.

- Determine the *minimum* changes necessary to reorganize along a product/service or market/customer line. Try to avoid major shifts in employee work assignments, management, and so on. Your purpose in redesigning the organizational structure is to undertake the least changes necessary to ensure that the structure of the organization supports the new strategies. Rather than overhauling the entire organization, explore with your management team how you can approximate an ideal structure with a limited number of changes.

- As you conduct your review, some existing functional groups might not fit into the new structure because they no longer have strategic significance. Plan to dissolve these groups and transfer their employees into other components under the new structure. For employees who cannot be placed elsewhere, determine how to treat these employees consistently with your value statement.

- Other existing functional groups might not fit the new structure because they perform functions that must be centralized for economic control, security, or other reasons. Include these groups in the new structure as functions that *service* or *support* the components with direct product/service or market/customer responsibilities. Such service or support groups should be shown in the structure as *subordinate* to groups with direct product/service or market/customer responsibilities.

*Organization Meeting #3: Assigning Missions
and Key Accomplishments*

- For each of the components established in the previous meeting:

    1. Prepare a *mission* statement (see examples earlier in this chapter);

    2. Identify competitive requirements and restate these requirements as critical accomplishments (that is, the critical accomplishments for each component are to meet the competitive requirements for the product/service or market/customer for which that component is responsible); and

    3. Identify the key capabilities each component will need to fulfill its competitive requirements.

- For each of the support or service components you have included in the structure, prepare a mission statement, statement of competitive requirements, and statement of key capabilities.

- The result of your third meeting should be a new organizational chart with statements regarding mission, competitive requirements, and key capabilities for all components in the new organization.

Summary

In this chapter, we have discussed the first step in implementing values and strategies developed in chapter 3. We discussed the gap between strategies and behavior and talked of the importance of clearly defined missions and accomplishments as a way of bridging that gap. We discussed the necessity of restructuring the organization to align the structure with strategic objectives. Finally, we showed how, as a result of this restructuring, clear missions and accomplishments are identified for each organizational unit. In the next chapter, we will show how *measures* can be developed from these missions and accomplishments.

Chapter 5

How to Develop Performance Measures

In chapter 3, we discussed how values and strategies are developed and communicated. In the last chapter, we took the discussion further to the development of a performance organization where each component or unit had a clearly defined mission and key accomplishments to attain. With values, strategies, missions, and accomplishments identified and understood by employees at every level, we have provided the basic information necessary to support exceptional performance. But this information alone is rarely sufficient to guarantee superior performance. As we noted in chapter 1, employees need to know not only what must be done and why but also what is currently being done and how current performance compares to expectations. To support the latter, we must develop measures of performance; we must set goals and create an information system to provide regular feedback on performance. In this chapter, we discuss the first of these final steps toward providing employees with adequate information—developing measures.

The Failure of Measurement

"What gets measured gets done." "If you can't measure it, you can't manage it, because you won't know if it improves." These two axioms of management are widely known, understood, and accepted by all experienced managers. Of course we need measurements. How can we manage without them? Measures provide direction—what gets measured gets done. Measures also provide confirmation—you know if it improves. All of us as managers accept the importance of measurement, and we do measure—but poorly.

We have heard much about the importance of measurement, and we see a lot of reports containing a lot of numbers. But we meet very few managers who have good measurement systems. If performance measurement is so widely accepted and so important, why is it so poorly done? We actually see two types of problems with measurement, depending upon whether our client is manufacturing or service oriented.

Why Measurement Fails in Manufacturing

Manufacturing clients inevitably use lots of measurements. Everything at every point is measured—efficiency, scrap, rejects, first quality, costs, absenteeism, turnover, uptime, downtime, maintenance, on-time shipments, customer returns, department efficiency, shift efficiency, line efficiency, materials usage, waste, parts usage, changeovers, direct labor costs, labor cost variance, overtime, indirect cost, fringes, parts cost, material costs, operator efficiency, machine utilization, rework, first quality after rework, energy usage, and so on. Manufacturing managers stack reams of computer printouts and manual reports in front of us when we ask for measures. Not infrequently, at least one person, and sometimes a whole staff, at a plant does nothing but compile and publish these numbers for today, this week, this month, this quarter, this year, compared to yesterday, last week, last month, last quarter, last year. The one thing manufacturing managers don't lack are measures (or more precisely, numbers). What is wrong with them?

We see several problems. First, most manufacturing managers have too many measures. Though a few manufacturing managers can quote from memory an amazing array of statistics on their operations, most are simply overwhelmed. Key measures are buried in a mass of detail and scattered throughout numerous isolated reports. Often, these reports were prepared by different people at different times, cover different reporting periods, and possibly conflict with each other. There is no systematic focus for the piles of paper and columns upon columns of numbers. As a result, most of what is produced goes completely unused or is underutilized. To sort out the important from the less important, manufacturing managers tend to give serious attention only to a fraction of what is produced. This month or quarter, their primary concern might be for quality indicators. As a result, the quality reports get excessive scrutiny. Next month or next quarter, their attention shifts to financial reports and cost indicators. At another time, the focus is on production volume and efficiency indicators. The focus changes from month to month, quarter to quarter, year to year, and usually it changes based upon upper management's most recent area of concern. The classic example is the manufacturing manager who knows his production and efficiency numbers by heart but gets yelled at in the senior managers' meeting about his quality. The next month, this manager knows his quality numbers by heart and has prepared elaborate excuses for his poor quality, only to be admonished about runaway manufacturing costs. For this manager and for many manufacturing managers, what is going to be important to upper management next is a constant guessing game.

But more is wrong with the typical manufacturing measurement and reporting system than just the overwhelming volume of numbers. Many, if not most, of these numbers (or at least the calculation methods) are outdated. They might have little direct relationship to current corporate strategies. It is not unusual to find that the strategic emphasis has changed but that the measurement and reporting systems have not. Since measurement and reporting systems are inevitably developed in isolation and over a period of time, the various extant systems most likely reflect different assumptions and different concerns. In the worst cases, no one knows why or how a report was first created. Even those who produce the report (particularly automated reports) might not fully understand how some numbers are derived. It is not unusual to find that the only person who fully understood the report has long since left the company. Even if that person was still available, in all likelihood he or she is a lower level employee with limited knowledge about current business strategies and with excessive concern about mathematical precision and sophistication. Operating from limited knowledge concerning what is really important, this person creates elaborate routines for data collection and manipulation that yield final totals so abstract that they bear little, if any, relationship to the real objectives of the business.

Why Measurement Fails in White-Collar/Service Companies

In sharp contrast to manufacturing managers, white-collar/service industry managers are forced to run their businesses with little beyond basic financial measurements. Those who have attempted to develop meaningful measures of performance, particularly for knowledge-worker professionals, have met considerable resistance from employees and other managers. As a result, most have given up. These efforts fail for two reasons. First, these white-collar managers attempt to apply measures that have been used successfully in manufacturing but are totally inappropriate for a white collar/service environment. Typically, there is excessive concern with developing input/output productivity or efficiency measurements at the level of individual employees, yet data to support individual measures rarely exist in the white-collar area. Most white-collar work is not performed by individual employees but by employees working in groups, thus individual measurement is inappropriate. Also, except in low level clerical jobs where the work performed mimics the conversion or processing of a manufacturing environment, input/output productivity ratios are inappropriate. For the white-collar/knowledge-worker employee, the only input is "information" and the only output is "judgment," neither of which is easily quantifiable. Finally, in white-collar/service organizations, attempts at measurement fail because of an obsessive concern with finding a single, all-encompassing measurement of performance when, because of the nature of white-collar work with its variety and complexity, no such single measure is possible.

In our opinion, the failure of white-collar/service managers to develop meaningful measures of performance can be attributed to a number of myths about measurement that appear almost self-perpetuating. Until these myths are destroyed, we will never be able to develop significant and meaningful measures in white-collar environments. Here are some of the myths that continue to stand in our way.

Myth No. 1: "You can't measure creativity or judgment, therefore a meaningful measurement of what we do can't be developed." It is true that "creativity" and "judgment" are extremely difficult to measure, if they can be measured at all. Yet few, if any, businesses exist for the purpose of providing "creativity" and "good judgment." Almost all businesses exist to provide a product or service to meet the needs of a customer. Though "creativity" and "good judgment" might be invaluable in providing the product or service, they are by no means an end in and of themselves. Performance measures should be designed to report changes in the product or service provided, particularly as these changes relate to the satisfaction of the customer, whether the customer is the ultimate "external" customer or an "internal" customer within the company.

Myth No. 2: "It isn't possible to develop a measure that will truly reflect the performance of this group." No single measure is likely, in and of itself, to be satisfactory in the white-collar arena. All measures are only indicators of performance. Usually, it is necessary to have a "family of measures," which taken together provide meaningful information about current levels of performance. The search for a single, ideal measure will inevitably result in no measure being developed.

Myth No. 3: "This measure is misleading. It fails to consider those things beyond our control." All measures are only useful for indicating changes in level of performance. Rarely is it possible to develop a measure that excludes all extraneous factors. A measure cannot be expected to explain a change, only to indicate when a change occurs. Any attempt to charge every measure with not only the responsibility for reporting changes but also with explaining why they occur dooms the measurement program to failure at the start.

Myth No. 4: "We need a more sophisticated measure." Though complicated measures are elegant and intellectually stimulating for some, most of us find them frustrating and confusing. It is important to keep measures as simple as possible, particularly when the results of the measurement will be shared with large numbers of people. We advise our clients to keep measures as close to the real world as possible. The best measure is simple, easy to understand, and easy to relate to what employees do (behavior) on a day-to-day basis.

Myth No. 5: "Measurement is easy when the job is manufacturing widgets. Then you have something to count. But our job is to provide a service. There is nothing to count." Obviously it is easier to measure performance when there is a product that can be physically counted. Yet it is incorrect to say that service delivery results in no countable by-products. Schedules are met or not met. Complaints are received or not received. Customers are served or not served. Costs are controlled or not controlled. There are many "results" from providing services that are countable and that can serve as indicators of the level of service provided. The provision of service involves doing something. That's why we pay people. Whenever people do something, there is an action, event, or behavior that can be counted.

Myth No. 6: "Since all measures are corruptible, it is a waste of time to develop them. Somebody will always find a way to beat the system." There is no measure sufficiently pure that no one can find a way to corrupt the numbers to his or her own benefit. Yet it is usually possible to make the effort required to corrupt the measure more trouble than it is worth. Also, when measurement is used in a positive and constructive manner rather than in a negative or punishing way, most people quickly lose their fear of being measured. Rather than wanting to trick the system, most want fair, objective measurement of their performance. Most of us really do not like to cheat, and we resort to cheating only when we believe the measurement will be used unfairly or to punish us.

Myth No. 7: "It's just not possible to measure what we do. There are undefined or intangible aspects of our job that cannot be measured." Almost every job has components that are difficult, if not impossible, to measure without resorting to considerable trouble and expense. This does not mean that the measurable components should be ignored. Measures should be developed when it is possible to do so. Also, often the intangible or difficult to measure parts of jobs lead to results that can be measured, and results are more important.

Guidelines for Developing Measures of Performance

So far, the discussion paints a rather bleak picture of the status of measurement, both in manufacturing and in the white-collar/service sector. Yet we know that having meaningful measures of performance is critical if we are to get maximum performance from employees. How, then, do we develop the measures we need when our previous efforts have failed? A place to start is with some fundamental guidelines for measurement.

Measurement Guideline No. 1: "All measures should be accomplishment based." In the previous chapter, we discussed the importance of having clearly identified missions and key accomplishments for each organizational unit. The mission of every component in the performance organization, as you will recall, was to provide products or services to meet the needs of identified markets or customers, either internal or external to the company. The key accomplishments of each unit were to fulfill the competitive requirements for those products/services it provided and markets/customers it served. Having developed values, strategies, missions, and accomplishments, we now have a starting point for developing measures. In the past, values, strategies, missions, and accomplishments were not clearly identified, and we were developing measurements before we knew what we wanted to measure. With clearly identified accomplishments, developing measures becomes simply an effort to quantify the extent to which each key accomplishment is or is not achieved. Later, we will see how, given a clearly identified accomplishment, we can move easily and naturally to one or more measures of the achievement or the failure to achieve that accomplishment.

Measurement Guideline No. 2: "Develop group or team-oriented measures, not measures of individual employee performance." In both manufacturing and white-collar/service companies, the difficulty of developing and maintaining measures of performance has been exaggerated due to our insistence upon measures of the individual employee. In the past, when work was performed by individual employees, measures at the employee level made sense. Now, however, measuring the performance of individual employees no longer makes much sense. Most American workers today are white-collar or service workers, and there are few, if any, white-collar jobs where the work of an individual employee doesn't impact and isn't impacted by the work of other employees. Even in manufacturing environments, with increased levels of automation employees no longer work in isolation. In fact, today most of us work with other employees as members of a team. It is through team effort that meaningful results are achieved. Thus, it only makes sense that we measure at the level where results are achieved—at the team or group level. When we move to the team level, measurement becomes easier since data is more readily available, fewer calculations have to be performed, and employees more readily accept measures because measurement is no longer personal.

Measurement Guideline No. 3: "When developing measures, seek a level of precision sufficient for the purposes of the measurement, and use a family of measures rather than try to force one measure to serve as the ultimate indicator." What level of precision do we need in a measure? We need a measure adequate for its intended purpose. If that measure is a single indicator, then we need a high level of precision to ensure we are not misled by some aberration in the underlying data or calculation algorithms. However, if we have a family of measures (multiple measures), and if these measures are easy to calculate and easy to understand, then no single indicator in the family need be as precise since the other measures will confirm or deny the results suggested by any one indicator.

Measurement Guideline No. 4: "As with the organization structure, measures should be reviewed and changed, if necessary, when strategies change." No set of measures will last forever, and we should have no reluctance to discard measures when our business changes or we discover a better measure. In our work with managers, we are constantly amazed at the almost mystical quality measurements developed and the reluctance to change or discard a measure. Yet a measure has value only to the extent that it supplies information enabling us to make better decisions. You should review all your measures in light of your current strategies, missions, and key accomplishments at least annually. Ask yourself if these measures are still the best indicators of the accomplishments that are now important. Discard or change any measures that do not pass this test.

A Guide to Developing Accomplishment-Based Measures

In previous chapters, you worked with your management team in developing strategies, defining missions, and identifying key accomplishments. We recommend you involve this same team for developing measures. In addition, we suggest that you also involve three to five employees in the measurement development process. Involving employees at this stage is important since the measures you develop will be a major vehicle for communicating with employees, and in most instances you will depend upon employees to generate the raw data necessary to support the measures. If you successfully involve employees at this stage, you are more likely to develop measures that will be widely accepted and understood.

As with developing strategies, missions, and so on, your work in developing measures will be accomplished through a series of meetings that you will conduct. For most of the members of your measurement development team, attending these meetings will be routine. By this time, hopefully your team has developed its own style of working together. Also by this time, you have probably become more comfortable with your role of coaching and facilitating these meetings. But don't let your level of comfort overshadow some major differences between the measurement development meetings and those you conducted earlier.

With the measurement development meetings, you have not only increased the size of the group, but you have also introduced employees into the group. If you followed our suggestions, your previous meetings involved five to nine members, most of whom were managers or supervisors. Given the three to five employees you are adding to this team, you are now conducting meetings with eight to fourteen people. Because of the increased number of people, the meetings will be longer, and it may be more difficult to reach a consensus. Try to resist the temptation to "move things along" by taking over the meeting and making all the decisions. You shouldn't allow the meetings to wander aimlessly off track, but neither should you cut off discussion prematurely. As long as the discussion is related to the question at hand, allow it to continue so that consensus can be reached. Our experience is that the time allotted for discussion and agreement up-front is more than recouped during implementation.

Also, you must recognize that, since employees are being added to the meeting, you will have to create an open climate to ensure their active participation. If your company's culture emphasizes status or levels or discourages informal communication between levels, you might find that employees are reluctant to voice their opinions and that higher levels dominate the discussion and even actively exclude employees from the discussion. To reap the benefits of employee involvement and participation, however, you must break down these barriers. Some ways to do this are:

1. Set the expectation at the first meeting that you want everyone's full participation regardless of level or position.

2. In selecting employees to participate in the measurement development process, pick employees who are experienced, have a good reputation for performance, want to participate, and are likely to be secure in their positions and willing to voice their opinions.

3. During the meetings, encourage employees to talk by asking specifically for their opinions and by probing for more detail if the answers to your questions are short "yes/no" responses. When you get responses, reinforce the behavior by thanking them for their suggestions and comments.

To develop measures, we suggest that you conduct five meetings, each of which can extend over several days.

Measurement Meeting #1: Introduction and Planning

- Review progress to this point:

    1. Values

    2. Strategies

    3. The new performance organization structure

    4. Missions

    5. Accomplishments

- Review the information in this chapter on:

    1. The failure of measurement

    2. Myths about measurement (for white-collar/knowledge-worker applications)

    3. Guidelines for developing measures

- Review the purpose of measurement development: To develop a series of indicators that we can track to determine if we are achieving or failing to achieve our key accomplishments.

- Review the process of measurement development and the agenda for the measurement development meetings outlined in this chapter.

- Ask the measurement team to assemble and bring to the next meeting copies of any reports or other documents that contain existing measures of performance. These should include both automated and manual reports. (This could be a sizable volume of information, but you need to assemble these reports at some point, if for no other reason than to inventory what you already have.)

Measurement Meeting #2: Identify or Develop Measures

There are many ways to develop accomplishment-based measures of performance. Having experimented for a number of years, we recommend the following three methods. The first method is the simplest and easiest, the second is more difficult and time consuming, and the last is the most difficult and time consuming. Therefore we suggest you start with the first method and proceed to the second and third only if you are unable to reach consensus on a measure.

Regardless of the method you use, we suggest you first develop measures for the highest level of the organization and proceed down from there. At each level, you should take one key accomplishment at a time (as you developed them in the last chapter) and develop one or more measures for that accomplishment before moving on to the next accomplishment. Thus, by developing measures accomplishment by accomplishment and level by level from the top of the organization down, you will develop a complete set of measures linking each organizational unit.

In order of difficulty (easy to more difficult), our three methods of developing measures are as follows:

Method #1: Selection from Existing Measures

Our first method simply involves reviewing existing measures to see if any are sufficient to serve as indicators for a particular accomplishment. To do this, we suggest you use a modified Nominal Group Technique (NGT). The Nominal Group Technique is a process for facilitating group discussion and decision making that has gained popularity in recent years because it overcomes some of the common problems of traditional group meetings. Among these problems are the tendency of a traditional group to focus on solutions before problems are clearly identified, to engage in endless discussion and debate, and to be dominated by strong personalities. The advantages of NGT are that it increases the creative productivity of the group, facilitates decision making, stimulates the generation of ideas, provides a method for reaching group consensus, and leaves participants with a sense of satisfaction. To use a version of NGT to select among possible measures, we suggest you proceed as follows:

1. Arrange to have at least two flip chart stands, plenty of flip chart paper, and markers in the room.

2. Explain this method of selecting measures (from existing measures) to the measurement team members.

3. Pick one organizational unit for which measures will be selected. We suggest you start at the top of the organization and work your way down.

4. From the list of accomplishments for this organizational unit, take one accomplishment at a time and write it at the top of a flip chart page.

5. Go around the room and ask each person to suggest one existing measure with which they are familiar and that they feel indicates achievement or failure to achieve this accomplishment. "Existing measures" are those that appear on a report currently produced.

6. During this first round, ask team members not to evaluate or discuss measures as they are suggested.

7. Repeat these rounds, asking each person to suggest one measure until all ideas for measures are exhausted.

8. As each possible measure is suggested, write the measure on the flip chart page underneath the accomplishment. Number the suggested measures (1, 2, 3, etc.) as they are suggested. If there are no existing measures that the team members feel are appropriate for this accomplishment, set the accomplishment aside and go on to the next accomplishment.

9. When everyone has had an opportunity to suggest possible measures, ask if anyone would like clarification about a measure that was suggested. Ensure that everyone understands the meanings of the measures that have been selected.

10. When you are sure everyone understands the suggested measures, ask if anyone would like to suggest eliminating or combining any of the suggested measures because they overlap others or are not true indicators of achievement or failure to achieve an accomplishment. Eliminate or combine measures only if there is complete consensus among the group that this should be done.

11. When you have completed steps 4 through 10, you should have a list of possible measures for this accomplishment. If there is only one or a small number of measures suggested for this accomplishment, ask the group if they are in agreement that these are the measures that should be used. If there is agreement, you have selected measures for this accomplishment. If the group is not totally satisfied with these measures, set

the list aside for use with one of the remaining two methods of developing measures. If too many possible measures have been suggested, proceed to the next step.

12. At this point, you have a list of possible measures, but more than you wish to use. Explain to the group that they need to select a small number of measures from this list by voting and ranking the suggested measures. Prior to voting and ranking, ask if anyone would like additional clarification about any of the suggested measures.

13. Once you are sure that everyone understands the remaining suggested measures, distribute a number of blank three-by-five cards to each team member, equal to the number of final measures to be used. For example, if you want everyone to rank their top ten choices, distribute ten cards to each team members.

14. Ask each member to write the measure they want to rank and its number on the cards, one measure to a card.

15. When they have finished writing the suggested measures on the cards, ask each team member, working alone, to rank the measures from most to least preferred by assigning weights to the measures. For example, if there are ten measures to be ranked, they should write and circle the number 10 on the card they *most prefer* as the measure for this accomplishment. They then set that card aside. From the remaining nine cards, they then select the measure they *least prefer* as a measure for this accomplishment, write and circle the number 1 on that card, and set it aside. From the remaining eight cards, they should select the measure they *most prefer*, write and circle the number 9 on that card, and set it aside. From the remaining seven cards, they should select the measure they *least prefer*, write the number 2 on that card, and set it aside. They should continue this process—most preferred, least preferred, most preferred, and so on—until all the measures have been ranked. If there were ten measures to rank, when finished, each member of the team should have ten cards. Each card should contain the

number of the measure, the measure, and the rank for that measure (a *circled* number from "1" to "10").

16. When each team member has finished their voting and ranking, collect the cards and tabulate the results. You might want to allow the group a ten-minute break at this time. To tabulate the results, sort the cards from all of the team members by measure (all of the cards for a given measure in one stack), and then record the ranks given to that measure on the flip chart page next to the measure. When you have finished the tabulation, next to each measure should be the *ranks* given that measure by each of the team members.

17. Reassemble the measurement team and review the results of the voting and ranking. Ask the team, based upon the rankings, if any of the suggested measures can now be eliminated. Attempt to reach consensus on a small number of measures for this accomplishment. If, even after eliminating measures that received low ranks, there are still too many possible measures, repeat the voting and ranking process for the measures that remain.

Method #2: Selection from Sample Measures

Our second method for developing measures also involves reviewing a number of possible measures and selecting those that seem appropriate for a given accomplishment. This time, rather than selecting from measures that already exist in your organization, you select from a list of generic measures. To use this method, you follow the same NGT process described for the first measurement development method. Here are some sample measures to get you started:

- *Production Planning/Scheduling:*

    1. % deviation from actual/planned schedule

    2. % on-time shipments

    3. % utilization of manufacturing facilities

4. % manufacturing facilities at maximum utilization

5. % overtime attributed to production scheduling

6. % earned on assets employed

7. Ratio cost consumables supplies to cost production materials

8. Ratio cost parts and materials to production costs

9. % on-time submission master production plan

10. Time lost waiting on materials

11. Days receipt of work orders prior to scheduled work

12. % turnover of parts and material (annualized)

13. % accuracy order status checks

14. % reduction cost of inventory from previous year

15. % on-time issuance of daily status report

16. No. times actual shop operation starting time greater than X minutes passed scheduled time

17. No./lbs./cost delayed orders

18. % usage of internal sources for semi-finished materials on components

19. % back orders

- *Personnel:*

1. Personnel costs/average no. of employees

2. Recruiting costs/no. recruits retained

3. Training costs/average no. employees

4. Cost of wage increases/average no. employees

5. Cost of lost production due to labor problems/average no. employees

6. No. man days lost in production due to labor problems/no. man days worked

7. No. man days lost to absenteeism/no. man days worked

8. No. employees who leave/average no. employees

9. No. employees one year service/no. employees one year ago

10. No. employees more than one year service/total no. employees

11. Training costs/training days

12. Training days/trainees

13. Recruiting costs/recruits interviewed

14. Recruits selected/recruits interviewed

15. Recruits accepting/offers made

16. No. recruits remaining on job twelve months/no. recruits accepting employment

17. No. accidents or time lost due to accidents

18. Ratio supervisors or managers to work force

19. Benefit cost as % of compensation

20. % implementation of performance appraisal recommendations

21. % accuracy of employee answers on company knowledge test

22. % sick leave utilization

23. % errors in processing personnel records

24. No. requests for transfer

25. Cost of testing applicants

26. % tardiness

27. Ratio of employees available for promotion to total employees

28. % adherence to job classification/reclassification schedules

29. % new hires completing orientation within X days

30. % supervisors and managers having completed basic supervisor training

31. % new supervisors or managers completing basic supervision training within X days of promotion or appointment to position

32. Cost hours of outside training

33. % assessments of outside training submitted on time

34. % insurance claims processed on time

- *Marketing/Sales:*

  1. Total dollar sales

  2. Ratio of actual to projected sales

3. % new account sales

4. % new product sales

5. Total no. new orders, accounts, new product orders

6. Total no. accounts

7. Gross margin

8. Marketing and sales expense

9. Total sales/quotations

10. Total sales/orders

11. Total dollar sales/sales expense

12. Sales expense as % of dollar sales

13. No. sales per salesperson per day

14. Total sales/calls

15. Total quotations (contracts presented)/total sales calls

16. New account presentations/new account calls

17. New product presentations/new product calls

18. Sales expenses/total calls

19. Profit as % of total sales

20. Sales this year/base year sales

21. % previous year sales

22. Sales growth in real (inflation adjusted) terms

23. Accounts receivable/average daily sales

24. Selling man-hours/dollar sales

25. No. units sold/man weeks

26. No. new customers gained

27. Dollar revenues/dollar sales costs

28. Dollar revenues/dollar sales quota

29. No. prospects per week (month)

30. Average quality rating of prospects

31. Profit before tax (PBT)—YTD

32. Capital turns—YTD

33. Number rebuys

34. Return of capital—YTD

35. Sample (demonstration) expense—% of sales

36. Travel and entertainment—% of sales

37. Cost/no. invoices past due

38. % accuracy sales forecast

39. % pricing variations to standard

- *Research and Development:*

    1. Actual/budget costs

    2. R&D costs/company profit contribution (actual or estimated)

3. No. or dollar value of new products developed (last year, five years)

4. No. or dollar value of process improvements (last year, five years)

5. No./% hours overtime

6. No./% hours on scheduled assignments

7. R&D total cost as % of gross (or net) sales

8. % cost reduction objectives met

9. % product development delivery (target) dates met

10. No. years payout of research investment (actual or projected)

11. % product development actual/planned costs

12. Ratio no. R&D managers to no. R&D employees

13. Ratio no. R&D technical/R&D nontechnical personnel

14. Ratio R&D postgraduate/R&D graduate (or nongraduate) staff

15. Ratio R&D support/R&D technical staff

16. % turnover (technical personnel)

17. Dollar value (actual or estimated) new products or process improvements to total R&D cost

- *Purchasing:*

  1. Dollar purchases made

  2. % purchases handled by purchasing department

3. Dollar purchases by major type

4. % purchases/dollar sales volume

5. % "rush" purchases

6. % orders exception to lowest bid

7. % orders shipped "most economical"

8. % orders shipped "most expeditious"

9. % orders transportation allowance verified

10. % orders price variance from original requisition

11. % mail not metered

12. % "personal" mail

13. % orders "cash discount" or "early payment discount"

14. % major vendors—annual price comparison completed

15. % purchases—corporate guidelines met

16. Elapse time—purchase to deliver

17. % purchases under long-term or "master contract"

18. Dollar adjustment obtained/dollar value "defective" or "reject"

19. Purchasing costs/purchase dollars

20. Purchasing costs/no. purchases

21. Dollar value rejects/dollar purchases

22. % shortages

23. Dollar value orders over due/average daily value purchases

24. Dollar value orders outstanding/average daily value purchases

25. % dollar inventory/dollar sales

26. Average cost per requisition

27. Average lead time for purchases

28. Average time purchase request to issuance of purchase order

29. Ratio of no. requisitions received to forecasted

30. Vendors or suppliers % on-time performance

31. Vendors or suppliers quality rating

32. Vendors or suppliers % standards comformance

33. Stock outs per time period indexed to inventory costs

34. % purchase order changes

- *General Manufacturing:*

  1. % downtime by machine type

  2. % reworkable waste

  3. % nonreworkable waste

  4. % operator efficiency to standard by type of operation

  5. % quality checks different from standard by type of check

6. No. investigated accidents

7. No. first aids (minor accidents, uninvestigated)

8. % machine efficiency to standard by type of machine

9. No. machine stops due to operator errors

10. Direct labor dollar variance to planned

11. Total dollar variance to planned

12. % attendance/absenteeism

13. % turnover

14. % shrinkage over standard

15. Lbs. production

16. % lots completed on time

17. % lots late due to plant

18. % maintenance hours

19. % reworks or rehandles

20. % scrap by type of scrap

Method #3: Developing New Measures

If neither of the first two methods we have suggested generate appropriate measures for the accomplishments you have identified, you must develop new measures. To do so, we suggest you proceed as follows:

- Explain to the measurement team that there are only four possible types of measures that can be developed. These are:

1. Counts—The *number* of times an accomplishment is achieved.

2. Ratios—The *number* of times an accomplishment is achieved divided by the number of times the accomplishment could have been achieved (i.e., the *opportunities* we had to achieve the accomplishment).

3. Percentages—The *number* of times the accomplishment is achieved divided by the *number* of times it could have been achieved out of one hundred *opportunities*.

4. Dollar amount—The dollar impact of achieving or failing to achieve an accomplishment.

Regardless of whether the measure we ultimately develop is a count, ratio, percentage, or dollar amount, we cannot develop a measure until we have identified something we can count (i.e., we must be able to determine the *number* of times the accomplishment was achieved or not achieved). In order to have something to count, we have to identify two things: (1) an *event*, the occurrence or failure of occurrence of which indicates that the accomplishment was achieved or not achieved, and (2) since measurement is always performed "after the fact," we need a *record* that is made when the event occurs or fails to occur. It is from this record that we develop the counts necessary to support the measures we develop.

- Ask the group to brainstorm for possible events for each accomplishment that would signal (or constitute evidence) that this accomplishment had been achieved or not achieved. Here is how to facilitate this brainstorming session:

1. Arrange to have a flip chart stand, plenty of flip chart paper, a roll of masking tape, and markers in the room.

2. Review with the measurement team the following "rules for brainstorming":

The purpose of brainstorming is to generate as many ideas

as possible without regard to the quality of these ideas. Our focus during brainstorming is on *quantity*, not *quality*.

Everyone is expected to participate in the brainstorming session.

During the brainstorming session, no one is allowed to criticize or evaluate ideas that are generated (either their own or someone else's).

No idea is too unusual or too silly. We are going for *quantity*.

As the session progresses, try to build upon previous ideas. Does an idea that has already been suggested make you to think of another related idea? (This concept is called "hitchhiking.")

3. Your role is to rapidly record ideas on the flip chart paper as they are expressed and to reinforce people for their participation. Be sure that you *reinforce* participation and that you do not evaluate or judge the quality of the idea. You should reinforce *quantity* and not *quality*, since your objective is to generate as many ideas as possible.

4. State the problem to be brainstormed: "For this accomplishment, what events would signal to us that this accomplishment was achieved or not achieved?"

5. Say, "Let's roll. Whatever you say, I'm going to write down."

6. Write down ideas rapidly on the flip chart paper. As you fill a page, tear it off, tape it to the wall, and start a new page.

7. Keep encouraging people to generate ideas. The result of your brainstorming session should generally be twenty to fifty ideas of possible events.

8. After you have finished brainstorming, ask the group to review the ideas that were generated and see if any of the ideas can be eliminated or combined with others.

9. Once you have eliminated or combined ideas, hand a marker to each of the team members and ask them to go up to the flip chart pages posted around the walls and place a check mark next to the five ideas they think are the best.

10. Once everyone has selected his or her five best ideas, total the check marks for each idea and record the number of check marks next to each idea. Strike off ideas that received no check marks.

11. If, after eliminating ideas with no check marks, there are still too many ideas remaining, use the NGT process (as described earlier in this chapter) to narrow the list further.

12. Continue this process of refining and eliminating until the group has reached consensus on a small number of events, the occurrence or nonoccurrence of which they feel will signal that the accomplishment has been achieved or not achieved.

- Once you have a list of events, ask the measurement team what *record* exists or could be created that will show that each event occurred or failed to occur. If necessary, use brainstorming to generate ideas about possible records.

- Once you reach consensus on records, ask the measurement team to suggest *measures* that could be derived from these events and records. Recall that a measure is a count, ratio, percentage, or dollar amount.

- Continue this process of developing measures through all of the organizational units and all of the accomplishments until you have developed one or a small number of measures for each accomplishment.

- Once you have a final set of measures, prepare a list of the proposed measures for each accomplishment and circulate this list to both senior management and employees for comment.

Measurement Meeting #3: Review Comments and Revise Measures

With the conclusion of measurement meeting 2 (which usually extends over a number of days, and in some cases, weeks), you will have reached agreement on a number of critical performance measures tied to key accomplishments. You now have a list of proposed measures for each accomplishment, and you have circulated this list to senior managers and at least a sample of employees for comment.

In this third measurement meeting, you should review with the measurement development team the comments you have received from senior management or employees, and you should reach agreement on any necessary adjustments to the measures. To reach agreement, we suggest you use a consensus decision-making process such as the following:

- List the proposed changes on flip chart paper.

- Quickly review each proposed change with the group and ask if there is unanimous agreement to accept or reject the change. Check off any changes that are acceptable or unacceptable to everyone.

- For the remaining proposed changes, take one change at a time and ask the group to list the "pros" (advantages) and "cons" (disadvantages) of making the change. List the "pros" and "cons" in columns on a separate sheet for each change.

- Encourage everyone to participate in developing the "pro/con" list.

- Once the pros and cons are listed, check to see if there is agreement to accept or reject the change.

- At this point, it is likely that you will reach consensus. If it is necessary to break a deadlock, have the team vote on whether to accept or reject the proposed change.

Measurement Meeting #4: Developing Calculation Formulas and Identifying Sources of Data

In this meeting, decide how you will document the methods to be used in calculating the scores for each measure. You should choose a format for documentation that is simple to prepare and that will be easy for a clerk to follow in developing a report. We suggest the documentation show the following:

- The organization or unit responsible for the measure.

- The accomplishment to which the measure relates.

- The exact wording of the measure you plan to use.

- A narrative description of how the measure is to be calculated. For example, "divide first quality units by total units produced and multiply the result by 100 to get percentage first quality or (first quality units/total units) x 100."

- A list of source documents.

- An example of the actual calculation with marked samples of the source documents containing the raw data.

Since developing this documentation will take some time, you should assign responsibility to team members for developing calculation formulas and documentation for specific measures. The process of developing calculation formulas and identifying sources of data can be tedious and time consuming; therefore, we suggest the work be divided up among the members of the measurement team. Team members should work in groups of two or three on specific sets of measures. For example, a two or three member work group might work on all measures for one or more organizational units or on all measures of a certain type (i.e., quality measures, financial/cost measures, etc.).

In addition to developing calculation formulas, performing sample calculations and preparing documentation on how measures are to be calculated, this work group should also be responsible for developing any necessary worksheets, data collection forms, record-keeping procedures, and so on for supplying the raw data required to support the measures it has been assigned. Thus, in assigning measures to a team, consider whether data currently exists or whether a new data collection system must be developed, and try to balance the work load among the groups. If a new source of data must be created, developing the new system will add to the work load of the group.

Agree upon a target date for completion of this documentation development and schedule the next measurement meeting.

Measurement Meeting #5: Review of Measurement Documentation and Test Calculations

In this final measurement meeting, you should review the documentation and test calculations prepared by the work groups. Each work group will present the results of its efforts, and the entire team should review the calculation formulas and results of the sample calculations to ensure that the formulas are clear and the results are as envisioned by the measurement team. If new data collection procedures have been developed, the entire measurement team should review these to determine if they are reasonable, cost effective, and likely to yield accurate data.

The result of your efforts in this final measurement meeting should be complete documentation on the measures you will use to monitor performance on the critical accomplishments you identified in the preceding chapters.

Summary

In this chapter, we have taken the process of providing information to employees one step further to the development of accomplishment-based performance measures. We have shown why traditional efforts at measurement in both manufacturing and service industries have too often failed. We suggested some myths about measurement that stand in the way of developing meaningful measures of performance, and we provided guidelines for developing measures. Finally, we outlined a process for developing measures at every organizational level and for producing measures tied directly to key accomplishments, business strategies, and values.

In the next chapter, we turn to the development of an information system that will meet your needs for monitoring and controlling performance on these measures and that will provide meaningful feedback to your employees on performance.

Chapter 6

How to Develop an Effective Management Information System

In the previous chapters, you identified values, developed business strategies, created a new performance organization structure to support these values and strategies, determined the mission and critical accomplishments for each new organizational unit, and developed measures to track performance on these accomplishments. You expended considerable time and effort in determining precisely what has to be done and how to measure performance in these critical areas. Yet, if you are unable to create information systems through which managers and employees can receive timely and accurate reporting on these measures, all this work will be wasted. You should be able to rely upon your enormous investment in computer technology (both mainframe and micro) and your data processing (DP) or management information systems (MIS) department to meet the need for this type of information. However, you perhaps have already realized that your MIS department doesn't, and perhaps can't, meet your need for information on performance. You discovered this when you developed measures and went searching for data to support these measures. Data on a number of critical measures probably did not exist on any report or in any automated database. If it did exist, it was probably scattered throughout numerous reports and was difficult to extract and use. If you were fortunate enough to find the information you needed, if it was accurate and up-to-date, and if it was readily available in a format you could use easily, count yourself lucky. Praise your MIS department. Most of us are not so lucky. In fact, most of us find that our MIS department falls far short of providing us with the information we need to manage performance.

In this chapter, we examine the status of information for performance management in most companies today from the manager's perspective. We suggest some reasons why the information you need to manage performance might not exist. Finally, we outline the type of information system you must create to support the MPM performance organization.

What Is Wrong with Existing Information Systems?

When we work with managers to help them improve performance, we examine the information available to them. We discuss with them how they use (or don't use) this information, and we listen to what they have to say about the information that is available (or not available). Here is a composite of what we hear from managers:

My biggest complaint is that I just receive too many reports. And I still don't get the information I really need to manage the business.

Look at the reports they send me! Most of this stuff isn't relevant to what I really do to manage the business. These reports don't lead me to action. They don't provide me with any new insight about my business. They don't show me how we are doing in the areas that really matter. Oh, I guess I could dig it out. But I don't have the time for that.

I will admit that some of these reports used to be valuable, but not anymore. The business has changed. My needs have changed. But these reports? They're just like they have always been. Forget trying to get any new reports or getting the existing ones changed. It'll take years. By then the business will have changed again and I'm right back where I started.

Another thing, why can't my reports be more concise? Can't they give me a summary about what is important? The things I really need to know are always scattered throughout page after page. Sometimes I think the people who design these things know nothing at all about running a business. They use the shotgun approach. They pepper me with a mass of detail I can't possibly use. If I want to get to what is really important, I have to weed through all of the junk first. I don't have time for that. You know what I do with some of these reports? Well, I put them on the side of my desk, and sometime during the day I gently tip them off into the waste can. That's where they belong anyway.

Believe it or not, in spite of all the reports I get, critical information I need is still missing. And if it isn't missing, it will not only be hard to find but will be inconsistent with other information. Most of what I get is just bits and pieces collected at scattered locations and at different points in time. No one ever seems to take the time to pull these bits and pieces together into something that makes sense. How am I to know what to believe when three different reports say three different things? Instead of explanations, I get excuses. I just want to know the real story.

Accuracy is a big problem. Half the time I can't trust the information I do receive because I don't know where it comes from. Sometimes my people don't even trust the information themselves. On the other hand, we spend so much time getting some numbers perfect that it's too costly or I get the information too late.

Why can't they understand that being timely is important? If I get the information after I have already had to make the decision, it doesn't do me any good. But then, it doesn't do me any good either to get the information so often that I can't see the trends. It's like I need it when I need it—not too often and not too late.

When they give it to me, why can't they give me some help in seeing the patterns? Isn't it possible to point out the exceptions? Most of the time I don't get exception reports at all. But if I do, I can guarantee they will be only the negative things. No wonder my people think I only know what they have done wrong. That's all I ever see. Aren't there some good things going on out there?

To go along with the exceptions, let's build some accountability into the reporting system. I can't monitor and control everything myself. Can't we make sure that my managers and supervisors get what they need to see and that I get what I need to see? Why does everybody have to get everything? You wouldn't believe the reports we generate around here. Sure, I want to know if something is out of control, but can't we set it up so that I can see just what I need to see and when I need to see it?

And when you bring it to my attention, make it visible. Make it jump out. Can't I see some graphs and charts instead of just columns of numbers? Speaking of columns of numbers, why is it that every computer report I see is filled with numbers—bottom to top, right to left. Totals are always on the last page. Subtotals are scattered throughout the reports. Why is it that the first thing I look for is always the hardest thing to find?

I guess the biggest thing is that it is just all too complicated, cumbersome, and time consuming. If I want information, I have to dig through piles of paper to find it.

Their answer to all of this? Well, they've given me a personal computer and terminal to the mainframe. As soon as I can dig through that stack of manuals and learn how to use the things, maybe I can get the information myself. But I doubt it.

Why Information for Managing Performance Doesn't Exist

For most managers, the situation is not as bad as this composite suggests. But it is almost as bad. Why are things this way? Well, we think there are several reasons:

1. Most of the information received by managers is the by-product of transaction systems that were never designed to serve managers. Our information systems were originally designed to support day-to-day operations such as preparing the payroll, posting accounts, entering sales orders, inquiring about the status of specific orders, and so on. These systems were not designed to support decision making, problem solving, or performance management.

2. Because our systems have been devoted almost exclusively to transaction processing, record keeping, and standard business reporting, MIS/DP employees are more comfortable with and

experienced in meeting these types of needs. Few system designers are experienced in decision making or performance management. Is it any wonder they have trouble understanding, much less anticipating, managers' needs?

3. Most managers have little experience with information systems and have difficulty communicating exactly what information they need. Many are not sure what they need. All they know is that what they get is not what they need.

4. Most MIS departments have difficulty just maintaining and enhancing existing systems without undertaking the development of new and innovative systems for managers. For many companies, backlogs in applications development are tremendous. Maintenance of the existing applications consumes a substantial portion of MIS resources, leaving little available for new development. Many of these applications lack adequate documentation and are poorly understood by those responsible for maintenance. Some applications critical to the basic operation of the business are so poorly documented that major changes (and in some cases any changes) are avoided at all cost. Those who maintain such applications recognize that, since no one really knows how (or even why) a program operates as it does, any change has the potential for disastrous consequences. Upper managers, if they are aware of the tenuous nature of such applications, ignore the problem and hope for the best. Often even the basic repositories of corporate data are significantly flawed. Tape and disk libraries are frequently a mass of redundant and chaotic data. In the face of severely aging and crippled information systems, MIS departments are under a state of siege and have little time to address managers' needs for performance information.

The above paints a gloomy, but we believe accurate, picture of the current status of information support for performance management. Five years from now, we might find the situation improved. By choice and competitive necessity, we believe companies will have found or will be well on the way to finding a solution to many of these problems.

There is growing interest in and promise for new software development tools that should improve programmer productivity, shorten development time, and simplify software maintenance and enhancement. In addition, there is growing concern for upgrading the management (people) skills and business knowledge of MIS managers. Though these developments promise better days ahead, your efforts effectively to manage performance cannot (and should not) wait. To have an effective management information and performance feedback system, you must create that system yourself. In the next section, we will suggest the minimum components of such a system and how it can be created.

A Guide to an Effective Management Information and Performance Feedback System

The management information and feedback system you create should provide you with at least an interim solution to the problems presented thus far. The system you create should consist of four basic parts: Scorecard Database, Scorecards, Exception Summaries, and Graphs on Performance. Let's look at each of these.

1. *The Scorecard Database.* The scorecard database is a central repository for scores on the measurements you defined for each organizational component. In the previous chapter, you developed key measures of performance for each component of the organization. You also determined how scores would be calculated for each of these measures. Now you need to create an automated or manual system for keeping track of these scores over time. Since the data to support your calculations and scores on the measures are most likely scattered throughout numerous reports, you need to bring the scores for each organizational component together into a single location—into the scorecard database. In its simplest form, this database might be nothing more than a ledger sheet for each measure showing the name of the measure and scores for that measure by week, month, quarter, and so on. Alternatively, you can set up a spreadsheet for each component with rows for separate measures and columns for different scoring periods. Regardless of whether the scorecard database is manual or automated, there should be one central location for current and historical scores on performance for each measure you are tracking.

2. *Scorecards*. What we call scorecards are the basic reports of current scores on the measures of performance you identified in the previous chapter. Scorecards are one of the major vehicles you will use to provide feedback to managers, supervisors, and employees on a regular basis. The frequency with which these reports are produced (weekly, biweekly, monthly, etc.) depends upon the availability of data to support the measures you are tracking. However, the more frequently these reports can be produced, the better. There are a number of possible formats for your scorecard reports. We suggest that the report for each component contain the following information:

- Performance measure—A list of the performance measures that component must monitor and control.

- Current period score—A current period score for each measure— the actual score for that week, month, quarter, and so on.

- Reporting frequency—The reporting frequency for each measure. Here we assume that the data to support the different measures you are tracking are not available at the same frequency. Thus you will report scores on some measures weekly, some biweekly, some monthly, and so on.

- Goals—In the next chapter, we will discuss the importance of goals, how you set goals, and why we feel you should set three levels of goals (what we call the management minimum, short-term goal, and long-term goal) for each measure. For now, we note only that a space for recording goals should be provided on the scorecard.

- Trend—An indication of the trend in performance over time. There are a number of possible ways of calculating the trend. For example:

    1. Base the trend on a comparison of the score for the current period with that of the previous period. If the current score is better than the score for the previous period, then the trend is good.

2.   Base the trend on a moving average. Here you calculate the average score for a number of periods (i.e., four, six, or eight periods). Each time a new score for that measure is calculated, you calculate a new average score for the most recent four, six, or eight periods. You then compare the new average to the previous average. If the new average score is better than the previous average score, the trend is good.

3.   Base the trend on a statistical "trend analysis." Here you use a statistical formula (for example, the least square linear regression) to determine if the trend for a given number of periods is good or bad. Any good textbook on statistics will provide the formulas you need.

An example of a scorecard is included here (figure 5).

SCORECARD
ASSEMBLY DEPARTMENT
Performance on Key Indicators

TEAM LEADER: Tom Drake   P/E: MM/DD/YY

PERFORMANCE MEASURE	CURRENT PERIOD SCORE	RPTG FREQ	GOALS			TREND
			MGMT MIN	SHORT TERM	LONG TERM	
I. EFFICIENCY						
% Labor Efficiency	99 %	W	95	98	100	GOOD
Units per FTE	50	W	45	50	60	GOOD
II. QUALITY						
% Reworks	7.48 %	W	7.00	5:00	2:00	BAD
% Off Quality	10.00 %	W	8.00	4:00	3:00	BAD
III. COSTS						
$ Unit Cost	$ 200	M	220	180	160	GOOD

Figure 5

3. *The Scorecard Exception Summary.* In addition to the scorecard report we have just described, prepare an *exception summary* each time scorecards are produced. The exception summary is a separate report for each organizational component that highlights both *positive exceptions* (where current performance is equal to or better than the short-term goal) and *negative exceptions* (where current performance is equal to or worse than the management minimum). By highlighting exceptions, you focus on areas of performance that should be of greatest concern—on positive exceptions, where goals have been met and good performance should be rewarded, and negative exceptions where minimum performance expectations have not been met, signaling the need for some type of problem solving. In addition to reporting positive and negative exception, the exception report should also report the number of consecutive times/periods the exception has occurred. By showing consecutive occurrences of exceptions, we can provide the most recognition/reward for repeated occurrences of positive or good performance and can focus problem solving efforts on repeated occurrences of problem performance. A suggested format for the exception summary is included here (figure 6).

SCORECARD EXCEPTION SUMMARY
ASSEMBLY DEPARTMENT

TEAM LEADER: TOM DRAKE   P/E: MM/DD/YY

POSITIVE EXCEPTIONS	CURRENT SCORE	SHORT TERM	CON SEC PER	RPTG FREQ	REPORTED TO	TREND
% Labor Efficiency	99 %	98	5	w	Tom Purser	Good
Units per FTE	45	50	2	w	Tom Purser	Good

POSITIVE EXCEPTIONS	CURRENT SCORE	MINIMUM	CON SEC PER	RPTG FREQ	REPORTED TO	TREND
% Reworks	7.48 %	7.00	3	w	Tom Purser	Bad
Units per FTE	10.00 %	8.00	2	w	Tom Purser	Bad

Figure 6

4. *Graphs on performance*. In addition to maintaining a scorecard database and producing scorecards and exception summaries on a regular basis, you should produce graphs on performance for the measures you are tracking. If you maintain your scorecard database on one of the popular microcomputer spreadsheets, you should be able to produce on-screen and printed graphs directly from this software. If you are maintaining the scorecard database manually, you will have to produce graphs by hand. Regardless of how you maintain the scorecard database, we recommend that you produce graphs for all of your measures (or at least for your exceptions) on a regular basis. We recommend you make graphs a part of your regular performance feedback for the following reasons:

1. Graphs provide a picture of performance over a long period of time that is easy for your people to read and interpret at a glance.

2. With graphs, it is easy for your people to see and analyze trends, cycles, improvements, and other changes in performance.

3. In addition to providing information on performance, for most people graphs serve as a prompt (to get performance started), as well as a consequence, for performance.

4. With graphs, it is easy for people to compare current performance with past performance, and such comparison encourages competition with past performance.

5. Graphs provide a neutral source for negative feedback when the data shows that performance is not improving.

Regardless of how graphs are produced, they will be more effective if you follow a few guidelines:

1. Place the title of the graph (name of measure being graphed) in large type at the top or bottom of the graph.

2. Place the periods covered (days, weeks, months, etc.) along the horizontal axis at the bottom of the graph.

3. Place the scale for the performance measure along the left vertical axis.

4. Show "baseline data" to encourage comparison of current performance with previous performance. Baseline data is the performance on a measure before any effort was made by the work group to change the level of performance on that measure. Though there is no "rule of thumb" concerning how much historical data on performance on a given measure is required for a valid baseline, usually you need scores for a least four consecutive periods and perhaps more if there are seasonal fluctuations or cycles in performance. At any rate, there must be sufficient baseline data to show the typical level of performance before improvement efforts were started. In addition to plotting the actual baseline data on each graph, you should also draw a horizontal line through the baseline data at the level of the "baseline average" and a vertical line to separate the baseline from the graph of performance after an effort is made to improve performance.

5. Once goals have been set, show the short-term and long-term goals for the measure, drawn as solid horizontal lines from the end of the baseline period to the right-hand side of the graph.

A sample graph is shown in figure 7.

A clerk or administrative assistant should create and maintain the management information and feedback system we outlined in this chapter. Avoid adding staff to perform this function. Instead, look for a secretary, clerk, or assistant, etc. can assume responsibility for this performance reporting along with their regular duties. Many of our clients assign such duties to the principal secretary or administrative assistant of each operating component.

Once you have selected a person(s) to be responsible for this reporting, see that she/he is provided with the measures and calculation formulas you developed in the previous chapter. In addition, you should arrange for the measurement team to review measures, calculation formulas, test calculations of scores, and sources of data

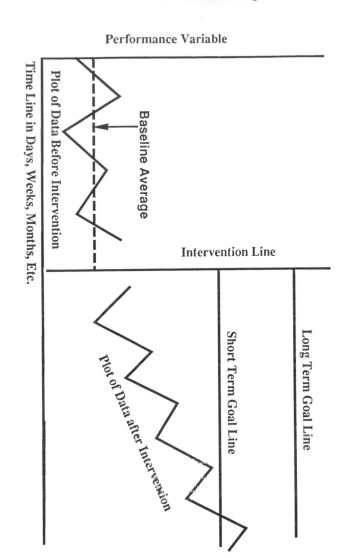

Figure 7

with this person. Finally, you should arrange to have the data needed to calculate scores sent to this person on a regular basis.

Summary

In this chapter, we examined the status of reporting performance information as it exists in most companies today. We suggested why, for most managers, the information they require to manage performance is not readily available. And we suggested what an effective management information and performance feedback system should look like. In the next chapter, we turn to the final step in providing information to employees—setting goals.

Chapter 7

How to Set Performance Goals
and Objectives

In the previous chapter, you created an information system to track performance on key measures and to provide feedback to managers and employees. We noted in that chapter that to be effective, this system should not only consolidate and summarize performance data from many sources, but should also compare performance to goals and provide managers and work teams with reports showing both positive and negative exceptions. To provide this exception reporting, you must negotiate several levels of performance goals for each measure being tracked by the system. In addition to being necessary for an effective management information and performance feedback system, goals also have significant motivational value.

In this chapter, we discuss the purpose of goals and how to develop the types of goals you need for MPM. We also suggest a process for negotiating goals.

The Purpose of Goals and Their Impact on Performance

Besides the need for goals to support the information and perfor-

120

mance feedback system we outlined in the previous chapter, why are goals important? First, goals give meaning to scores on the measures you are tracking. Without goals, you have no way of determining the meaning of a particular score. In short, goals serve as benchmarks or reference points against which performance on a measure can be compared. For example, what does a Direct Labor Efficiency of 97 really mean if there is no goal against which it can be compared? Is 97 "good or bad," "better or worse," movement "toward or away from" the level of performance that is desired? If our goal is to improve Direct Labor Efficiency to 95 or better, because we had been performing at the level of 92 or 93, then a score of 97 means one thing. But, if we traditionally perform at or near 100, and our goal is to surpass 100, a score of 97 means something totally different. Thus, a measure without a goal to serve as a benchmark and reference point is meaningless, except for showing a trend.

Goals are important for another reason though. Research has repeatedly shown that the process of setting goals and the existence of goals has a significant relationship to improvement in the performance of individuals and groups. (See Gary P. Latham and Gary A. Yukl, "A Review of Research on the Application of Goal Setting in Organizations," *Academy of Management Journal,* December, 1975, pp. 824-45.) In particular,

1. Specific goals ("improve performance by x percent") result in a higher level of performance than general goals ("do your best") or no goals at all.

2. Difficult/hard goals will result in higher performance than easy goals, provided the difficult goal is accepted as worthwhile and perceived to be attainable (whether or not it is ever actually attained).

3. Although employee participation in goal setting does not necessarily result in higher performance and improvement in goal attainment, participation does increase acceptance, particularly of difficult/hard goals.

Requirements for Meaningful Goals

Based upon the research on goal setting and our own experience in working with managers in setting goals, we feel there are several requirements that must be met if resulting goals are to be meaningful and motivational:

1. Goals should be challenging. They should represent a significant improvement of current/typical levels of performance.

2. Although challenging, at the same time goals should be perceived as attainable. There must be a balance between the level of difficulty and the achievability of goals. Goals that are perceived as too difficult or too easy lose their motivational value.

3. Although participation in and of itself will not guarantee that performance will improve or goals will be attained, there should be widespread employee participation in setting goals. Such participation will result in greater acceptance of more difficult goals and in a higher commitment to goal attainment.

4. The level of difficulty of a particular goal should correspond to its relative importance in meeting compelling business needs. Employees will accept (and quite often find a way to meet) extreme challenges when as they see a direct relationship between the goal and a compelling business reason that justifies the sacrifice to attain that goal.

5. Multiple goals should be set for each measure to establish a range within which performance on a given measure can be expected to vary. We know that scores on any given measure will vary from reporting period to reporting period simply as a result of random fluctuation. Regardless of how well we manage, we can never completely eliminate some variation. Even the most highly sophisticated and highly automated manufacturing processes are inherently variable. No two products produced using the same process will be exactly the same. Fortunately for us as managers, a certain degree of variation is accepted in any work product. It is thus acceptable for scores on any measure to vary to some

extent from reporing period to reporting period, as long as that variation stays within certain predefined limits. Additionally, since we know that scores on measures will always vary to some extent from reporting period to reporting period, minor changes do not necessarily mean that performance is "better" or "worse." Multiple goals are important because they specify the limits within which performance is expected to vary.

Why the Typical Method of Setting Goals Doesn't Work

The above requirements specify some simple rules of setting goals—make them challenging but attainable, allow ample participation by employees in setting goals, ensure that the level of difficulty corresponds to the relative importance of the measure, and set multiple goals to provide a range within which a certain degree of variation is acceptable. Yet typically we find that most (and in some cases all) of these requirements are violated.

Frequently, particularly in manufacturing environments, we find standards rather than goals. The work process has been studied by an industrial engineer, and a standard rate has been set. Usually this standard is the "normal pace." How much can an average worker produce on an average day?

If no standards have been set through some type of formal study, then a "national" or "industry" standard rate might have been selected as the goal. The goal might be to match a competitor's performance. Alternatively, upper management might have arbitrarily set a goal at 2, 5, or 10 percent higher than last year's average.

Regardless of how goals are typically set, they usually violate the basic requirements for meaningful and motivating goals, for there is little or no participation or involvement by employees. The goals are imposed by management. As a result, there is little, if any, employee ownership, acceptance, or commitment to meeting the goals. Frequently, the goals are either not challenging or are perceived by employees to be unattainable.

Engineered time standards usually represent the normal or average pace for many employees and fall far short of what potentially could be attained. Depending upon current levels of performance, national or industry standards might be no more challenging than engineered standards or might be perceived by employees as so challenging that they are impossible to attain. Similar problems are associated with dictated percentage improvements based on previous years.

In defense of traditional practices, the task of setting goals has always been difficult. Most of us would agree with the research findings that goals must be challenging but attainable; yet how do we determine what is a challenging and/or attainable level of performance without engineered standards, national or industry comparisons, and/or comparisons with previous years? Most of us would agree (at least in theory) that participation is good, but how do we control that participation? If we allow employees too much control in setting goals, won't they have a vested interest in holding goals/standards to minimum levels? How do we gauge the relative difficulty of any goal, much less match levels of difficulty with the importance of a given measure? Finally, if we have difficulty just setting challenging but attainable minimum standards, how are we to set a range of goals?

All these problems are real. Perhaps we can simplify the process of setting goals if we make some assumptions:

1. We could begin by agreeing that our purpose in setting goals is to obtain continued improvement over the long term. Certainly, given the competitive business climate of the 1980s and 1990s, we cannot assume that we will ever reach a level of performance beyond which further improvement is unnecessary. In short, we must continue to get better and better.

2. We might agree that, at least over the long term, we must strive for a level of performance that is equal to or better than that of our competitors.

3. We might agree that the only way to gauge how challenging or attainable a goal is would be to compare the goal to our previous performance. At a minimum, a challenging goal for us must be something better than our current or typical performance. And we could probably agree that a goal is attainable if we have reached that level of performance at least once in the past.

4. We might agree that since performance improvement must be continuous if we are to be competitive, our minimum expectation should be that performance over the long term does not

deteriorate, and that over the short term our performance is not worse than any we have experienced in the past, except for normal fluctuations, seasonality, and the like.

5. We might also agree that since our performance organization is designed to help us achieve our competitive requirements (as discussed in chapter 3), we should look to these requirements to gauge the relative importance of each measure and the relative difficulty of the goals associated with each measure. In short, if better performance on the measure helps us be competitive, it is then more important to set challenging goals for that measure.

6. Finally, we might agree that participation should be limited by the above five assumptions. We then need not discuss all possible goals that could be set, only those alternatives consistent with these assumptions.

We suggested the above assumptions about goals because we have found that they simplify the process of setting goals. Additionally, we have found that when we present these assumptions, most managers, supervisors, and employees accept them as a valid starting point for goal setting. Also, these assumptions allow us to meet most of the requirements for meaningful goals that we listed earlier in this chapter. By agreeing to these assumptions, we have a basis for determining if a goal is challenging and attainable; we can allow for meaningful participation; and we have some guidelines for deciding the relative importance of a measure and the resultant difficulty of the associated goals. You will notice that we still have not addressed the requirement for multiple goals. In the next section, we look at that requirement.

Why Multiple Goals Are Needed for Each Measure

Traditionally in setting goals, most of us have focused on reaching agreement on one goal for each measure of performance. Sometimes this goal was really the standard or minimum level of performance expected. Any performance better than the standard was good, any worse than the standard was a problem. Sometimes, instead of a standard, we focused upon reaching agreement on a single goal for each measure we hoped to attain during a year, quarter, and so on. There was no minimum level of performance, only a goal for something better than current performance. Regardless of what type of goal we set—a minimum standard, a short-term goal for a month or quarter, or a long-term goal for a year or more—we only set one goal.

As we noted earlier, the problem with a single goal for each measure is that it ignores random fluctuations in scores. With a single goal, we have no way of determining whether fluctuations mark significant changes in performance. We might be fooled by this random variation into believing that performance has improved or deteriorated when, in fact, there has been no change. Because of random fluctuation, then, we listed multiple goals as one of our five requirements for meaningful goals. But what are these multiple goals, and how do they work?

The concept of multiple goals requires setting three levels of goals for each measure of performance. These three levels are:

1. *The long-term goal*—The long-term goal is the level of performance sought over a period of one to two years. Usually this level is significantly better than current performance. In some cases, the long-term goal is the ultimate level of performance, such as "zero defects" or "zero absenteeism." Unlike the other two goals (described below), the long-term goal can be dictated by management without regard to past performance or to whether the long-term goal is currently perceived as attainable.

2. *The short-term goal*—The short term goal is the level of performance desired and perceived as being attainable with some effort within a period ranging from three months to one year. At the end of that time, short-term goals are reevaluated based upon performance. The expectation is that when the short-term goal is consistently being met, it will be moved closer to the long-term goal. The short-term goal must conform to the following criteria: (1) it must be less than or equal to the long-term goal; (2) it cannot be better than the best performance ever achieved; and (3) it must be better than the current average or typical performance. Short-term goals are negotiated. Usually employees and lower level managers recommend and develop short-term goals subject to approval by upper management.

3. *Minimum or standard*—The minimum or standard is the cut-off point for signaling the existence of or potential for a performance problem. Like short-term goals, minimums or standards are set for a limited period but for longer duration—perhaps one to two years. At the end of that time, minimums/standards are reviewed based upon performance experience, with the expectation that they will be raised. Minimums/standards are negotiated like short-term goals and must conform to the following criteria: (1) they must be less than or equal to current average/typical performance; and (2) they cannot be worse than the worst performance for any previous period.

The purpose of the three levels of goals for each measure—long term, short term, and minimum/standard—is to specify the ultimate level of performance desired by management and to define a range of performance within which scores on measures may fluctuate without triggering an exception situation, either positive or negative. The long-term goal is the ultimate level of performance set by upper management. The short-term goal and minimum/standard are positive and negative cut-off points negotiated by managers and employees. If performance equals or is better than the short-term goal, then a definite improvement has occurred. If performance equals or is worse than the minimum/standard, performance has declined and some corrective action is required.

In chapter 6, we suggested a management information and performance feedback system consisting of two types of reports for each component—scorecards and exception summaries. We recommended that you reserve space on the scorecards for goals, and our sample scorecard showed space for minimums/standards, short-term goals, and long-term goals. We explained that the exception summaries were intended to show positive and negative exceptions. After you set short-term goals and minimums/standards, you can create an exception report by doing the following each time scorecards are produced:

1. Compare the current score on the scorecard to the short-term goal. If the current score is equal to or better than the short-term goal, that measure is a positive exception and should be shown as such on the exception report.

2. Compare the current score on the scorecard to the minimum/standard. If the current score is equal to or worse than the minimum/standard, that measure is a negative exception and should be shown as such on the exception report.

3. If the current score for a measure on the scorecard is neither positive nor negative, then any change in the current score from previous performance is a random variation and can be ignored. In other words, there has been no significant change in performance on that measure.

A Guide to Setting Goals

We suggest that you work with your measurement team (the same people who developed measures) to set goals. Again, you will be conducting a series of meetings with this team.

Goal Setting Meeting #1: Introduction and Planning

- Review the following information from this chapter with your team:

  1. The purpose of goals

  2. The requirements for meaningful goals

  3. Assumptions about goals

  4. The concept of multiple goals

  5. Guidelines for short-term goals and minimums/standards

  6. The agendas for goal-setting meetings outlined here

- Discuss with your team and reach agreement on the following:

  1. The assumptions about goals

  2. The desirability of multiple goals

3. The guidelines for developing short-term goals and minimums/standards

- Decide upon the period of time for which goals will be set. We recommend you initially set goals for three months, with the intention of reviewing and revising the goals you have set at the end of that time. After your initial experience with setting goals, we recommend you make it a practice to review and revise goals according to the schedule mentioned earlier for each type.

- Starting at the top of the organization and working down, review and assign priorities to the measures you have set. As a result of your work on developing measures, you already identified as many as twenty to thirty measures for each component of the organization. Probably not all these measures are equally important, given the competitive requirements you identified. Our experience in working with many organizations suggests that there are usually five or six measures that are the most critical. Since the difficulty of attaining a goal should be relative to the importance of the measure, your first task in setting goals is to identify your five or six *priority* measures. To do so, have your team review the measures in light of your competitive requirements. If you cannot reach agreement on the five or six priority measures for each component, try using the ranking and voting steps of the NGT process described earlier.

- Discuss and reach agreement on long-term goals for each of the measures you are tracking. As we discussed in this chapter, the long-term goal is the ultimate level of performance you would like to attain over a period of one to two years, regardless of your current level of performance or the feasibility of attaining the long-term goal within that time frame.

Goal Setting Meeting #2: Review of Baseline Data

To set challenging but attainable short-term goals and minimums/standards, you must determine your current level of performance. To do that you must collect baseline (historical) data on performance for each measure.

Prior to this second goal-setting meeting, then, you need to collect baseline data on all the measures you have developed. If a measure is new and no historical data exists, you should set temporary goals (your best estimate) for that measure until you have a baseline.

As we noted in the previous chapter, for a valid baseline, you need data for at least four consecutive periods. Though there is no absolute standard for how many periods are ideal, our recommendation is that you have twice as many periods as the number of periods for which you will be setting the goal. For example, if your goal will be reviewed after three months, you should try to collect baseline data for six months. Additionally, if performance is likely to be affected by business cycles (for example, seasonal fluctuations), you should attempt to collect baseline data for at least two business cycles (i.e., through two seasons) and use temporary goals (your best estimate) until you have collected this data.

In addition to raw baseline data on each measure, you need to calculate the following basic statistics for each measure:

1. The best and worst performance during baseline—Sort the scores during baseline into ascending order. The two most extreme scores are the *best* and *worst*.

2. The median score during baseline—The median score is the score that occupies the middle position in your sorted list of baseline scores (that is, half of the scores are higher and half lower than the median score). We suggest you use the median rather than the perhaps more familiar arithmetic mean (average) because the median is less affected than the mean by any extremely high or low values in your baseline scores. For example, if your baseline scores were as follows, the median would be "73" and the average "78":

99
98
73
73   Median = 73.0
73
72
71
70

─────

629/8 = 78.6 Average

Armed with the raw baseline data, the high and low scores and the median score, you are now ready to conduct the second goal-setting meeting to review the baseline data and set the guidelines for lower level managers and employees to follow in developing short-term goals and minimums/standards. To prepare these guidelines, you can use the worksheet for setting goals we have included here (see figure 8).

For each measure, you should provide the following:

1. Worst score ever attained—Enter the worst score from the baseline period.

2. Typical score/baseline average—Enter the median score for the baseline period.

3. Best score ever attained—Enter the best score from the baseline period.

4. Long-term goal—Enter the long-term goal your team or top management established for this measure.

5. Priority—Note for each measure whether or not the management team has determined that measure to be a priority measure.

Goal Setting Meeting #3: Component Level Goal Setting

This goal-setting meeting should be held at each component level of the organization. The purpose of these meetings is for the managers, supervisors, and employees in each component to develop recommendations for short-term goals and minimums/standards for their measures.

The senior manager of each component should conduct these meetings, and all persons with supervisory responsibility should attend. If the component is small, all employees should attend. However, if by including all employees you will exceed ten to fifteen people, we suggest you select employees to participate in the goal setting, as you did for measurement development.

The component team should have the freedom to recommend short-term goals and minimums/standards at any level, provided their recommendations follow these guidelines (see figure 8):

1. A short-term goal cannot be *worse* than typical baseline performance nor *better* than the best ever attained during the baseline period.

2. A minimum/standard cannot be *worse* than the worst score ever attained during the baseline period, nor can it be *better* than typical baseline performance.

3. A minimum/standard for a priority measure must be set not *worse* than the typical baseline performance.

Goal Setting Meeting #4: Review of Component Recommendations

At this meeting, the management team will review and approve the recommendations for short-term goals and minimums/standards developed by the components. Generally we suggest the management team accept the recommendations whenever possible. Exceptions would be when the recommendations of the component do not follow the guidelines or when the management team strongly disagrees with the recommendations for business reasons. If a recommended goal is rejected by the management team, it should be returned to the component with an explanation of why the recommendation was rejected and with instructions for the team to develop a new recommendation.

As goals are set for individual measures, they should be given to the clerk responsible for performance reporting. This person should

WORKSHEET FOR DETERMINING GOALS

Performance Measure: _____

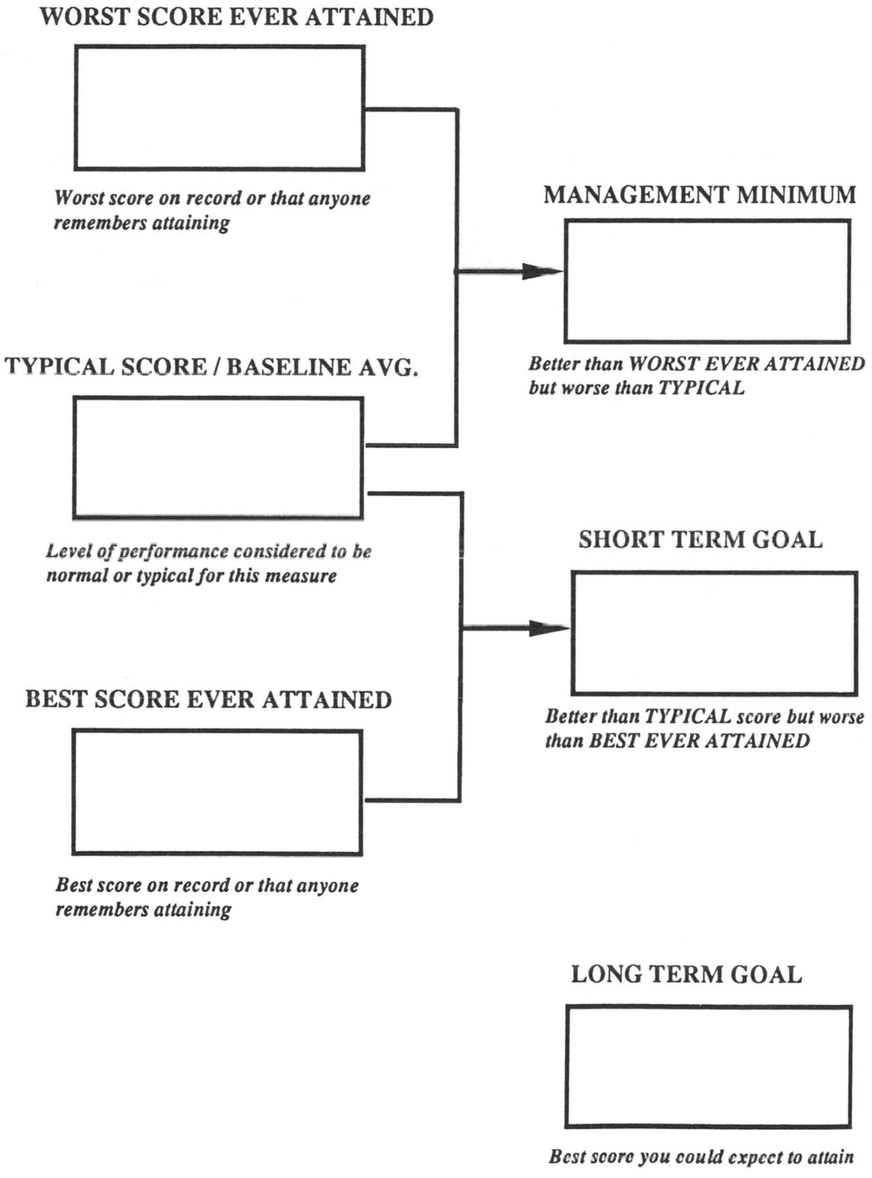

WORST SCORE EVER ATTAINED

Worst score on record or that anyone remembers attaining

MANAGEMENT MINIMUM

Better than WORST EVER ATTAINED but worse than TYPICAL

TYPICAL SCORE / BASELINE AVG.

Level of performance considered to be normal or typical for this measure

SHORT TERM GOAL

Better than TYPICAL score but worse than BEST EVER ATTAINED

BEST SCORE EVER ATTAINED

Best score on record or that anyone remembers attaining

LONG TERM GOAL

Best score you could expect to attain

Figure 8

begin producing scorecards and exception reports on a regular basis. These reports should be distributed to managers and supervisors for their use in their regular meetings with employees to provide feedback on performance.

Summary

With this chapter, we conclude our discussion of the first task of management under MPM—providing information for direction and confirmation. In this chapter, we examined the purpose of goals, discussed some of the traditional problems in setting goals, and outlined a goal-setting process that overcomes these traditional problems.

In the next section, we turn our attention from providing information to the second task of management—providing consequences for performance. As we said in chapter 1, by providing good information we clarify for employees what must be done and why. Now we have to make it important for them to do what is required. Our next chapter discusses how this task can be done.

PART 3

Consequences

Chapter 8

The Impact of Consequences on Employee Behavior

In the preceding chapters, we examined values, strategies, missions, and accomplishments. We discussed the link between employee behaviors and accomplishments for the organization. We said that each accomplishment is the result of employee performance on a set of behaviors. Theoretically, if we knew all the specific behaviors required of employees to achieve the performance results (accomplishments) we desire, and if those behaviors were always exhibited by employees, then the accomplishment we desire would always be attained. Obviously we can never know all of the specific behaviors required for any given accomplishment, since to do so would require that we know possibly hundreds of thousands of behaviors and are able precisely to link these with each accomplishment we desire. Yet it is possible for us to know a number of key behaviors and, by encouraging their repeated performance, to strengthen the chances that a given accomplishment will be attained.

In this chapter, we will discuss the link between behaviors and accomplishments in more detail. In addition, we will summarize what is known about employee behavior and how as managers we can arrange the work environment to increase the likelihood that employee behavior will be consistent with the accomplishments required for strategic success. In this chapter, we will also look at what is known about the impact of consequences on employee behavior. Unlike previous chapters, in this one we do not suggest specific actions you should take to change employee behavior; rather, we lay the groundwork for our discussion of financial and social consequences and their application which follows in the next two chapters.

Having read this far, it should be obvious that each chapter is building on each preceding one. We began our detailed discussion with chapter 3 on values and business strategies. In that chapter, you defined fundamental beliefs and constructed strategies consistent with those beliefs. Your strategies were built around the products/services you provide and the markets/customers you serve. You identified your major or potential competitors and the competitive requirements for being successful. In chapter 4, we examined the gap between values/strategies and what employees do. In that chapter, we made several important points that bear repeating:

1. Values and strategies are necessary to provide general direction but are too far removed from what your employees actually do on a day-to-day basis to be sufficient for excellent performance.

2. If most of your employees are to achieve (or at least approximate) excellence, then they must change their behaviors—what they say or do—employees are only able to change directly their own behaviors.

3. A gap exists between employee behaviors and the values/strategies critical for the success of your business.

4. To bridge this gap, we suggested you reorganize along product/service or market/customer lines and that you clearly define a mission and critical accomplishments for each organizational component. We discussed missions and accomplishments as the link between behaviors and values/strategies.

In chapters 5, 6 and 7, we discussed how measures, feedback systems, and goals can be developed based upon the missions and accomplishments you have identified. At this point, values/strategies and missions/accomplishments are being clearly communicated to all of your employees. They know what results are important and why they are important. Additionally, you have created systems to provide your employees with information on how they are performing in these areas. Yet, actual improvement in performance will only occur when employees change their behavior consistent with achieving the desired accomplishments. How do you get employees to change their behavior? You do so through your control of consequences.

Types of Consequences

Consequences have a strong (some would say controlling) influence on behavior. The nature of this influence is well established in basic and applied research on human behavior in a wide variety of settings conducted since the early 1900s. Although there has been considerable debate about the efficiency and practicality of managing employee behavior by arranging consequences, there is agreement that consequences do influence behavior and that managers are well advised to consider these influences. (A good summary of the debate can be found in Donald B. Fedor and Gerald R. Ferris's, "Integrating OB Mod with Cognitive Approaches to Motivation," *Academy of Management Review* 6, no. 1, 1981, pp. 115-25.)

To understand the influence of consequences on behavior, it is important to distinguish between two types of behavior, only one of which is of primary significance to managers in the work environment. These two types of behavior are reflex behavior and voluntary (operant) behavior. Reflex behavior follows a stimulus (something that happens to the person) in the environment. A classic example of reflex behavior is salivation (a behavior) in the presence of food (a stimulus). A characteristic of reflex behavior is that the person has no control over it. If hungry, the person will salivate in the presence of food. The behavior (salivation) is not planned or initiated by the person but is simply an automatic, physical response to the stimulus (food). In contrast to reflex behavior, voluntary (operant) behavior occurs when the person acts in order to operate on (influence) the environment in some way. Examples of voluntary (operant) behavior include walking, writing, talking, lifting, and so on. Practically all work behavior is voluntary, and it is this voluntary behavior that managers can influence by arranging consequences.

By definition, consequences are what follow behavior and determine the likelihood that a behavior will be repeated. Thus, consequences always result when voluntary behavior occurs. As a manager, you cannot eliminate consequences. They will occur regardless of what you do, even if you do nothing. Consequences are continually at work altering and influencing the behavior of your employees. What you can do is arrange consequences so that desired employee behavior is encouraged and undesirable behavior is discouraged.

When you arrange consequences to influence employee behavior, you have two types of consequences to choose from—reinforcement and punishment. As used here, the terms reinforcement and punishment have very specific meanings.

Reinforcement is anything that follows a behavior and *increases* the likelihood that the behavior will be repeated. The two possible types of reinforcers are:

1. Providing something the employee wants after the behavior is performed. For example, if the employee values (wants) increased personal time, providing a day off with pay if performance and/or quality goals are met for the week, month, or quarter would be a reinforcer.

2. Removing something the employee does not want after the desired behavior is performed. For example, if an employee wants to continue working for the company, placing the employee on probation and later removing the probationary status, provided performance improves, is reinforcing. In this case, removal of the undesirable consequence—continued probation or dismissal—is the reinforcer.

Punishment is anything that follows a behavior and *decreases* the likelihood that the behavior will be repeated. As in the case of reinforcement, there are two types of punishment:

1. Providing something the employee does not want after the behavior occurs. For example, if the employee wants to continue

working for the company, placing the employee on probation for excessive absenteeism is punishing.

2. Removing something the employee wants after the behavior occurs. For example, if the employee wants to keep a particular job assignment, removing the employee from that assignment after poor performance is punishing.

Of the two types of consequences, positive consequences have repeatedly been shown to be the most powerful and effective, yet positive consequences are the least frequently used by traditional managers. There is a seeming contradiction in this. All managers provide consequences to their employees in some way. All managers presumably want good performance from their people. Yet the very type of consequence least likely to result in excellent performance is the most frequently used, while the type of consequence most likely to lead to excellence is typically ignored. Why?

We think the reason has much to do with the timing of employee responses to these two actions by management. Negative consequences (punishment) produce a relatively immediate, although short-term, response from employees. In most cases, employees alter their behavior in the direction desired by management. Managers are fooled by the immediacy of the response into believing they are seeing meaningful changes in performance. In fact, they are seeing only transitory changes. When punishment is withdrawn, performance returns to old levels.

The arguments against the use of punishment are as follows:

- It is not likely to have a long-term effect unless it is severe and consistently applied.

- It frequently has undesirable results such as avoidance (increased absenteeism), complaining, fear, anxiety, resentment, and so on.

- It usually indicates only what an employee should not do and does not provide information about what should be done; therefore, it is not likely to result in increases in desired performance.

- It may become habit forming to the manager in spite of the above, since punishment frequently produces immediate, although short-term, stoppage of undesired behaviors on the part of the subordinate, and cessation of such behavior is in itself rewarding to the manager.

The arguments in favor of reinforcement are:

- It is likely to have a long-term effect when used correctly.

- It produces other desirable side effects such as greater involvement and participation on the part of employees, increased feelings of job security and job satisfaction, and enhancement of employees' self-image and self-worth.

- It provides instruction/information to employees about what constitutes good performance.

- Though frequently uncomfortable for managers, it eventually results in a more constructive work environment and long-term performance gains.

Notice that both reinforcement and punishment follow behavior and are distinguished by their effect on the future frequency of that behavior. If the behavior increases in frequency, then it was reinforced. If the behavior decreases in frequency, then it was punished. In short, whether a consequence is reinforcing or punishing depends entirely on its effect on the behavior, not what is intended by managers.

This rather strict definition of what is reinforcing and what is punishing presents some obvious problems for managers. If we cannot know whether a consequence we arrange is a reinforcer or a punisher until we observe its impact on the frequency of the behavior, then how can we hope to make practical use of consequences to manage employee behavior? Can we never know in advance whether we are reinforcing or punishing a given behavior? In fact, we cannot know for certain. We can, however, predict with a fair degree of accuracy the probable response to a consequence if we approach the selection of consequences from the employee's viewpoint rather than from our own.

All the above examples of different types of reinforcers and punishers cited what the employee wants or does not want. If the employee does not care what shift he or she works on, providing choice of shift assignment based upon performance is not reinforcing. If the employee does not want to continue working with the company, is confident of finding equal or better employment elsewhere, or does not truly believe that he or she will be fired for poor attendance, then placing the employee on probation for poor attendance is not punishing.

Our continued reference to employee needs or wants in our examples is important. It is this consideration of needs and wants that makes it possible to predict employee responses to different consequences and therefore to make practical use of consequences in managing employee behavior. Employees respond to consequences in a predictable manner and in a way that makes sense to them. The key is knowing "what makes sense to them." What matters is how each individual employee perceives the consequence. If, in the employee's view, the consequence satisfies a need the employee has, then the consequence is reinforcing for that employee. As managers, we often fail to alter the behavior of employees because we assume they perceive consequences the same way we do. As a result, we use rewards that are not reinforcers, and we use discipline that is not punishing, at least from the employees' viewpoint which is, after all, the only viewpoint that matters.

An example of this occurred with one of our clients. In an effort to recognize and reward good performance, the management team arranged to take the most outstanding (highest producing) employee each month to dinner at company expense. Each month, a different senior executive took the chosen employee and his or her spouse or friend to an expensive local restaurant. When employees were asked about this reward, most found the dinner to be punishing rather than reinforcing. As one young woman told us, "I'm not sure I would have the right thing to wear, and anyway, I would find it uncomfortable trying to make conversation all evening with an executive I don't even know. I hope I never win." In this case, the offered reward for good performance was not reinforcing and, in fact, might have been punishing—just the opposite of what was intended by management.

How to Determine What Employees Want

If our use of consequences to influence employee behavior is dependent upon employee needs and wants, a natural question is, What do employees want? What employee needs can serve as a foundation for positive and negative consequences?

There has been considerable debate in management literature about employee needs. For example, in the early 1900s proponents of scientific management argued that employees were primarily motivated by money and would work to maximize what they could earn. In the 1920s and 1930s, a human relations school of thought argued that social relationships at work and the attention employees received from management were as important or more important than money. In the 1940s, Abraham Maslow argued that there was a hierarchy of employee needs ranging from physiological needs (food, clothing, shelter) to safety concerns (job security, safe working conditions) to social needs (friendships on the job, acceptance by coworkers) to esteem (praise, recognition), to self-actualization (sense of accomplishment, challenge). According to Maslow, employees first seek to meet their lower level needs such as physiological and safety needs. Once these are met, the successively higher level needs—social needs, esteem, and self-actualization—become important. At about the same time as Maslow, H. A. Murray argued that multiple needs can motivate employee behavior at any given point in time and that there is no specific hierarchy of needs as proposed by Maslow. In 1972, Clayton Alderfer argued that employees had three basic types of needs: existence (similar to Maslow's physiological and security needs), relatedness (similar to Maslow's social and esteem needs) and growth (similar to Maslow's self-actualization). Like Murray, Alderfer argued that more than one type of need can be important to an employee at the same time.

All these "needs" theories represent attempts to answer the question, What do employees want/need? Each theory does provide a perspective on what needs are important, yet not one of them has been shown by research to be absolute. What does appear to be supported by research on employee needs is the following:

1. Employees do have needs, and they attempt to satisfy these needs in the workplace.

2. Although employees have a wide variety of needs that they attempt to meet in the workplace, those needs usually include the following: (1) the need for personal and financial security; (2) the need to be accepted as part of the work group; and (3) the need for a sense of accomplishment or achievement in the work they perform.

3. There is probably no neat hierarchy of needs but rather a variety of needs that employees are attempting to meet at any given time.

Our review of the research on employee needs, along with our own experience with managers in arranging consequences for performance, suggest the following as the best practical advice:

1. Since most employees need personal and financial security, social relationships on the job, and a sense of accomplishment from the work they perform, as a manager you should arrange and take advantage of naturally occurring consequences that effect these types of needs. For example, tying the positive and negative consequences of compensation and job security to objective measures of job performance appears important, since compensation and job security affect the ability of employees to satisfy their needs for personal and financial security. Similarly, you should consider how naturally occurring and arranged consequences for performance affect social relationships on the job, since most employees seek friendships and acceptance from their peers. Finally, you should consider how the consequences available for performance affect employees' sense of accomplishment and self-worth, since most employees do seek to fulfill these needs through work.

2. Since most research suggests that employee needs differ from employee to employee and work group to work group, perhaps the best advice is to know your employees. We are not suggesting here that you conduct some type of clandestine investigation, but rather that you simply interact with your employees on a daily basis. Normal exchanges during the business day and your observation of what people say and do will tell you much about what is important to them. For example, what are their personal and professional goals and objectives? Do they have any specific plans about what they want to achieve for

themselves? What are their personal likes and dislikes? What do they volunteer to do, and what do they complain about having to do? What do they spend their free time doing? What hobbies, sports, or other outside interests do they have? What attracted them to this job or your company in the first place? Was it the money they could make, the company's reputation, the work environment, how people are managed? The more you know about your employees, the easier it will be for you to arrange consequences that will influence their performance.

3. Since consequences always result from behavior, pay attention to the effect naturally occurring consequences and those you arrange have on employee behavior. Pick an employee behavior you are attempting to understand. For example, why does the employee come late to work, or why doesn't the employee perform the quality checks required? From what you know or think you know about that employee, make a list of the positive and negative consequences for that behavior. From the employee's viewpoint, what are the good and bad things that result from that particular behavior? Often you will find that, from the employee's viewpoint, the behavior makes sense. For example, you will probably find that, if the employee is frequently absent from work, the reason has much to do with the balance of positive and negative consequences. In short, the positive consequences of being absent outweigh any negative sanctions you might impose. By first understanding the existing balance of consequences influencing the behavior, you are in a better position to rearrange consequences— positive and negative—in order to encourage the employee to change his or her behavior.

4. Recognize that the power of any given consequence to influence an employee's behavior is dependent upon a number of factors, such as:

1. The employee must believe that the behavior will lead to the consequence (that is, the employee must see a connection or relationship between the behavior and the consequence).

2. The employee must believe that the consequence offered for the behavior will satisfy a need he or she has.

3. The need that will be satisfied by the consequence must be more important than a competing need at the time of the behavior.

4. The effort required to perform the desired behavior must be perceived by the employee as less than the effort required to perform some other behavior(s) that would lead to the same consequence.

5. The effort required from the employee to perform the desired behavior must be perceived as less than the effort required for performing different behaviors that would lead to different consequences satisfying the same need.

If you are providing consequences and they are not working—you are not getting the desired behavior—ask yourself:

1. Does the employee see the connection between the behavior and the consequence I am offering?

2. Does it matter to the employee? Does the employee believe that the consequence will satisfy a need that is important?

3. Is it worth the effort to obtain the consequence by performing the behavior, or is there an easier way?

Your answers to these questions should reveal much about why an offered consequence does not work.

A Guide to Using Consequences to Manage Performance

Positive and negative consequences have a powerful influence on employee performance. But to use them successfully, it is important that you follow a few basic guidelines. The following suggestions are based upon research conducted on the use of consequences and on our own experience.

1. You must continually monitor the impact of consequences on performance. Never assume that any given consequence will have the same impact on performance each time it is used. Over time,

some consequences lose their effect. Also, employee needs change and, as a result, what was once a positive consequence can become negative, a negative consequence can become positive, and any consequence—positive or negative—can lose its effect. The only sure way to know the effect of a consequence is to observe its effect on behavior. If that effect has changed, you must change the consequence.

2. Always arrange positive consequences for accomplishment. You will recall that accomplishments are the desired end product of behaviors. Since what you are really trying to gain is accomplishment (something valuable to the organization) and not behavior (which really is a cost to the organization), you should always positively reinforce accomplishment.

3. Always provide positive consequences for steady improvement in an accomplishment measurement. Again, it is the accomplishment you are after, and steady progress toward that goal should be recognized and reinforced.

4. Never provide negative consequences for failure to attain an accomplishment. The attainment of an accomplishment (some end result that is desirable) requires that employees perform a wide variety of behaviors. When an accomplishment is not attained, usually the failure to get the desired result was caused by poor performance of only a few of the required behaviors. If you provide negative consequences (punishment) for failure to attain the accomplishment, you also punish the behaviors associated with that attempt, both desirable (correct) behaviors and problem behaviors. The danger of using negative consequences when an accomplishment is not attained is that you may inadvertently suppress desired/correct behavior. Additionally, since attaining meaningful accomplishments in organizations usually requires group behavior, the employee might view the negative consequence as unfair since, in the employee's view, it was the behavior of others that resulted in the failure. When an accomplishment is not attained, your first response should be to identify the set of behaviors that are most likely to lead to attainment of the accomplishment. Then use positive and

negative consequences to shape that desired set of behaviors.

5. When using positive and negative consequences to shape behavior, emphasize positive consequences to encourage correct behavior rather than negative consequences to discourage incorrect behavior. To shape their behavior, employees must learn to perform desired/correct behavior. Negative consequences teach people what not to do. They don't teach people what they should do. Rather than punishing undesired behavior, it is far more preferable to eliminate the undesired behavior by reinforcing an incompatible desired behavior. For example, rather than punishing a salesperson for not making sales calls, reinforce the salesperson for making sales calls. If you must use negative consequences to correct problem behavior, try to ensure that you also provide positive consequences for desired behavior. A good rule of thumb is to use positive consequences about four times as often as negative consequences, at least until the new pattern of behavior is learned.

6. Time the delivery of the consequence for maximum impact. The timing of consequences has been repeatedly shown to be extremely important. The shorter the time between the occurrence of the behavior and the consequence, the more powerful the consequence is in respect to its influence on behavior. Perhaps the best example is the "thank you" that comes days or weeks after the performance of the behavior we want to reinforce. We meant to express our appreciation to the project team for the extra effort, sacrifice of personal time, and quality of performance, but somehow we never found the time. Days or weeks later, we finally get around to telling the team what a good job they did, only to be met with icy stares. Worse, we are accused of being insincere.

7. Ensure that the consequences you arrange are truly contingent on performance. Even when we provide recognition for a job well done, we often fail to make the recognition contingent on good performance. To be nice to employees, we fund birthday parties, company picnics, and holiday parties. We treat employees "Oh, so nice" and "Oh, so well." Yet these ungrateful people don't perform any better. The problem with parties, picnics, and

so on is that they are not contingent on performance. Everyone can attend regardless of how well or poorly they have performed.

Even when we create a formal program to recognize good performance, the program frequently becomes noncontingent over time. For example, the "Employee of the Month" award, originally designed to recognize superior performance, eventually loses any relationship to performance. We discover that Jane has won the award three times in a row. Sure, she still has the best performance, but we don't want to be accused of playing favorites. Maybe we will pick the second best this time. Soon, for the same reason, we are picking the third best and fourth best. Eventually, everyone (or nearly everyone) gets the award, not because they earned it but because it is finally their turn. The reward is no longer contingent on performance. Even if we don't rotate the award, chances are that the criteria for getting the award are not clear. In fully half the companies we have worked with who had "Employee of the Month," "Team of the Month," or similar awards, the recipients of the award were not able to tell us precisely why they got the award or what specific behaviors they should perform to get the award again. Unless the employee sees a direct relationship between day-to-day behavior and obtaining a consequence that matters, that consequence is not truly contingent, and the behaviors we desire cannot be strengthened.

Summary

In this chapter, we examined the impact of consequences on employee performance. We described two types of consequences used by managers in managing employee behavior—positive consequences or reinforcement, and negative consequences or punishment. We defined reinforcement as anything that follows a behavior and *increases* the likelihood that the behavior will be repeated. Punishment was defined as anything that follows a behavior and *decreases* the likelihood that the behavior will be repeated. We pointed out that whether a consequence was reinforcing or punishing depended upon how the employee perceived its effectiveness in satisfying a need. We reviewed some of the research and theories about employee needs and provided some practical advice on selecting consequences that respond to those needs. Finally, we reviewed some guidelines for using consequences to manage performance.

In the following chapters, we examine positive and negative consequences and their use in greater detail. First we look at social reinforcement as a positive consequence. Then we examine financial incentives and their role in reinforcing good performance.

Chapter 9

How to Use Positive Consequences to Encourage Performance

In the preceding chapter, we discussed the impact of consequences on performance. We said that consequences (what occurs after behavior) have repeatedly been shown to have a powerful, and perhaps controlling, influence on future behavior. We discussed two types of consequences that occur in the workplace—positive consequences (reinforcers) that increase the likelihood that the behavior will be repeated, and negative consequences (punishers) that decrease the likelihood of behavior repetition.

In this chapter, we examine positive consequences—reinforcement. We explain why positive reinforcement works best for encouraging performance, even though it is used least frequently in the workplace. We discuss some rules for delivering reinforcement, show how to schedule the delivery of reinforcement, and provide a menu of positive reinforcers. Finally, we discuss how to maintain reinforcement over the long term and how to troubleshoot your reinforcement system. Let's start by reviewing what we already know about positive consequences or reinforcement.

Types of Reinforcement

In the previous chapter, we indicated that reinforcement was anything that followed behavior and *increased* the likelihood that the behavior will be repeated. We said in that chapter that reinforcement can take two forms:

1. Positive reinforcement provides something the employee wants as a means of encouraging future desired behavior. For example, praising good performance is a positive reinforcer.

2. Negative reinforcement removes something the employee does not want as a means of encouraging future desired behavior. For example, removing an employee from a probationary status, provided certain performance is obtained, is a negative reinforcer.

Of these two types of reinforcers, negative reinforcement is the most frequently used in organizations. Yet it is the least effective type of reinforcement and the most misunderstood.

Why Negative Reinforcement (Do It or Else) Doesn't Work

Here is a typical example of negative reinforcement: John, the plant manager, discovers that, given the current level of production, the monthly production quota for his plant will not be met. He calls a meeting of his managers and supervisors and threatens dire consequences if someone doesn't get busy and do something. To ensure movement, he announces that there will be a production review meeting each morning for the rest of the month to review the previous day's performance, and that daily production goals had "better be met or else." As a result of the "get tough" policy, production goals are met. Once again, John made the monthly goal—just barely. John used negative reinforcement only and only managed just to reach production goals—a typical result from negative reinforcement.

For most managers or supervisors, the above example will probably sound familiar. We have often used such meetings and threats to get the performance we want. For many of us, this is our primary style of managing performance. To understand negative reinforcement in more detail, let's look at what the plant manager in our example really did.

First, John, the plant manager, became concerned about low production. The accomplishment he wanted was for the monthly production quota for the plant to be met. This task required a number of specific behaviors on the part of managers, supervisors, and employees that, in John's opinion, were not being performed. The action the plant manager took was reinforcement, not punishment, because he attempted to *increase* the frequency of behaviors that would lead to meeting the production quota.

Second, the inducement John offered for success was removal of a punishing situation. In this case, the punishing situation was the threat of "dire consequences" if the monthly production goal was not met and the daily production review meetings, which presumably the managers and supervisors would prefer not to have.

Finally, John's action is a reinforcer because the behavior of his managers, supervisors, and employees apparently did change and the production quota was met. Reviewing this example, we might ask, "What's wrong with what John did?" After all, the production quota was met. Additionally, John demonstrated that he is a strong and forceful manager who can "get the job done." It sounds, then, as though negative reinforcement is an effective method for managing performance. But let's look at its advantages *and* disadvantages.

On the plus side, negative reinforcement frequently works over the short term. John got the performance he wanted; the production quota was met—if only barely. Second, John probably received some personal satisfaction from what he did. He took charge, gained control, and demonstrated that he could be tough. Very likely John modeled his behavior on what he had seen many times from his boss and other managers he admires. John saw himself as finally acting like a manager.

Because negative reinforcement so often works over the short term, and because administering negative reinforcement frequently gives us personal satisfaction as managers, we often overlook its shortcomings. What are the disadvantages of negative reinforcement?

First, as in this example, when we use negative reinforcement, usually the performance we want is just barely attained. It is characteristic of negative reinforcement that we get performance just sufficient to remove the punishment, no more. In our example there was no incentive for managers, supervisors, and employees to produce in excess of the quota, so they didn't. If we are only after minimum performance, then, negative reinforcement works.

Second, the plant manager will probably find that the production level obtained during that short term will not be sustained. As soon as the production quota is met, everyone goes back to "business as usual." Another characteristic of negative reinforcement, then, is that people work to remove the punishment. Once that punishing situation is removed, there is no longer any reason to continue performing. In our example, the plant manager will have the same production crisis each month.

Also, because negative reinforcement depends upon the existence of a punishing situation (the threat of unpleasant meetings/confrontations), it shares many of the problems of punishment. First, it usually causes employees to focus on escaping or avoiding the punishment rather than on performing. In the plant manager's example, we might see managers, supervisors, and employees manipulating production reports, sacrificing quality, and/or taking unsafe production short cuts just to meet the production quota.

Finally, in all likelihood morale will sharply decline, and there might be emotional outbursts. Employees might become angry, aggressive, and even destructive. Others might withdraw and become noncommunicative. Absenteeism, tardiness, and turnover might increase as employees seek to escape the punishment.

On balance then, negative reinforcement—what has been called the "do it or else" style of management—gets us minimally acceptable performance over the short term. In its wake, it leaves an angry and frustrated workforce composed of people who do, or fake doing, the minimum. Managers who consistently use negative reinforcement usually describe their employees to us as people who "have a bad attitude," "just don't care," and so on. These same managers wish for employees who "do care," "have a desire to succeed," "are willing to do a little extra to make sure the job is done right," and "can be counted on." Yet few of these same managers use positive reinforcement to encourage the employee behavior they want.

Why Positive Reinforcement (Do It and You Get . . .) Does Work

Positive reinforcement provides something the employee wants to encourage the employee to repeat the behavior. Positive reinforcement can be as simple as a "thank you" or as complex as a monetary reward. It is a form of recognition for good performance that most managers think they use much more often than they actually do.

The advantages of positive reinforcement are straightforward:

1. It works. In research and in the day-to-day experience of managers who use it, positive reinforcement has repeatedly been shown to produce significant gains in performance.

2. It not only works, but it works over the long term. Unlike negative reinforcement, performance gains with positive reinforcement are sustained over time. Performance improves and continues to improve, or it increases to a high level and is sustained at that level. There is a continuous improvement mindset.

3. Not only does positive reinforcement work over the long term, but it works exceedingly well. Compared to negative reinforcement, positive reinforcement typically results in performance that is 20 to 50 percent better. Occasionally with positive reinforcement, performance is hundreds of percentage points better.

4. In addition to improving measured performance, positive reinforcement typically improves morale, job satisfaction, and relations between managers, supervisors, and employees. People have a much more positive attitude about their jobs, feel a heightened sense of satisfaction and self-worth, and are much more positive about their company.

5. These positive attitudes frequently find expression through increased employee involvement and commitment to the company. Employees are much more willing to exert extra effort, to be creative, to share their ideas, and to become actively involved in making the business successful.

All these advantages of positive reinforcement, and more, have been extensively documented and proven through research and practical experience. Yet, even today, positive reinforcement is rarely used. Why? Let's look at some possible reasons.

Why Positive Reinforcement Isn't Used

Why don't managers use positive reinforcement more than they do? We believe there are several reasons. First, positive reinforcement hasn't been used in the past. Most of us have few, if any, role models of managers who used positive reinforcement. Most of us probably work for bosses who don't use positive reinforcement now. Not only do we not have a model to follow—someone to demonstrate what positive reinforcement is and how it works—but most of us resent having to reinforce our employees when we aren't being reinforced ourselves. Why should they be treated any differently from us? We did our jobs. We produced, and we got ahead. They can do the same.

Without a role model and without receiving positive reinforcement ourselves, we reject its use. If we were honest with ourselves we would probably admit that, at least in part, our rejection of positive reinforcement stems from our bitterness that we never received such reinforcement ourselves. It seems unfair that, after we have struggled along in our career, the rules are changed for those who follow. Additionally, our very success is testimony that it is possible for people to perform well without positive reinforcement. We did. However most of us forget that many others did not. Of course, we had the internal drive and ambition to succeed, and they didn't. It is as simple as that. But, is it?

If we were honest, most of us would have to admit that our success can be at least partially attributed to luck. We were in the right place at the right time. We got the right assignments. We made the right contacts. Maybe we even had that occasional manager who did recognize and positively reinforce our performance when it counted most. It is likely we were in the right job at the right time. Perhaps we were fortunate enough to hold jobs where we were in the top 5 percent because we had the right knowledge and skills or abilities. Also, performing those jobs might have been fun. The jobs themselves might have been reinforcing.

Looking back over our careers, we might have to admit that, although we have been successful, others just as capable or perhaps more capable than us failed. Their performance fell far short of their potential, and the lack of competition helped our careers. But at what cost to the organization? Could those other employees have performed better had they worked for managers who used positive reinforcement instead of negative reinforcement? Most of the research indicates that many would have. Our job as managers should be to get the best performance from every employee and not just from the select few who might succeed regardless of our management skills.

A second reason we believe positive reinforcement is not used as much as it should be is because of its association with a "soft" school of management. Somehow positive reinforcement is associated in many manager's minds with being nice to people. Many see it as "country club management," where "the happy employee is the productive employee." When we interview some managers about their use of positive reinforcement, we hear about company picnics, employee birthday parties, Christmas bonuses to every employee, and so on. Yet none of these events constitute positive reinforcement, since none are contingent upon performance. The difference is simple. Being nice is not sufficient. Happy employees do not necessarily work harder or smarter, but employees will work harder and smarter if they know they will be recognized and reinforced for their efforts. Positive reinforcement is not being nice; it is giving people what they are due— what they have earned and have a right to expect.

Finally, some managers reject positive reinforcement because they feel it is just bribery or manipulation. In fact, positive reinforcement is neither. Perhaps the problem in this instance is one of definition. According to Webster's dictionary, *bribery* is "the act or practice of giving or taking a bribe." A bribe is "money or a favor given or promised to a person in a position of trust to influence his judgement or conduct." Especially, bribery refers to anything promised or given as an inducement for others to do something illegal or wrong. *Manipulation* is "to manage or handle skillfully, especially in an unfair way." Both bribery and manipulation imply that the purpose of the inducement is to encourage an unethical or illegal act by another or to inflict an act upon another. Like bribery and manipulation, positive reinforcement involves an inducement or reward for the performance of some act; but positive reinforcement is not bribery or manipulation unless the behavior you are trying to encourage is unethical or illegal or your intention is to treat your employees in an unethical or illegal manner. Hopefully your reason for using positive reinforcement is to encourage employee performance that is in your employees' and company's best interest. The behavior you are encouraging is both ethical and legal. If your intentions are not such, remember our warning at the beginning of this book: you can't fool people for long. If what you are doing is bribing and manipulating your employees rather than reinforcing good performance, it just won't work.

Hopefully, based upon our discussion of the advantages of positive reinforcement and our discussion of objections to its use, you now accept it as a valid tool for managing performance. If you do, you probably have many questions about it and its use. We will try to answer some of these questions in the remaining sections of this chapter.

When and How Often You Should Reinforce Performance

One question you might have is, "Just when should you reinforce performance and how often should you reinforce?" As we noted in the previous chapter, positive reinforcement is a consequence. It should thus be provided *after* performance, and it should be *contingent* on performance. Here are some events that should be followed by positive reinforcement:

1. In chapter 5, you identified some measures of performance. In chapter 7, you negotiated goals for these measures. If the short-term goal you set for a measure of performance is met or exceeded, then you should provide some type of positive reinforcement.

2. If the goals you set for these measures are not met, but there is steady progress or improvement toward meeting these goals, then you should provide some type of positive reinforcement.

3. Regardless of whether goals on performance measures are being met, you should reinforce correct behavior or approximations of correct behavior. For example, suppose you are measuring quality and you have set minimum, short-term, and long-term quality goals. If your quality objective is not being met, you should work on improvement by making sure your employees understand how their behavior impacts the quality indicators. Suppose one behavior you feel leads to quality problems is the failure of employees to perform the necessary quality checks at their work station. Once you are sure that employees understand

the importance of the checks and know how to perform the checks, then you should reinforce employees for any increase in the frequency with which quality checks are performed.

In summary, you should reinforce (1) when goals are met, (2) when there is steady progress toward meeting goals, and (3) when you are working on a performance problem and observe the correct behavior or approximations of the correct behavior.

In respect to how often you should reinforce performance, you have two choices. You can reinforce on a continuous basis or on an intermittent basis. Continuous reinforcement means you provide reinforcement every time the goal is achieved, when there is evidence of steady progress toward the goal, or when you see correct behavior or an approximation of the correct behavior. The classic example of continuous reinforcement is receiving candy from a candy machine each time a coin is inserted. The reinforcer (candy) is provided each time the behavior (inserting the coin) is performed. The advantage of continuous reinforcement is that you normally get a high level of performance quickly. As long as the candy is provided when a coin is inserted in the candy machine (the behavior is reinforced), and as long as the person wants candy (the candy is reinforcing), then we can expect the person to continue the behavior. The disadvantages of continuous reinforcement are that it requires a lot of reinforcers and a lot of your time to deliver the reinforcement. You have to catch every instance of the accomplishment or desired behavior and provide reinforcement. Additionally, people can quickly receive so much reinforcement that the reinforcing event loses its effect. For example, with the candy machine a person would quickly receive so much candy that the behavior of putting coins in the machine would stop. A period of time would then elapse before the behavior reoccurs—not until he or she once again becomes hungry.

Under an intermittent schedule, reinforcement is provided only after multiple instances of performance or after a lapse of time since the previous reinforcement. The classic example of intermittent reinforcement is that of the slot machine. Unlike the candy machine, the slot machine does not pay off (provide reinforcement) each time a coin is inserted. Instead, the payoff is variable, and multiple coins have to be inserted. There are actually four types of intermittent reinforcement, of which the slot machine example is one. The four types are:

1. *Variable ratio*. The reinforcement is provided after a variable number of instances of the performance. For example, the slot machine might pay off twice in a row but then not again until a substantial number of additional coins are inserted (as any of us who have played slot machines know only too well). Of the four types of intermittent reinforcement, variable ratio reinforcement is usually considered the most powerful. Its power can be largely attributed to the uncertainty about when the reinforcement will be given. For example, the slot machine player is never certain when he/she might win the jackpot. This uncertainty about exactly when the reinforcement will be provided usually sustains high levels of performance even after the reinforcement has stopped completely. For example, even when the slot machine stops paying off, the player will continue putting coins into the machine. Contrast this scene with a person putting coins into a candy machine. Since the expectation is that candy will be provided each time a coin is inserted, one or two instances of the machine failing to provide the candy is sufficient to stop the behavior.

2. *Fixed ratio*. Under a fixed ratio schedule, reinforcement is provided after a given number of instances of performance. For example, under a piece rate compensation system, employees are paid after producing a specified number of units. A characteristic of fixed ratio schedules of reinforcement is that there is a pause in performance after the reinforcement is provided. Thus, employees working on a piece rate might work hard to reach a daily quota of production, then slack off for the rest of the day.

3. *Fixed interval*. Under a fixed interval schedule, reinforcement is provided after a specified period of time regardless of the number of instances of performance. A characteristic of fixed interval schedules is that the level of performance peaks just prior to reinforcement, then drops off considerably after the reinforcement is provided. Annual performance and salary reviews are examples of fixed interval reinforcement. Frequently,

employees will work hardest just prior to the appraisal and return to lower levels once the appraisal period is over. For example, one employee told us in an interview, "I work hard just two months out of every year—September and October. The rest of the time, I just take it easy and coast." Why September and October? He explained, "You see, my annual review is in November."

4. *Variable interval.* Under a variable interval schedule, performance is reinforced after varying lengths of time. An example of a variable interval reinforcement schedule in the work environment might be visits to the work site by upper management (assuming that a visit by top management is reinforcing). Such visits might average once per month; however top management might visit twice in one month but none in others. Variable interval schedules usually produce high levels of performance that are fairly consistent over time.

Of the various schedules of reinforcement that are available, research and practical experience suggests the following:

1. If you want to start reinforcement where it has not been widely used before and/or you want people to learn new behavior, you should reinforce performance continuously until a pattern of performance is established.

2. Once employees are accustomed to reinforcement and/or have learned the new behavior, you should gradually move to an intermittent schedule. Preferably, this intermittent schedule will be a variable ratio schedule where performance is reinforced after a random number of performance occurrences.

The advantages of beginning with continuous reinforcement and later moving to intermittent reinforcement are:

1. Continuous reinforcement has consistently been demonstrated to be the fastest method for starting new behavior. However, if used over an extended period, performance will decline if, for any reason, expected reinforcement does not occur. Additionally,

there is a danger that after repeated and frequent use, the reinforcer will lose its effect.

2. If you gradually move from continuous to intermittent reinforcement by slowly lengthening the time and/or number of performance instances that occur before you again reinforce performance, you have a greater chance of sustaining high levels of performance over time. Although you will need to continue reinforcing performance, an intermittent schedule demands less of your time and attention. Additionally, fewer reinforcers will be required, and those that are used will retain their effect on performance longer.

How to Find Positive Reinforcers

So far in this chapter, we have discussed the differences between positive and negative reinforcers, why positive reinforcers are preferred, and when to use reinforcers. But we haven't discussed how you identify possible reinforcers. What exactly can you use to reinforce good performance?

Unfortunately, the correct answer to this question will probably not help you much in selecting reinforcers, for anything you do, say, or provide that follows behavior is only potentially reinforcing. A smile, a handshake, a word of praise, another assignment, a note or letter, a cash award, a trophy—any or all of these items are reinforcing to many people. But they are not reinforcing to all people. In short, there are an enormous number of things you can do, say, or provide to your employees that could be reinforcing; the trick is finding the ones that are actually reinforcing. Your task, then, is to select from the large number of possible reinforcers those that are right for your employees. To help, we will provide (1) some examples of things you can do, say, or provide that are reinforcing to many employees, and (2) some guidelines for determining whether or not these suggested reinforcers will work for you and your employees.

First, here is our menu of possible reinforcers:

1. Physical gestures such as:

   a smile
   a nod
   a handshake
   a pat on the back
   eye contact

2. Verbal praise such as:

   Thank you.
   Good job.
   I am pleased with . . .
   Fantastic, I like the way you . . .
   It is a pleasure to have you working for me.
   All right!
   Way to go!
   Beautiful!
   That's a winner!
   That is really exciting!
   Excellent!
   You amaze me!
   Let me see you do that again.
   I don't see how you do it.
   Nice going!
   What a (performance, etc.)!
   Wow!
   Will you show (name) how you did that?
   I'm really proud of you.

3. A letter of commendation

4. Asking a person for their advice or opinion

5. Providing an award, plaque, or trophy

6. Offering help

7. The person's picture on the bulletin board or in the company or local newspaper

8. An article about the person in the company or local newspaper

9. Your initials or positive comments on a graph, chart, or report

10. Letting the person report his/her results to significant others

11. Excusing the person from having to attend a meeting they don't want to attend

12. Allowing a person to attend a meeting they want to attend

13. Giving the person advanced information on a procedure or policy change

14. Giving the person increased responsibility

15. Allowing the person to make decisions affecting their own work, organization, strategies, plans, etc.

16. Giving the person a choice of work assignments

17. Providing a status symbol, such as title, special furniture, parking spots, etc.

18. Posting the names and results of people who have improved the most

19. Providing the opportunity for special training

20. Providing a special introduction to VIP's

21. Bonus

22. Promotion

23. Company car

24. New office

25. Free meals

26. Trips

27. Tickets to entertainment, sporting events, etc.

28. A party

29. Appliances

30. Tools

31. Clothing: special shirts, caps, jackets, etc.

32. Jewelry

33. Sports equipment

34. Prizes/gifts

35. Points or tokens that can be exchanged for merchandise or services

How to Select Positive Reinforcers

All of the above have been used in work settings to encourage good performance. As you reviewed this list, you probably thought of many other reinforcers you could use. But how do you select those you should use? How do you determine if any given reinforcer is right for you and your employees? Here are some guidelines:

1. Consider the age, interests, values, likes, and dislikes of those you wish to reinforce. What do you already know about them? If you think about it, you probably already know a great deal about the people who work for you. Use this information in

deciding what kind of reinforcer will be appropriate. In effect, selecting reinforcers is much like selecting a gift for someone. The more you know about their likes and dislikes—their preferences—the more likely you are to select something they will appreciate.

2. Consider what you wish to reinforce. What reinforcers match the level of behavior or results you are trying to encourage? It is important that the reinforcer be proportional to the value of the behavior or results you are trying to reinforce. Just as a large cash award would not be appropriate for reinforcing someone for coming to work on time, a word of praise is hardly sufficient to reinforce a suggestion that saved the company thousands of dollars.

3. Observe what people do frequently or what people talk about frequently. If you observe what people do of their own volition and listen to the topics of conversation they choose, you can learn much about their interests. All of us constantly send out clues about our desires, needs, wants, interests, and preferences. Try to pick up on these clues. For example, if your people talk about sports and/or attend sports events on their own time, reinforcers tied to that particular sport or team might be appropriate.

4. Ask people what they like or what would be appropriate. Sometimes the best method for finding out what a person wants and likes is simply to ask. We have sometimes had employees brainstorm possible reinforcers and, as a result, have been able to develop a number of novel and creative ideas. However, if you do ask employees, be aware that sometimes the responses you receive will only be those employees think you want to hear. If you ask, check out the answers with some of the other methods of selecting reinforcers we have suggested.

5. Look for reinforcers that occur naturally in the workplace. Special job assignments, increased or decreased responsibilities, choice of shift assignment, and so on can all be reinforcers.

A major advantage of such naturally occurring reinforcers is that they are readily available and don't require money.

6. Use trial and error. As we have said before, you never really know if something is reinforcing until you observe its impact on behavior. Thus, one method for choosing a reinforcer is to pick something you think might work and observe how the person or group responds. If the behavior you wish to increase does increase, then you have successfully identified a reinforcer. If the reinforcer you chose doesn't work, pick something else and try again at the next opportunity. Eventually you will identify reinforcers that do work for your employees.

7. To the maximum extent feasible, choose reinforcers that are readily available. The best reinforcers are those easy for you to obtain and to use. A word of praise, a thank you, a smile, a small token gift can be used immediately and require little effort. Most importantly, such reinforcers cost little or nothing and don't require any higher level approval.

8. Choose reinforcers that can be used frequently without losing their appeal. In particular, use a lot of social reinforcers such as physical gestures and verbal praise. Often, a considerable amount of reinforcement is required to permanently change behavior. Some researchers have argued that thousands of instances of reinforcement might be necessary for a person to learn one new behavior. Thus, it makes sense to reinforce desired behavior or approximations of desired behavior often. Since you must use so much reinforcement, you should choose reinforcers that will continue to have an effect even after repeated use. Generally, social reinforcers are the most enduring and the least subject to loss of appeal over time.

Never underestimate the power and enduring effect of social reinforcement even after repeated use. Verbal praise and physical gestures (smiles, nods, pats-on-the-back, etc.) respond directly to the needs most people have for affection, approval, attention, acceptance by others, and so on. In fact, most other forms of reinforcement such as awards, trophies, plaques, T-shirts, and even money lose much of their power to influence behavior if they are not paired with social reinforcers. The best advice is to use a lot of social reinforcement and to follow up with other types of reinforcers as special, added incentives.

How to Deliver Positive Reinforcers

Regardless of the type of reinforcer you select, the method in which you deliver the reinforcer has enormous impact on its effect. The most appropriate reinforcer loses much of its power to influence behavior if it is poorly delivered. How do you deliver reinforcers so that they have maximum effect? Here are some guidelines:

1. Individualize not only the reinforcer, but the words and style you use in delivering the reinforcer. The words and mannerisms you use as you are delivering the reinforcer add or detract from the reinforcer. With some employees, you can kid and joke. With some, you can even be mildly sarcastic or even use profanity. For others, kidding, joking, sarcasm, profanity, and so on is offensive.

2. Put variety into your reinforcement. No one likes the same thing over and over. Mixing the types of attention and approval you give people keeps them interested. Don't always use the same words or phrases; don't always deliver reinforcers at the same time of day or in the same location. A certain amount of variety, mystery, and surprise helps make the reinforcer something special.

3. Consider whether it is better to reinforce in public, private, or some of both. Some people will do anything to be in the limelight; others find public praise or compliments embarrassing. Ask yourself what kind of attention will work best with the person you wish to reinforce.

4. Be specific. Each time you reinforce employees, make sure you describe exactly what they did or what they accomplished (the behavior or result) that you liked. If you fail to be specific, the employee might assume that you are reinforcing a different

behavior or result (even a behavior or result you don't wish to reinforce).

5. Be sincere. Never give reinforcement unless you really mean it. Regardless of how good an actor you think you are, you won't fool anyone for very long.

6. Personalize your message. Express your approval in terms of how you feel. Why did you like what they did? What did it do/mean to you? Remember, for most of us it is what we do for others that matters, not what we do for a cold, impersonal institution.

7. Make your reinforcement proportional. The words and style you use should match the significance of the accomplishment. Don't make "a big deal" over a minor achievement. On the other hand, don't—as a result of your voice, mannerisms, and style of delivery—minimize the importance of what was done. Sometimes a simple "thank you" is enough. Other accomplishments call for a major celebration.

8. Don't mix reinforcement with punishment or asking for more. When you reinforce, just reinforce. Don't punish the high performers by immediately asking for more. Employees have learned to be wary of reinforcement. Too often they are praised only to be set up for criticism or to be asked for something more. Don't say, "I really like the way you . . ., but . . .", or "I really appreciate the fact that you . . ., now could you . . .", or "You've done such a good job on this report that I'm going to assign this one to you also."

9. Be consistent. Don't just reinforce when you feel like it. Once you have determined what behaviors or results you want to reinforce (and be sure you do!), then reinforce those behaviors when they occur. Also, be consistent over time and across people. Don't reinforce just some people and not others, and don't send mixed messages by demanding more or less behavior or results in an unpredictable way as a condition for delivering the reinforcement.

How to Troubleshoot Your Reinforcement System

Sometimes, in spite of your best efforts, the reinforcement you are providing does not work. Perhaps there is no increase in the behavior you are trying to encourage, or, more likely, you are seeing only marginal improvement. You might find yourself becoming frustrated and discouraged. What do you do?

First, and most importantly, don't give up on reinforcement. It will work. Remember, you cannot change behavior—particularly behavior that has to be conditioned over a lengthy period—overnight. You might see immediate results with some people, others may change only gradually over three months, six months, or even a year. As we said at the beginning of this book, this management technique takes time and patience.

Second, ask yourself the following questions. The questions getting a "no" answer will indicate where you need to do something differently.

Reinforcement Troubleshooting Checklist

1. Have you described the behavior or result you want in precise language so that you know what you are looking for and your employees know exactly what you expect from them?

2. Did you make the reinforcement truly contingent upon performance of the behavior or upon attaining the result you desire?

3. Did you reinforce improvement, particularly if you are asking for a significant change in behavior or a challenging result?

4. Did you provide reinforcement immediately following the behavior or result?

5. Did you individualize the reinforcement so that it really matters to the person?

6. Did you use a variety of reinforcers?

7. Did you make the right decision regarding the use of public as opposed to private reinforcement?

8. Were you specific about the behavior or result you were reinforcing?

9. Were you sincere—did you really mean it or were you just going through the motions?

10. Did you personalize your delivery of the reinforcement?

11. Was the reinforcement you provided proportional to the behavior or result—not over or under done?

12. Were you completely positive and consistent in the way you provided the reinforcement?

If you answered "no" or were unsure about your answer to any of these questions, we suggest you re-read the portion of this chapter dealing with those particular questions. Then decide how you can improve your method of providing reinforcement.

A Guide to Creating a System for Reinforcing Performance

At the end of previous chapters, we provided you with one or more exercises to help you implement some of the ideas presented in the chapter. In many cases, they were one-time activities you will not have to repeat or will repeat only once per year or so. Providing exercises to implement positive reinforcement is more difficult, since you must reinforce good performance on a regular basis for it to be effective. Reinforcement is not just something you do once, but something you have to do repeatedly. Yet we need to give you some way to get started.

Perhaps the best way to start is for you to accept personal responsibility for providing a positive work environment. You can and should have the employees who directly report to you read this chapter and perhaps attend some formal training on the use of positive reinforcement. But in the final analysis, much of what they learn about the use of reinforcement will come from observing you. Some of the managers who use reinforcement best never attended any formal training. They learned simply by working for a manager who used reinforcement effectively and was a good role model for this type of management. In effect, we are suggesting that the best way to get your company actively reinforcing is for you to be the role model. How do you become a role model?

First, decide what it is you want to reinforce. If you have completed the exercises we provided in the previous chapters, this task should be easy for you. You have already identified what your group should accomplish and how such accomplishment will be measured. You have established a reporting system that will track performance over time on these measurements, and you are preparing graphs on performance. You know to reinforce (1) when goals are met, (2) when there is steady progress toward meeting goals, and (3) when you are working on a performance problem and observe the correct behavior or approximations of the correct behavior.

Second, you need to decide when you will reinforce. What will signal you to reinforce good performance? We think a good signal is the performance reports. Each time you receive a new scorecard and exception summary, you should review the report and make notes concerning who needs to be reinforced, and why. You will be reviewing performance in a regular (at least monthly) staff meeting, where you go over the reports and display any graphs you are producing. Set aside time during this staff meeting to recognize and reinforce good performance. Obviously you must not restrict reinforcement to just the staff meeting, but if you get in the habit of reinforcing performance during these meetings, you are more likely to make reinforcement a part of your regular contact with employees outside them.

Third, you have to decide how to reinforce good performance. In this chapter, we provided a number of suggestions and guidelines for selecting reinforcers. Perhaps the most important thing you can do, however, is to inventory what you know about the background, training, experience, aspirations of the people in your organization. For example, what are their interests or hobbies, what kind of work do they like most, what kind of recognition or reinforcement have they responded to in the past?

Fourth—and most important—you must reinforce good performance. We have already suggested that you set aside time in staff meetings to reinforce, but there are other opportunities to use reinforcement as well. For example, each time you receive a memo, report, or note from one of your employees, ask yourself if the document covers something that should be reinforced. Make a habit of jotting a word or two in the margin of the report or memo to reinforce people for what they did. A simple "Thank you," "Good," "Excellent," "Great!" written in the margin can go a long way and takes very little of your time. (It also proves that you actually *read* what they wrote! That's reinforcing too!) Finally, whenever you find yourself thinking, "I liked that . . . that was good," tell the relevant persons immediately! Pick up the phone and call them. Walk down the hall and see them. If you wait to reinforce, chances are you won't do it.

Fifth, review any formal recognition programs you currently have in place to ensure that they follow the guidelines for reinforcement provided in this chapter. In particular, take a close look at any contests or "Employee of the Month or Year" awards. Contests are notorious for being poor reinforcers, particularly if they set up destructive competition, become noncontingent, are unfair (only one person can win, or some have an unfair advantage), or guarantee that only a few people will win and most will lose. (We want as many winners as possible.) If you do retain a recognition or award program, ensure the following:

1. Everyone has a fair chance to win the award

2. Winning is a result of scores on objective measures, not subjective evaluation

3. Everyone knows exactly what it takes to win (what score it takes) and exactly what they can do to win (what behaviors are required)

4. The award does not encourage destructive competition

5. Performance that results in the award directly supports implementation of business strategies

Finally, continually review your use of reinforcement and your reinforcement systems. Nothing works forever. Test everything you do to reinforce performance against the guidelines we provided in this chapter, and if something doesn't seem to be working, use our troubleshooting questions to decide what you need to change.

Summary

In this chapter, we examined how you can use positive consequences—in particular, positive reinforcement—to encourage behavior you desire. We discussed the differences between positive and negative reinforcement and why positive reinforcement is the better of these two choices. We suggested when and how often you should use positive reinforcement and provided numerous examples of workplace reinforcers. Finally, we provided some guidelines on how to deliver reinforcers and how to troubleshoot reinforcers when they don't seem to be working.

We have focused thus far on social reinforcers—praise, a thank you, a small token, and so on—because these types of reinforcers are not only the most readily available but in many respects the most powerful. In the next chapter, we turn to pay-for-performance systems—how you can, and eventually must, tie compensation to performance. As we turn to money as a reinforcer, we leave you with one note of caution: you cannot buy performance. If monetary rewards are used exclusively without the social reinforcement base we discussed in this chapter, they will not work. But when monetary rewards are added to a culture where positive social reinforcement is frequently used, the power of the entire reinforcement system is increased dramatically. In short, you must first provide the types of social recognition and reinforcement we discussed in this chapter, then add monetary incentives. It doesn't work the other way around.

Chapter 10

Pay-for-Performance: An Overview

Throughout this book, we have tried to provide you with practical information you could put to work in your organization to begin managing for maximum performance. Hopefully, so far we have succeeded. But this chapter is somewhat different. Your ability to readily apply what we present in this chapter depends greatly upon your position in your organization. If you are the CEO or division general manager, you should be able to put these ideas to work right away. But if you manage at lower levels, you probably don't have control over compensation practices. Most of us are stuck with pay practices dictated by someone else. If you are in this group of lower level managers, you might be tempted to skip over this chapter completely. Please don't.

Though you might not be in a position to set compensation practices for your company, we think you will find the information presented in this chapter of interest for two reasons. First, in this chapter we present some recent findings about the direction of compensation practices in the United States today. If you are not in a company that has adopted one of the nontraditional compensation systems we describe in this chapter, you might be soon. This chapter will give you some idea about how your own pay might be determined in the future.

Second, though you might not directly influence your company's compensation practices, you might still be able to have some indirect influence. If nothing else, this chapter gives you ideas worth discussing with those who do have the ability to initiate changes.

We will be describing here some of the major pay-for-performance systems that are currently being tried and outline some of the issues surrounding the movement to nontraditional methods of compensation. At the conclusion of this chapter, we suggest some of the reasons your company might consider adopting a pay-for-performance system and show how to determine when and if such a system will work for you. In the next two chapters, we discuss two types of pay-for-performance systems that have generated considerable interest in recent years and that we feel are well worth considering as part of Maximum Performance Management because of their documented impact on performance.

Why You Should Pay for Performance and Only Performance

In the last two chapters, we discussed the impact of consequences on performance. We said that consequences have a strong and perhaps controlling influence. Most of us will agree that one consequence for performance should be higher pay. But is it? Apparently, in the opinion of most American workers, it isn't.

In his book, *Vanguard Management*, James O'Toole summarizes the results of numerous opinion polls conducted during the 1970s. O'Toole says (Doubleday, 1985, p. 183).

Pollsters found remarkable consistency among the responses of working Americans to two interrelated questions:

When asked if they could work harder if they tried, between 70 percent and 80 percent of American workers would reply, yes, they could be more productive.

When then given a list of reasons why they are not more productive, roughly 75 percent of workers would indicate that "all the benefits of harder work go to management and owners, and not to workers.

O'Toole goes on to cite a 1983 Public Agenda Foundation national poll in which "only 22 percent of American workers said they saw any link between how hard they worked and how much they were paid, and . . . 73 percent conceded that they personally exerted less than full effort because there was no such link" (O'Toole, p. 184).

In 1986, the American Productivity Center, in its report on *People, Performance and Pay* said (p. 5):

Reward systems have a key role to play in sustaining a motivated and committed workforce. But according to many national surveys, there is a major reward systems problem in this country:

The majority of people at work do not find their "reward systems" rewarding.

Most employees see little relationship between pay and performance.

Most employees believe they will not benefit from productivity improvement in their organizations.

Increases in salary and wage levels have exceeded our productivity, hurting competitiveness.

The attitude of most American workers about the relationship (or lack of relationship) between pay and performance should not be surprising. In fact, traditional compensation plans make little, if any, effort to tie pay to performance. Traditionally, pay is a function of position or status in the organization, not performance or contribution to company goals. Market demand and equity considerations are far more important factors in establishing pay levels. Even when a company adopts a merit pay system meant to tie increases to some judgment about performance and contribution, in reality managers and supervisors often fail to make true performance distinctions when deciding about increases. In practice, under most merit pay systems the range of percentage increases is relatively narrow—varying only a few percentage points—and most employees ultimately receive increases at about the mid point of the range. Also, the amount of the possible increase (even at the high end of the range) tends to be relatively low.

Under traditional compensation systems, employees quickly learn two things. First, there is no meaningful relationship between performance and pay. Substantial increases come from promotion to a higher paid job, not from higher performance in your current job. Second, everyone should expect an increase every year regardless of company, group, or individual performance, and the amount of everyone's increase will be about the same.

The prevailing attitude of American workers toward the lack of a meaningful relationship between pay and performance, plus increased competitive pressures, have forced many American corporations to rethink their compensation systems. American business now competes in a world market. Foreign wages are significantly lower than those of American workers, and wage increases can no longer be automatically passed along to consumers in the form of price increases. Competitiveness, and in some cases survival itself, depends upon the ability of American businesses to improve productivity, reduce costs, improve quality, and increase overall consumer satisfaction with goods and services. Standing in the way of these performance gains are antiquated compensation practices that fail to provide employees with any financial stake in company performance. As a result, employees resist the introduction of new methods and technology because any productivity gains will go to owners and managers, not to workers. Employees are typically not concerned about reducing costs, improving quality, or satisfying customers because they see no direct benefits to themselves. Recognizing that something has to change, a number of companies are undertaking at this writing a wide range of nontraditional compensation systems intended to provide for employees a financial stake in improving company performance. In our opinion, these nontraditional compensation practices will be the "typical" practices of the future; thus as an employee, your compensation—if not now—will soon be in line with one of these nontraditional schemes. Additionally, to manage for maximum performance, you will eventually have to arrange employee compensation along one or more of the lines we present below. What are some of these nontraditional compensation systems? Let's look at a few.

Types of Nontraditional Pay Systems

In 1986, the American Productivity Center and the National Compensation Association conducted a national survey on nontraditional reward and human resource practices. This survey covered 1,598 organizations or operating units of organizations, representing approximately 10 percent of the American civilian workforce. The purpose of the survey was to determine if organizations were tying pay to performance, why they were making such changes, and what results they were achieving.

How were these companies tying pay to performance? According to the APC/NCA survey, they were adopting one or more of the following practices:

1. *Gainsharing*. Under gainsharing plans, employees earn bonuses tied to unitwide performance as measured by a predetermined, gainsharing formula. Companies either adopt one of several standard gainsharing formulas (Scanlon, Rucker, or Improshare) or develop their own formula. Employees and the company share in any productivity gains as measured by the formula. In addition to a formula, most gainsharing plans include some structured method for involving employees in generating performance improvement ideas.

2. *Small group incentives*. Small group incentive systems are similar to gainsharing plans, but in this case the bonus employees receive is based upon the performance of a small group instead of an entire department, division, or plant. As a result, the amount of bonus (or whether a bonus was earned at all) varies from small group to small group within the company. Small group incentives differ from gainsharing plans in that the incentive program is usually designed by the company without employee participation, and there is no formal employee involvement system.

3. *Individual incentives*. Under a system of individual incentives, all or a portion of an individual's compensation is tied to their performance. Although such incentives (standard hour, production, piece rate, etc.) have been used for some time in

manufacturing, there has been a major growth over the last five years in their use in the managerial, professional, and service sectors. During the same period, many companies in manufacturing have begun replacing individual incentives with small group incentives or gainsharing plans, as factories become more automated and greater emphasis is placed on teamwork and cooperation.

4. *Lump sum payment/bonus.* There are really two types of lump sum plans. In some instances, companies are replacing merit increases with one-time performance bonuses that do not increase the person's base salary. In other instances, companies are using lump sum payments across the board as an alternative to annual automatic percentage increases in base pay. The purpose of the latter use of lump sum payments is not so much to encourage performance as to slow growth in base pay levels.

5. *Pay-for-knowledge.* In this case, base pay or pay progression is tied to job knowledge. Two types of such systems exist. "Increased knowledge-based" systems base compensation upon the range of skills employees possess in a single speciality or job classification. "Multi-skilled-based" systems tie pay progression to the number of different jobs an employee can perform across the organization. Under these systems, the more jobs an employee can perform or the greater knowledge an employee has of one job, the higher his/her base pay, regardless of whether or not he/she is currently performing the higher skilled job. The purpose of these systems is to allow the company to reduce job classifications and encourage a more flexible workforce.

6. *Profit-sharing plans.* Under profit-sharing plans, employees receive an annual bonus or shares in the company based upon companywide performance. Employees are either paid in cash, or their earnings are deferred into a retirement plan.

All these plans have in common an effort by companies to slow the growth of base pay and to make a portion (perhaps a substantial portion) of each employee's total compensation variable and tied to companywide, group, or individual performance. This wave of interest in nontraditional systems suggests that compensation practices in most companies will probably be quite different in the future. Traditionally, most of us worked in an organization where we were paid on a straight hourly or salaried basis. We came to expect regular annual merit or cost-of-living increases and steady growth in our base compensation. Our own, our group's, and our company's performance had only limited impact on our income, if any. The growth of nontraditional compensation systems will change all this. In the future, growth in base pay will slow considerably, and base pay will become a much smaller percentage of our total compensation. A larger portion of our pay (perhaps eventually as much as 40 percent) will be variable—go up or down based upon our own, our group's, or our company's performance.

Some Examples of Pay-for-Performance Systems

There are no models or standards for what future compensation practices might be like in most companies, beyond a devotion to holding the line on automatic increases in base pay and to making a larger portion of total compensation variable. Our experience with companies implementing new compensation systems has taught us that each situation is unique. Also, as we have shown above, there is a great range in the types of nontraditional systems being tried. It might be useful to describe some nontraditional systems to illustrate how they work. For illustrative purposes, let's look at three examples, two in manufacturing and one in the service sector.

Lincoln Electric: A Manufacturing Example

Located in Cleveland, Ohio, Lincoln Electric is the world's largest manufacturer of electric arc welding equipment. Our choice of Lincoln Electric to illustrate nontraditional pay practices should come as no surprise. Lincoln Electric has been the subject of Harvard Case Studies and of numerous articles as a company in a highly competitive business that gets high performance from its employees, produces a high quality product, performs exceptionally well even during deep recessions, avoids layoffs, and still manages to pay employees at levels unmatched by any competitor. Lincoln's success has much to do with its management philosophy (which parallels much of what we have discussed in this book) plus its nontraditional approach to employee compensation. Since the company's management philosophy and compensation practices work hand in hand, we need to examine both.

Lincoln Electric's Management Philosophy

The management philosophy followed by Lincoln Electric was laid down by its founders, James F. and John C. Lincoln. The Lincoln philosophy, among other things, includes the following key points:

1. The belief that employees are the company's most valuable assets, and therefore the company should ensure that employees feel secure, important, and challenged; have control over their own destiny; are confident in their leadership; are treated with honesty and integrity; and have access to persons in authority with open lines of communication.

2. A belief in simplicity in policies, practices, methods, and structure.

3. A firm belief in competition being healthy and desirable for human beings as well as for businesses.

4. A belief that the company exists solely to serve customers by providing the best product at the lowest price to the largest number of customers.

5. A guarantee of at least thirty (30) hours of work per week for every employee who has been with the company for two years or longer. Employees are not laid off for lack of work. (Lincoln has not had a layoff in over thirty years.)

6. As part of its guaranteed employment program, Lincoln requires that all employees agree to being transferred at the company's request to other jobs to meet company needs (employees are guaranteed a job but not necessarily a particular position). For example, in 1982 when there was a downturn in orders and sales, Lincoln retrained groups of hourly employees for sales positions and sent them out to sell products.

7. A commitment to promotion from within. Practically all new hirings from outside the company are for entry level positions. All other positions are filled internally to the extent possible.

8. An expectation of lifetime employment. All full-time employees are hired with the expectation that they will work for Lincoln until they retire.

9. A belief in employee responsibility for quality. All employees are responsible for their own quality, and defects are normally fixed on the employees' own time.

10. The existence of a regularly scheduled advisory board. Every two weeks, groups of employees meet directly with top management to discuss any issues of concern to them. Minutes of each meeting are prepared and posted for all employees to see. Problems or issues are assigned to executives, who are responsible for investigating them and reporting back at the next meeting.

Lincoln's Incentive Compensation System

Lincoln's compensation system consists of two parts: base pay (which is normally piece work) and an annual bonus.

1. *Piecework.* Whenever possible, employees are compensated according to a piecework system. There is no salary or hourly wage for most jobs; rather, employees are paid a set amount for each item they produce, either individually or as members of small work groups. Rates are based upon time studies and cannot be changed by management unless methods, materials, or machinery used in the job are changed. To arrive at the actual pay for each piece, rates are multiplied by a factor (the Lincoln Electric Multiplier), which is tied to the Consumer Price Index for the Cleveland area. Thus, the payment for each piece is adjusted each year—up or down—so that pay for a "normal" production level is brought in line with wages in the Cleveland area. Employees can challenge the rates established if they feel they are unfair, and the job will be restudied and new rates set if appropriate.

Although piecework systems have been used by a number of industries in the past, Lincoln Electric's system is unique in several respects. First, every effort is made to ensure that piece rates are fair. For example, employees can continue to challenge rates repeatedly, as long as they are dissatisfied. Second, management cannot change rates just because employees are making too much money, even if an employee is earning two or three times the normal wage under the system. Rates can only be changed if there is a change in methods, materials, or machinery used to do the job. Of course, then employees can challenge the new rates if they wish. Finally, employees are paid only for quality work. Employees are not paid for defective work until they repair the defects on their own time.

2. *Annual bonus*. In addition to piece rates, employees can earn an annual bonus. The bonus is not guaranteed, is not a gift, and is not automatic. At the beginning of each year, a 100 percent bonus is budgeted. At the end of each year, the board of directors sets aside an amount to be shared based upon company performance that year. To determine how much each employee will receive from the bonus pool, a merit rating is given twice each year by the supervisor of each department. Employees are rated on four categories: ideas and cooperation, output, dependability, and quality. Each department is allowed 100 points per employee to distribute among all the employees in that department—some employees thus receive more than 100 points, and some less. Points for exceptional performance—above 110—are awarded from a special companywide pool subject to review by a corporate committee. Those points above 110 do not count against the department's allotted points. Regardless of points awarded, at least one senior executive reviews each employee's merit rating to ensure that it is fair.

As with its piecework system, Lincoln's use of merit ratings is not unique; however, Lincoln's use of such ratings differs from that of other companies in several respects. First, the rating process is taken very seriously since it has a direct bearing on the amount of bonus an employee can earn—which can be considerable. Second, ratings are given twice per year, not just once as is more typical. Third, the range of ratings given can vary greatly—from as low as 45 points to as high as 160 points.

There is little doubt that Lincoln Electric's system of compensation—for performance and only for performance—works. The company has been very successful, even during difficult economic periods, and so have its employees. Workers continue to earn substantial bonuses on the average and total compensation far above what they could expect elsewhere. For example, the company has paid bonuses every year since 1934, and during recent years, bonuses have averaged nearly 100 percent of wages and salaries. Additionally, most of Lincoln's employees seem to like the company and its systems, for Lincoln's turnover rate remains extremely low by industry standards.

Nucor Corporation: A Second Manufacturing Example

Located in Charlotte, North Carolina, Nucor Corporation produces steel and related products and is the largest producer of steel joists in the United States. Like Lincoln Electric, Nucor continues to perform exceptionally well, even during difficult economics periods (see "Nucor Corporation—Gainsharing Program Boosts Productivity for Steel Producer," Case Study 28, American Productivity Center, 1983). For example, between 1971 and the early 1980s, Nucor's sales rose 850 percent, and profits 1250 percent. Between 1972 and 1982, average return on Nucor stockholders' equity was 24 percent compared to typical performance in manufacturing companies of 10 to 15 percent. In 1985, the market value of Nucor stock was 207 percent of book value. Like Lincoln Electric, much of Nucor's success can be traced to its nontraditional compensation practices and to its management philosophy. Let's look at both of these.

Nucor's Management Philosophy

Nucor's management philosophy consists of four basic parts:

1. A belief that employees should have the opportunity to earn according to their productivity

2. A belief that management should run the company in such a way that employees can feel secure in the knowledge that if they do their jobs well, they will have jobs tomorrow

3. A belief that employees should be treated fairly

4. A belief that if workers feel they are not treated fairly, they should have the right to appeal

Nucor's organization has a flat structure with only five levels between the President/CEO and non-exempt employees. Lines of communication between levels are open and informal. Employees are told the "good" and the "bad"; management openly admits its mistakes; risk-taking is encouraged; and all levels share the same benefits. There are no executive privileges—no company cars, no executive dining room.

Nucor's Incentive Compensation Systems

Nucor actually has a range of compensation systems, each tying pay to group performance.

1. Production employees are organized in clearly defined and measured work groups of twenty-five to thirty and are paid based upon group performance. Incentive bonuses are based upon production of good quality above an historical base. For example, if the group's quality production is 50 percent above the base standard, then the group receives a 50 percent bonus as part of the next pay check. In effect, each production group is treated as a business unto itself and is paid based upon its production. Employees who are absent or tardy risk losing part or all of their bonus pay. As a result, there is little problem with absenteeism or tardiness.

2. Department managers and indirect employees who are not part of production teams earn incentive bonuses based upon division and/or corporate return on assets employed (ROAE). Such bonuses are paid according to a schedule (ROAE of a given percentage earns a bonus of X percent) and can run as high a 50 percent of base pay plus overtime.

3. For senior level officers, pay is tied directly to company performance. Base salaries are set at 70 percent of salaries for such positions in comparable companies. If the company

performs poorly, officers are paid only their base. However, if the company performs well, 10 percent of pre-tax earnings are set aside and paid to officers as incentive compensation.

4. While Nucor has no retirement plan, 10 percent of pre-tax earnings are placed in a profit-sharing account each year. Approximately 15 percent of profit-sharing funds is paid out as a cash bonus based upon the percent of each employee's earnings for the year, with the remainder placed in a trust. An employee's retirement income is thus dependent upon company performance.

5. Other benefits available to Nucor employees include shares of Nucor stock based upon years of service, a scholarship fund for children of Nucor employees seeking education beyond high school, and an "extraordinary bonus payment" during years of exceptionally high earnings. The latter is above and beyond any other incentive pay, profit-sharing, or other program.

As we noted above, Nucor's management philosophy and incentive compensation practices have resulted in extraordinary company performance. At the same time, Nucor employees have benefited from exceptionally high earnings. For example, a 1983 American Productivity Center case study on Nucor reported that the average income of hourly employees at Nucor's Darlington, South Carolina, mill was over twice that of other hourly manufacturing employees in South Carolina.

City of Loveland, Colorado: A Service Example

Located fifty miles north of Denver, Loveland experienced a fourfold increase in population in 1981, but its tax base did not keep up with its population growth and service demands. Streets and other city facilities were in need of repair. City voters turned down a tax increase by a margin of four to one, and Loveland faced a $500,000 deficit in 1982 if nothing changed.

In desperation, the city council asked the advice of area business executives to find ways to eliminate or cut services. Instead, these discussions resulted in an innovative pay-for-performance system for city employees. Largely as a result of this nontraditional approach, in 1982 Loveland had a $2.4 million surplus as well as improved services. By 1984, resident satisfaction with city services had reached 90 percent, and the operating budget was the lowest of any of the three previous years (see "City Boosts Productivity as Alternative to Tax Hikes, Service Cuts," *National Productivity Report* 14, no. 19 [October 15, 1985]).

Loveland's turnaround was accomplished with a new compensation system that tied pay to performance and with a gainsharing program that returned a portion of cost savings from productivity improvements to city employees. Traditionally, city employees were paid salaries with relatively automatic annual increases based upon length of service. Under the new compensation system, an employee's pay was tied directly to his/her rating on specific performance criteria. Average performers earned the going rate for their jobs in the community, but high performers could earn as much as 15 to 20 percent more than their counterparts outside the city government. Additionally, all employees were eligible for bonuses under a gainsharing program. With this program, employees shared a portion of productivity savings from the operating budget (the revenues that exceeded expenses) provided that the public was satisfied with city services. If less than 60 percent of the public surveyed was satisfied, no bonus was paid. If 60 to 70 percent were satisfied, city employees shared 2 percent of the net operating income. If 70 to 85 percent were satisfied, the gainsharing went to 3 percent and if more than 85 percent were satisfied, the gainsharing went to 4 percent.

Loveland's experience with Pay-for-Performance worked very well, but its success was not solely a result of changes in compensation practices. Management practices also changed. First, city departments were reorganized to improve accountability and reduce layers of management. Also, at least for the first year, employees were assured they would not lose their jobs as a result of productivity improvements (instead they would be retrained and transferred to other positions). Some city operations such as the golf course and cemetery were reorganized as profit centers; others were required to operate on a full cost recovery basis. Finally, a financial planning process was initiated to project revenues and expenditures three years into the future.

The Serious Implications of Pay-for-Performance

The growing trend in American business away from traditional compensation practices and toward systems where pay is more closely tied to individual, group, or company performance has tremendous implications for employees individually and for the work environment as we know it. Consider, for example, the following:

1. When a substantial portion of pay is tied to performance, that portion becomes variable—can go up or down—based upon individual, group, or company performance. This change is significant. Most of us are accustomed to receiving a straight salary or hourly pay that is reviewed and adjusted annually. We might work occasional overtime or sometimes receive a bonus, but bonuses and overtime pay—the variable portions of our income—represent only a small percentage of our total compensation. If we lose the overtime or don't receive the bonus, there is little impact on our standard of living. Under pay-for-performance systems, base salaries are likely to increase at a slower rate (no automatic or nearly automatic annual increases). Additionally, performance bonuses will probably become a larger percentage of our total compensation. Such systems place new responsibilities on employees for controlling their own personal finances. If employees rely too much on the bonus portion of their income, they may experience financial hardships in deficit months, should they occur.

2. A second implication of pay-for-performance systems is that the nature of authority relationships and status in the organization might change. Under some pay-for-performance systems, employees are routinely able make more than their bosses as a result of performance bonuses. Thus, the economic gap between boss and subordinate may narrow or even be reversed. Additionally, since pay-for-performance systems tend to rely more on objective measures rather than supervisor ratings, employees might no longer see the need to give their bosses "automatic" respect, deference and seek their "good will." Employees can become more independent and more entrepreneurial. In all likelihood, there will be more questioning of authority (particularly of decisions that might impact bonus payments) and increased demand on the part of employees to be consulted and to be involved in problem solving and decision making. Obviously, there is nothing wrong with

these changes; in fact, MPM supports such changes as necessary for a productive organization (see previous chapters). However, this breakdown in traditional authority relationships will be difficult for some managers and employees.

3. An additional implication of pay-for-performance systems is that employees will demand, and the operation of the systems themselves might require, increased sharing of information. What types of information? Employees will probably have increased interest in such areas as sales, profits, return on assets, customers, competitors, operating costs, marketing strategies, and capital expenditures. Much of this information might never have been shared with employees before, at least not in the detail that will be required under a pay-for-performance system. Information that was once tightly restricted to only those with "a need to know" might now have to be disclosed to everyone or at least reevaluated to determine if it could be disclosed. Employees who used to be just "workers," who only needed to know what was necessary for them to do their jobs, will become more like partners with a genuine stake in the business. Again, there is nothing wrong with this. Increased sharing of information is a primary task of management under MPM. Yet many managers will find these changes difficult to accept.

4. Finally, pay-for-performance systems will create heightened pressure for performance and cost containment within the organization. This pressure will come not just from managers, but from employees themselves. For example, an outcome of group-based incentive plans has been increased peer pressure on low performers to improve or leave. Mistakes, lost time and waste that costs the group in bonus money simply aren't tolerated by the group. At the extreme, concern for saving money may become so prevalent that, as Theodore Cohn, a compensation consultant, has said, "a paperclip can't hit the floor without a hand going after it to retrieve it and return it to the paperclip supply." Obviously, this heightened sense of concern about performance and controlling cost is the very intention of pay-for-performance systems. Yet some people are concerned that these systems will create self-imposed "sweat shops," with employees working themselves to exhaustion. While we don't expect that to happen, we do feel there will be more "sweat." At least this time, part of the results of that additional "sweat" will be returned to employees.

Summary

In this chapter, we presented a vision of how you might be compensated in the next decade. We described a quiet revolution that is underway and gathering steam. You may not have been personally touched by these forces yet, but it is very likely that you soon will be.

The adoption of a pay-for-performance system is a change in business management practices that should not be taken lightly. In this chapter, we outlined some of the significant implications of such a change. Yet more and more companies are moving toward pay-for-performance. Some are making the change for economic survival reasons. Facing stronger domestic and foreign competition, they can no longer afford increases in labor costs without corresponding increases in labor productivity. Other companies are adopting pay-for-performance because they see it as a method of compensation that is only right and fair. Still other companies view pay-for-performance as a logical extension of participative management and employee involvement programs. Finally, a few companies are moving to pay-for-performance just because other companies are doing it.

Regardless of the reason, in our opinion performance-based compensation will be a common practice in American business by the middle of the next decade. Even now some two thousand companies are experimenting with pay-for-performance, and over 20 percent of these are using performance bonuses as the only method for granting regular pay increases. Many of these companies will experience tremendous gains in productivity, performance, and employee commitment similar to the results obtained by companies such as Lincoln Electric and Nucor Steel. Other companies that experiment with pay-for-performance will be much less successful and in some instances the experiment will be a total failure. Success or failure hinges on the types of pay-for-performance systems that these companies adopt, and how these systems are implemented. Obviously there is no one system that is right for every company, however there is a system that will be right for many companies. Our next chapter discusses that system—what it is, how to determine if it is right for you, and how to install it.

Chapter 11

Gainsharing: How to Increase Team Performance

In the preceding chapter, we discussed some of the changes that were taking place in American business with respect to compensation practices. We described a number of performance-based compensation systems that were being tried. Among them was a system of pay-for-performance called "gainsharing." We are devoting this chapter to gainsharing because we believe it will become one of the most widely used pay-for-performance systems. In this chapter, we will examine some of the reasons gainsharing has become so popular, describe how various types of gainsharing plans work, and suggest steps you should follow in designing a gainsharing plan for your own company. Let's start by giving a little background on gainsharing.

What Is Gainsharing?

Although there has been a tremendous increase in the interest in gainsharing over the last few years, gainsharing itself is not new. It has been used successfully in the United States since at least the 1930s. The original concept was developed by Joseph Scanlon, a cost

193

accountant and union official at the Empire Steel and Tin Plate Company in Mansfield, Ohio. Faced with a company on the brink of bankruptcy, Scanlon persuaded company management and the union to cooperate in an effort to involve employees in generating ideas for improving productivity. Although there was no formal bonus system under the initial Empire plan, experience at Empire led to the application of union/management cooperative efforts at other companies and eventually to the addition of a bonus system to encourage employees to find ways to improve productivity.

In brief, gainsharing programs involve groups of employees in improving productivity through better use of labor, capital, materials, and energy. In return for their efforts, the company shares part of the resultant savings from productivity gains with employees in the form of a cash bonus, the amount of which is calculated according to some predetermined formula. Note that under gainsharing programs, employees earn bonuses based upon *group* rather than *individual* performance, and that employees are *involved* in finding ways to improve productivity and make gains. Thus, gainsharing includes both a program for involving employees and a *formula* for calculating gains. The involvement system and formula are both important and vital to the success and longevity of the program.

The Advantages of Gainsharing

In the American Productivity Center survey we mentioned in the last chapter, 81 percent of the companies using gainsharing reported that it had a positive or very positive impact on performance. In addition, based upon results of this survey, the use of gainsharing was expected to grow by 68 percent overall, 76 percent in manufacturing and 168 percent in service industries over the next few years. Thus, gainsharing is likely to become (in fact, is already) one of the most popular of the nontraditional reward systems. Why has gainsharing become so popular? We think the reasons are the significant advantages gainsharing has over other pay-for-performance systems.

You will recall from the previous chapter that, in addition to gainsharing, we briefly described five other pay-for-performance systems—small group incentives, individual incentives, lump sum payments/bonuses, pay-for-knowledge, and profit-sharing. You will also recall that companies were adopting pay-for-performance for two primary reasons: (1) to hold the line on base pay increases, and (2) to make a portion of each person's pay variable and tied to performance. Let's compare gainsharing to the other pay-for-performance systems in respect to these objectives.

Gainsharing versus Individual Incentives

Individual incentives have been used for a long time, particularly in manufacturing settings. Obviously, such incentives do tie pay directly to performance. Also, at least initially, they do result in increased productivity. As long as good individual measures of performance can be maintained and there is no need for teamwork or cooperation between employees on the job, individual incentives can work. However, over time companies have found that individual incentives become increasingly more difficult and costly to administer since base rate standards must be restudied and adjusted to keep them in line with changes in methods and technology. When such adjustments are made, they often result in employee complaints and/or intentional efforts by employees to restrict output to avoid a rate change. If adjustments aren't made or if they are inaccurate, pay can lose its relationship to performance, and inequities can develop.

Beyond the problem of administering individual incentives, most companies find that such incentives become inappropriate and even harmful as the nature of the work changes. Individual incentives encourage employees to focus on their own individual output without regard to the output of their plant, department, or unit. Under individual incentives, there is no inducement for employees to cooperate, work as a team, help each other, or place the interests of their company, plant, division, or unit over their own personal interest. As long as people work independently, teamwork and cooperation may not be so important. But what happens when jobs become highly automated and servicing the new high-speed technology requires a group effort?

For many companies, gainsharing is an attractive alternative to individual incentives because it overcomes both of these problems. First, since measurements used in gainsharing are usually based upon total group performance, companies do not have to set and constantly update standards, thus avoiding most of the administrative costs associated with individual incentives. Second, and perhaps most important, gainsharing is based upon group rather than on individual performance. Gainsharing plans thus encourage teamwork, cooperation, and a long-term interest in achieving group goals.

Gainsharing versus Profit-Sharing or Lump Sum Bonuses

Like gainsharing, profit-sharing plans and performance-based lump sum bonuses rely upon macrolevel measurements and are based upon group performance. Thus, profit-sharing and lump sum bonuses have the same advantages over individual incentives as gainsharing. However, profit-sharing and lump sum bonuses differ from gainsharing in some important ways. First, they usually make payouts only once or twice per year, and in the case of profit-sharing, part or all of the payment might be deferred into a retirement plan. In contrast, most gainsharing plans pay out monthly. This difference in frequency of payment is important since, as you will recall, a reinforcer is more powerful in stimulating performance if it occurs close to the time of occurrence of the behavior. A second problem with profit-sharing is that bonuses are tied to company profits, not employee performance. Thus, employees might perform exceptionally well but receive no bonus because the company was not profitable due to pricing policies, economic conditions, management decisions to write off losses, or any number of other factors over which employees have no control. Likewise, employees can receive a profit-sharing bonus even when there has been no productivity or performance gain. Under gainsharing, bonus payments are more closely tied to actual employee performance, particularly if the gainsharing formula is based upon physical rather than on financial measurements. In some cases, employees can earn bonuses even when the company is not profitable. Over the long term, gainsharing should contribute to profitability, but gainsharing is usually not dependent upon profitability. As a result, under gainsharing employees have more control over their own destiny and are prevented from reaping benefits from something over which they have no control.

Gainsharing versus Pay-for-Knowledge

Under pay-for-knowledge, base pay or pay progression is tied to job knowledge. The more jobs an employee can perform, or the greater depth of knowledge an employee has in a specialty, the higher his/her base pay, regardless of whether or not he/she actually performs the jobs. Pay-for-knowledge indirectly affects performance since it encourages a more flexible workforce, which should translate into reduced labor costs. Yet pay-for-knowledge systems do not tie pay directly to performance. This lack of a direct connection between pay and performance we feel limits the widespread application of pay-for-knowledge. However, pay-for-knowledge can be an important application if installed as an adjunct to gainsharing. In the next chapter, we will discuss this role for pay-for-knowledge and how it can be used to offset a weakness in gainsharing plans.

Gainsharing versus Small Group Incentives

Small group incentives have many of the same advantages as gainsharing. They are based upon macromeasures of group performance, they tie pay directly to performance, and they can be paid out frequently. Yet, we feel that small group incentives have a severe disadvantage compared to gainsharing in that they can result in significant pay discrepancies from group to group and can encourage unhealthy intergroup rivalry. In contrast, gainsharing plans can normally be constructed so that such destructive competition is minimized or avoided altogether. Also, small group incentives are generally designed by the company's industrial engineer without employee participation. They thus do not create the "partnership" between employees and the company that is characteristic of gainsharing.

In summary, gainsharing has these distinct advantages over other pay-for-performance options:

- It is based upon group, not individual performance.

- It encourages teamwork and cooperation.

- It is based on macromeasures, and thus is relatively easy to administer.

- It results in payouts relatively close in time to performance.

- It is based upon factors controllable by the group.

- It usually does not encourage destructive competition between groups.

- It promotes an employee/company partnership for improvement.

The Importance of Employee Involvement

Two factors are critical to the success of any gainsharing plan: a provision for some type of structured employee involvement and a formula for calculating gains. Both are equally important, although frequently more attention is given to developing or acquiring a gainsharing formula, with too little attention given to the creation of a structured system for employee development and implementation of improvement ideas—thereby realizing gains. Gainsharing often (as much as 40 percent of the time) fails when there is just a formula and no structured system for involving employees. For this reason, we urge you not to consider gainsharing unless you include a workable involvement system with a continuing structure.

Types of involvement systems that will work with gainsharing include any structured method for providing feedback to employees on performance and for allowing employees to identify and solve problems. Under one of the oldest gainsharing programs, the Scanlon Plan, the involvement system uses production committees at the work group level composed of managers, supervisors, and employees. These committees are responsible for soliciting, evaluating, and implementing employee suggestions. In addition, there typically is a plantwide screening committee that receives and acts upon suggestions the work group level committees cannot implement by themselves.

In gainsharing programs we have implemented, we normally focus on creating or improving work group teams as a basis for employee involvement. Usually the teams follow the organizational heirarchy, with the manager or supervisor serving as the team leader. All employees participate as members of the team on a nonvoluntary basis. These teams communicate information about the gainsharing program and about performance on a regular basis. They also identify opportunities for performance gains, and they design and implement solutions. Cross-sectional and cross-functional problems identified by the work groups are assigned to problem-solving task forces composed of managers, supervisors, and employees from all the work groups that could impact the specific performance problem under discussion.

In a later chapter of this book, we spend considerable time discussing employee involvement and the operation of employee teams. In that chapter, you will find numerous suggestions on establishing employee involvement systems that will work well with gainsharing. Because we cover involvement later, we will not spend further time on involvement at this point; however, don't let our brief treatment of involvement here minimize its importance as a part of gainsharing. With that said, let's turn to the formula.

Traditional Gainsharing Formulas

As we said above, developing an appropriate gainsharing formula is one of the two critical factors in the success of gainsharing. A good gainsharing formula should meet the following criteria:

1. *Fair to the company*—The first test of a gainsharing formula has to be whether it is a true measure of performance over time and whether success on that measure will enable the company to achieve its objectives. Financial incentives are very powerful tools, therefore you have to ensure that when gains are earned, the company benefits as well as employees. You don't want a formula where employees are making bonuses at the expense of the company, for in the long term, the company will be severely damaged, even destroyed, and no one—managers, owners, or employees—will win.

2. *Fair to the employees*—A second test is whether or not the formula is fair to employees. Employees need the opportunity to make gains, provided they work harder or smarter. They have to be able to make a difference through changes in their behavior. If the formula includes too many extraneous variables outside of employee control, the whole gainsharing effort can fail simply because employees quit trying.

3. *Understandable to employees*—A third test is whether employees will be able to understand how the formula works and how their behavior affects performance as measured by the formula. An extremely elaborate and sophisticated formula that is understood only by your comptroller will fail simply because the people

involved never understand how gains are derived. Ideally, the gainsharing formula should be tied as closely to possible to what people physically do. Employees should be able to predict whether or not they will obtain a gain for any given month simply by observing what is happening around them day-to-day. For example, if the formula is tied to some measurement of products shipped, employees will see the shipments occurring day-to-day. They will have a feeling in advance of any month-end calculation as to whether or not a gain will be made, based just upon the shipping activity.

4. *Easy to administer*—Fourth, a good gainsharing formula should be easy to calculate based upon information that is already available to you on a regular and timely basis. You do not want to create elaborate new accounting systems to support the gainsharing program. Additionally, in most cases you need to pay bonuses on a monthly basis and as soon after the end of the month as possible. Gainsharing bonuses are reinforcers, and they are subject to all the rules governing the effectiveness of reinforcers we discussed in previous chapters. You will recall that one of these rules is that the reinforcer must be given as close to the performance incident as possible.

5. *Flexibility*—Fifth, a good gainsharing formula should be flexible. The environment where most companies compete changes rapidly today. As a result, company goals, objectives, and priorities change. If the gainsharing formula is to last, it has to accommodate these changes and not lock the company into rewarding behavior and performance that was appropriate once, but is no longer consistent with company goals and strategies.

6. *Usefulness in isolating problem areas*—Finally, a good gainsharing formula should help employee problem-solving teams isolate potential problem areas and should provide useful information concerning the possible causes of low productivity. Ideally, the calculation itself will suggest particular product lines, materials cost, and so on that are causing or contributing to poor performance. As a result, the formula will help direct problem-solving efforts.

With these rules in mind, let's look at some types of gainsharing formulas that have been used, starting with a simple example. Suppose Company A's major cost is for labor (payroll cost plus fringe benefits), and a good measurement of its output is the sales value of production. Also, let's assume that neither the input measure (labor costs) nor the output measure (sales value of production) are significantly affected by extraneous factors, so that the ratio of labor cost to sales value of production is a good measure of performance over time. Given this situation, Company A could calculate any gains by first determining what the ratio of labor costs was to sales value of production during a base period, and then by using that ratio to determine an allowed labor cost during the current period. Any savings in actual labor costs when compared to the allowed labor cost for a given month would be a productivity gain and could be shared with employees. A sample calculation might be as follows:

First, Company A calculates what is called an "Historical Base Ratio." This is simply the existing ratio of labor costs to sales value of production prior to installing gainsharing. Let's say that Company A's Historical Base Ratio is the following:

Labor Costs	$ 1,180,000	
——————	——————	equals 59% Base Ratio
Sales Value of Production	$ 2,000,000	

Having established a Base Ratio, Company A then determines each month whether or not there is any gain. The monthly calculation might be something like this:

Sales Value of Production (plus or minus changes in inventories)	$ 2,500,000
Allowed Labor Cost (Sales Value multi Base Ratio) $2,500,000 x .59 =	1,475,000
Actual Labor Cost	1,200,000
Amount of Gain (Loss)	275,000

Employee Share of Gain (assume 50% of total gain)	137,500
Amount of Employee Share Held Back, to protect against negative periods (assume 20% held back)	27,500
Net Amount in Bonus Pool (Employee Share minus Amt. Held Back)	110,000
Current Employee Payroll	1,200,000
Percent Bonus to Pay Employees (Net Bonus Pool/Payroll)	9.2%

Notice several things about the above calculation. First, the gain (and therefore bonus) made by employees resulted from a true increase in productivity from the base period. Although labor costs went up by $20,000 (from $1,180,000 during the base period to $1,200,000 during the current period), the sales value of production increased by $500,000 (from $2,000,000 to $2,500,000). Given the Historical Base Ratio, Company A would have expected payroll costs to be 59 percent of the sales value of production, or $1,475,000 ($2,500,000 multi .59); however, labor costs were actually only $1,200,000, which represents a savings (or productivity gain) of $275,000 for that month. Employees thus produced much more for very little additional increase in cost. As a result, a bonus was earned.

A second thing to notice from our example is how the amount of any gain was calculated and how much of the gain was returned to employees. The amount of the bonus that was earned (the "employee share of the gain") in our example was equal to half the difference between the expected or allowed labor costs for that level of production and the actual labor costs. Many gainsharing plans divide any gains equally between employees and the company, however we have seen plans that allocate as little as 25 percent or as much as 75 percent of the gains to employees.

Third, note that not all of the employees' share of the gain was distributed. In this case, 20 percent was held back by the company. The existence of a "holdback" provision is common to many gainsharing plans. Essentially, the purpose of the holdback provision is to protect the company from short-term "spikes" in productivity, where large bonuses are made only to be followed by deficit months. Without such a provision, the company might be required to pay large bonuses during a few months when productivity was extremely high, yet have no gains in productivity (or even a loss in productivity) for the entire year. With a holdback provision, employees have a stake in long-term rather than in short-term productivity gains. Usually the amounts held back are placed in a reserve fund and paid out to employees at the end of the year, provided gains are made over the course of the entire year. If there are no such long-term gains, employees forfeit all or a portion of the amount held back.

Finally, note that in our example the amount remaining in the bonus pool after holdback is expressed as a percentage of the total employee payroll. In this case, the amount of bonus each employee receives will be equal to 9.2 percent of their total wages (regular plus overtime). Thus, employees with higher total wages receive a larger portion of the funds in the bonus pool. This practice is another common feature of gainsharing plans. Though many employees object to this particular feature (arguing that bonuses should be distributed equally), most companies end up with this distribution method since it is the easiest way to ensure that the plan is in compliance with the Fair Labor Standards Act.

The above example of a gainsharing formula is what is called a "Single Ratio" formula. We picked a Single Ratio formula for our example because it is one of the easiest types of gainsharing formulas to understand. However there are many formulas, as we suggested earlier. Most of these other formulas modify the input and/or output sides of the base ratio equation to overcome problems with the Single Ratio formula that can occur if, for example, the selling price of products and basic labor costs change at different rates, the mix of products changes over time making the original ratio invalid, or large capital investments are made. Some of these other formulas include the following:

Split Ratio Formula

Here the sales value of production and allowed labor costs are calculated separately for each different type of product. Thus, if the product mix changes over time, the Split Ratio formula will adjust for the increased value and/or increased cost of producing these new products.

Multi-Cost Ratio Formula

In the Single Ratio and Split Ratio formulas, only payroll costs are included. Other costs for such items as materials, supplies, energy, and so on are not included. The Multi-Cost Ratio, as the name implies, includes these other costs and therefore encourages employees to control costs in those areas.

Value Added or Rucker Plan

Named for Alan Rucker, an economist who first developed the formula in the 1930s, the Value Added or Rucker Plan calculates productivity gains according to the ratio of "Value Added" to labor costs rather than of sales value to labor costs as used in the formulas we listed above. Value Added is the difference between the selling price of items produced and the cost of materials, supplies, energy, and other outside purchases required to produce the items. For example, if the value of items produced (sales plus or minus changes in inventory) is $1,000,000 and the cost of materials, supplies, and other nonlabor items used to produce these items is $600,000, then the "Value Added" by employees is $400,000. The ratio of this "Value Added" amount to labor costs is then used to calculate the allowed labor costs, from which actual labor costs are subtracted to find the amount of any gain. An example might look like this:

Sales Value of Production	$2,500,000
Minus Outside Purchases	1,000,000
Value Added	1,500,000
Allowed Labor Costs (40% of Value Added based upon historical analysis)	600,000

Actual Labor Costs	500,000
Amount of Gain	100,000
Employee Share (assume 50%)	50,000
Holdback (assume 20%)	10,000
Employee Bonus Pool	40,000
Bonus Percentage (Bonus Pool/Labor Costs)	8.0%

Improshare Formula

Developed by Mitchell Fein, an industrial engineer, the Improshare Formula differs from all the preceding in that it is based upon employee hours rather than on sales dollars or labor costs. By eliminating both sales dollars and labor costs from the calculation, Improshare avoids many of the typical problems associated with dollar-based (or financial) formulas. For example, when sales dollars are included, the gainsharing formula is affected by pricing and other factors over which employees probably have little control. Instead of using dollars, Improshare calculates bonuses as the difference between "Improshare hours" that are earned or credited for a given volume of production and actual hours worked. If actual hours are less than the projected Improshare hours for a given volume of production, then a gain is earned and employees receive a bonus based upon the hours saved. Here is an example of an Improshare calculation.

As a first step, standards are developed based on the historical record of the "production hours" required to produce each type of product. For example:

Product	Production Hours/Units Produced	equals Std. Hrs. per Unit
A	400/400	equals 1 Hour
B	1000/500	equals 2 Hours
C	800/200	equals 4 Hours

The second step is to establish a "Base Productivity Factor," the ratio of total production and nonproduction hours (direct and indirect) to total standard value hours. For example:

Product   Units Produced multi Std. Hrs. Per Unit = Std. Value Hrs.

A 400 × 1	=	400
B 500 × 2	=	1000
C 200 × 4	=	800

Total Standard Value Hours Earned   2200

$$\frac{\text{Tot. Production \& Nonprod. Hrs. Worked}}{\text{Tot. Std. Value Hrs. Earned}} = \text{Base Productivity Factor}$$

$$\frac{2200 \text{ plus } 1000}{2200} = 1.45 \text{ Base Productivity Factor}$$

Monthly Bonus Calculation:

Product A = 1 Std. Val. Hr. × 500 Units × 1.45 =	725
Product B − 2 Std. Val. Hrs. × 550 Units × 1.45 =	1,595
Product C = 4 Std. Val. Hrs. × 250 Units × 1.45 =	1,450

Improshare Hours Earned for Month	3,770
Actual Hours Worked (Production & Nonproduction)	3,000
Hours Gained (Improshare—Actual)	770
Employee Bonus Hours (assume 50% of Hours Gained)	385
Bonus Percentage (Employee Bonus Hours/Actual Hours Worked)	12.8%

Gainsharing Formulas for the Service Sector

All of the above examples of gainsharing formulas illustrate how they operate in a manufacturing setting. In fact, all these formulas were initially developed for manufacturing environments. In each case, the formulas relate financial output product sales to labor costs or some measure of physical output (units of production) to employee hours of input. The experience with gainsharing plans in white-collar/ service organizations is much more limited than in manufacturing. The problem with traditional gainsharing formulas for the service sector is that output measures (particularly measures of physical output) can be difficult to identify and, even if identifiable, might be less important than measures of quality, effectiveness, or customer satisfaction. However, service sector employers continue to express considerable interest in adopting gainsharing plans for their employees (the American Productivity Center projects a 168 percent growth of such plans in the service sector), and innovative ideas are being presented for adapting gainsharing to the service sector.

One of the problems in adapting gainsharing to the service sector is the tendency to lump all service sector employees into a single group. In fact, white-collar/service jobs range from the highly repetitive, easily measurable "back room" operations, which have a predictable work flow and are very much like a factory environment, to the less repetitive and more creative "knowledge-worker" service environments, where outputs are more difficult to identify and the work performed is less tangible. In the more factory-oriented white-collar/service jobs, traditional gainsharing formulas (Single Ratio, Split Ratio, Multi-Cost, etc.) often work very well. Traditional formulas can also work well if the service component is a profit center rather than a cost center and employees have some measure of control over revenues and costs. For example, a Single Ratio formula might work for professionals who generate revenues from fees to clients or through charge-backs to internal operating components for services rendered, and where the primary cost is labor cost. A Multi-Cost Ratio might work for employees in branch banks, employment agencies, hospitals, hotels, and other service institutions where materials, supplies, energy, and other costs are at least partially controllable by employees. If standard costs exist or can be developed, for example in repair shops, maintenance groups or transaction-processing areas of banks, or insurance companies, then an Improshare formula based upon the ratio of actual to standard hours might work. Thus, the problem in adapting gainsharing to the service sector is not so much with the measurable, "factorylike" service sector jobs or with those who directly generate revenues from the provision of services, but with the less repetitive, less tangible, knowledge-workers, particularly those who provide internal support services as cost centers. To include this latter type of service workers in gainsharing, companies have generally followed one of two basic approaches.

First, knowledge-workers who provide internal support to operating or production components of a company can be included in gainsharing by being allowed to participate in the gains experienced by the components they support. Such an approach works well for employees in areas such as production planning/scheduling, purchasing, or engineering whose performance has a direct impact on the performance of the groups they serve in the short term. Such workers either can be included for gainsharing purposes as part of the operating component workforce (with their costs added to the input side of the formula), not included in formula calculations but allocated a portion of any gains, or have their own separate gainsharing program with output measures tied to the operating or production component(s) performance.

Though the above approach will work for many internal support groups, it is less appropriate for internal knowledge-worker groups such as research people, systems programmers, or public relations people whose work performance is not reflected in short-term operating/production performance. For these groups, one approach is to construct the gainsharing formula based upon an Objectives Matrix as proposed by the American Productivity Center (see Carl Thor, "Knowledge Worker Gainsharing," *APC Productivity Brief* [August, 1987]).

The Objectives Matrix works for internal knowledge-worker employees such as those described above because it substitutes the single measure input/output ratio used in traditional gainsharing formulas with a calculation derived from weighted scores on a variety of measures, such as the following:

- Client/user ratings of service quality/effectiveness

- Measures of compliance with internal procedures or quality standards

- Quality measures related to rework, errors, etc.

- Measures of on-time delivery of services

- Measures of service delivery cost to budget or estimate

- Equipment and/or staff utilization measurements

Once measures are established—preferably as the result of a group effort involving managers, supervisors, and employees—weights are assigned to reflect the relative importance of each measurement, and agreements are reached concerning service level goals and bonus points that can be earned for attaining each level. Table 4 is an example of an Objectives Matrix.

The Objectives Matrix is constructed and read as follows:

1. First, key indicators of performance are identified. In our sample, these are: Client Satisfaction, Staff Utilization, Service Delivery Cost, and On-Time Delivery.

2. Next, weights are assigned to the measures to indicate their relative importance, so that the total of all weights equals 100. In our example, Client Satisfaction and On-Time Delivery are assigned weights of 30 each, with Staff Utilization and Cost weights of 20 each.

3. Next, the Base Period performance level is determined for each measure by examining historical data and entering it on the matrix at Performance Level "3". The matrix is then completed, starting from the Base level and including seven levels of performance better than the Base and three levels worse than the Base. Performance Level "10" is used for the best performance possible or the long-term performance objective.

Sample Objectives Matrix—Internal Professional Services

Client satisfaction score	% Staff utilization	% Service delivery cost to budget	% On-Time delivery	Performance level (points)
97	93	95	97	Current
100	100	89	100	10
99	99	91	99	9
[97]	98	93	98	8
95	97	[95]	[97]	7
93	96	97	96	6
91	95	99	95	5
89	94	100	94	4
87	[93]	110	93	BASE
85	91	115	92	2
83	89	118	91	1
81	87	120	90	0
8	3	7	7	Score
30	20	20	30	Weight
240	60	140	210	Value

Total possible point value = 1,000

Current period point value = 650

Base period point value = 300

Bonus points earned   Value = $100 per bonus pt.
(Current − Base = 350   Bonus Pool = $35,000

Table 4

4. Each month, results are calculated on the key measures and entered on the Objectives Matrix. Reading down and across the matrix, performance levels are identified for each measure and entered at the bottom of the matrix as the current month's score. When matrix scores are multiplied by the weight for each measure, a point value is determined for the current period.

5. With this construction, the maximum point value that can be earned for any period is 1,000 points (Performance Level 10 multi total weights of 100). The point value at the Base Period level is 300 (Performance Level 3 multi total weights of 100), thus Bonus Points are earned if the Current Period Point Value is over 300. For example, in our sample matrix the Current Period Point Value was 650, so 350 Bonus Points were earned (650 minus 300 equals 350).

6. To calculate the amount of money in the Bonus Pool and available for distribution to employees, the Bonus Points Earned for the period are multiplied by some dollar value. In our example, each bonus point was worth $100, therefore the Bonus Pool was $35,000 (350 Bonus Points multi $100 per point).

7. As with other gainsharing formulas, a portion of the Bonus Pool would probably be held back to protect against deficit periods, and the remainder would probably be distributed based upon the percentage that the Bonus Pool was of total payroll costs.

As we said above, the advantage of the Objectives Matrix is that it allows you to construct a gainsharing plan based upon weighted scores on a variety of measures. Bonuses are paid only if the total of weighted scores across all measures improve from the level during the base period. Additionally, once established, the Objectives Matrix is relatively easy to maintain and easy for employees to understand. Finally, the company can limit its risk because it can establish the maximum bonus to be paid if exceptional performance levels are reached across all measures, since the maximum possible bonus points are known in advance.

An alternative to the Objectives Matrix is to assign bonus percentages that can be earned for different levels of performance on each measure.

Performance at the Base level for any measure would earn zero percent. Performance above the Base level would earn a percentage of total wages as a bonus, which varies based upon the relative importance of the measure and the level of performance actually obtained (Good, Very Good, Excellent, or Outstanding). For example, in our sample below the maximum bonus for outstanding performance on all four measures is 12 percent. The bonus actually earned for the current period was 6 percent (3 percent Client Satisfaction plus zero percent on Staff Utilization plus 1 percent on Service Delivery Cost plus 2 percent on On-Time Delivery).

Measure	Base	Good	Very Good	Excellent	Outstanding	Current	%
Client Satis. Score							
Level	87	91	95	99	100	99	3.0
Bonus %	0	1.0	2.0	3.0	4.0		
% Staff Util.							
Level	93	95	97	99	100	93	0.0
Bonus %	0	0.5	1.0	1.5	2.0		
% Serv. Delivery Cost to Budget							
Level	110	99	95	91	89	95	1.0
Bonus %	0	0.5	1.0	1.5	2.0		
% On Time Delivery							
Level	93	95	97	99	100	97	2.0
Bonus %	0	1.0	2.0	3.0	4.0		

Table 5

Bonus
Earned = 6.0%

How to Determine if Gainsharing Is Right for You

There are many possible reasons for considering gainsharing, and when properly implemented, gainsharing can benefit many companies. Based upon our description of gainsharing so far in this chapter (what it is, its advantages, the involvement required, and the range of possible formulas for calculating gains), you might be considering gainsharing as an option. Obviously, we think gainsharing has much to offer, but it is not right for every company. How then do you determine if your company should consider gainsharing? Here are some guidelines to follow in answering that question.

1. If you are concerned that costs in your company are rising faster than productivity (unit costs are increasing), and you see a need to tie compensation above some base level to productivity, then gainsharing is a good option to consider.

2. If indirect labor costs are growing, and fewer and fewer employees are covered by individual incentives, then gainsharing may be a method of creating a group incentive that can cover both direct and indirect labor.

3. If because of changes in technology and/or work processes you want to encourage cooperation and teamwork, then a group incentive such as gainsharing might be more appropriate than traditional individual incentives.

4. If you want to create a structure through which employees can become more involved in improving productivity and reducing costs, then gainsharing might be appropriate.

5. If standards for individual incentives have become more difficult to set and keep up-to-date, if pay rates are no longer tied to performance, if inequities exist in total compensation, and if employees are less flexible in the jobs they are willing to tackle, then a group incentive like gainsharing might be worth considering.

How to Determine if You Are Right for Gainsharing

If some or all of the criteria we listed above apply to your company, gainsharing could be right for you. However, your company might not be ready for gainsharing. To determine if it is, ask yourself the following questions:

1. Do your employees have the skills and interest to make gainsharing work? Improvements under gainsharing will only come when employees use their job knowledge and skills to find ways to improve productivity and reduce costs, resulting in gains.

2. Does the work to be performed require a high degree of teamwork and cooperation? Gainsharing is most appropriate in a work environment where you want to encourage group rather than individual performance.

3. Is your management philosophy and are your day-to-day management practices consistent with a participative/employee involvement MPM style of management? Such a style is required for a successful gainsharing program.

4. Do you have or are you willing to create a system for tracking performance on key measurements and for sharing information about performance freely and openly with employees?

5. Do you have production and financial information systems in place, or can they be developed to support the data and information requirements of gainsharing?

6. Are you willing to involve supervisors, employees, and the union (if there is one) in the design of the gainsharing program?

7. Do you have in place or are you willing to develop management systems to support communication, feedback on performance, and employee involvement in action planning and problem solving?

8. Is the level of trust between employees and management sufficient

to support a gainsharing effort? If not, are you willing to take the necessary steps to build that trust?

If your answers to the above questions were "yes," then you most likely have in place or can develop the management practices and systems necessary for a successful gainsharing program. If you answered "no" or were unsure about any answer, then special consideration should be given to those questions during the design phase of gainsharing so that you can correct any problems before the plan is installed.

A Guide to Designing and Implementing Gainsharing

Based upon the previous two sections, you should now have a fair idea about the appropriateness of gainsharing for your company. The question remaining is, How do you actually design and implement a gainsharing program? Fortunately, much is known about the design and implementation processes. The accumulated wisdom of those who have installed gainsharing over the last fifty years advises that you break the process down into five steps: Awareness Raising, the Feasibility Study, Formula and Involvement System Design, Implementation, and Evaluation. Let's look at each of these.

Awareness Raising

The implementation of gainsharing results in significant change for most companies. Not only are compensation practices changed, but the entire management culture is changed. For example, just consider the implications of pay-for-performance we discussed in the last chapter. If you are successfully to accomplish this degree of change, top level management commitment is essential; therefore, the first step toward implementing gainsharing is to secure that commitment. How do you get that commitment? Primarily through information and awareness-raising programs. Here are some things to do:

1. Compile a library of books and articles on gainsharing and circulate these among senior managers. The history of gainsharing is extensively documented, and you should have little problem locating materials at your local library. If you do have trouble,

contact the American Productivity Center in Houston, Texas. They have numerous publications on gainsharing and can supply you with a large number of case studies on its application.

2. Based upon the information you have collected, prepare short summaries describing gainsharing, and arrange briefings for key managers.

3. As you review the case studies you collected and other documentation, you will identify companies that have adopted gainsharing. Most of these companies are very willing to share their experiences with you and, if you wish, to arrange for some of your key managers to visit them and learn about gainsharing firsthand. For example, we have taken numerous senior managers to Lincoln Electric when they were first considering gainsharing.

Your objective in this step is to secure sufficient top level interest in gainsharing to commit resources (people, time, money) to a feasibility study.

The Feasibility Study

In our opinion, you should never proceed with gainsharing without first conducting a feasibility study. There are just too many issues associated with gainsharing and too great a risk of failure should the program be implemented poorly to ignore the need for a beginning assessment.

To conduct the feasibility study, we suggest that top management appoint a gainsharing task force consisting of the following:

- The president of the company (if the company is small) or a senior manager

- The plant manager or location manager where gainsharing will first be installed (the feasibility study will be conducted at this location)

- The company comptroller

- The personnel manager or human resources manager

- Several other key managers, such as the quality control manager or industrial engineering manager

Although it is not absolutely necessary to do so, we suggest you hire an outside gainsharing consultant to help you with the feasibility study and later with the design, development, and installation of gainsharing. We make this recommendation because you can save a lot of time and expense by having the advice of someone who has been through this process before. Also, you will need the objectivity an outsider can bring. About 90 percent of the gainsharing programs that have been installed successfully have had the benefit of consulting assistance.

The objectives of the feasibility study are fourfold:

1. To determine the attitudes of top management and other key people concerning the applicability of gainsharing to the organization

2. To determine if existing management-employee relations and management practices support the teamwork, cooperation, and employee involvement that will be necessary to support gainsharing

3. To evaluate the feasibility of using one of the standard gainsharing formulas (Scanlon, Rucker, or Improshare) or of developing a customized formula if no standard formulas are appropriate

4. To assess the potential benefits, risks, and cost of implementing gainsharing

The actual study normally involves interviews with managers, supervisors, and at least a sample of employees; at least cursory operations reviews (products/services, process flow, measurement, reporting systems, current incentive plans, etc.); limited collection of historical data (productivity and financial); and the preparation of a formal report. Feasibility studies that we conduct normally include the following:

- Interviews with senior management about strategic issues and concerns. In particular, we seek to identify the critical areas of performance that should be emphasized by any gainsharing formula.

- A cursory examination of operating procedures and process flow. We look for major inputs/outputs and the interdependence of functional units.

- Interviews with middle management, supervisors, and a sample of employees covering the following areas:

  1. Knowledge of and reaction to gainsharing.

  2. Knowledge of company strategic direction and departmental/unit mission.

  3. Nature of and reaction to organizational change that has occurred in the last few years, such as changes in management, work methods, technology, human resource management practices, and so on. We seek to determine whether the change was successful and, based upon prior experience, the receptivity of managers, supervisors, and employees to change.

  4. Top down communication.

  5. Communication across functions and shifts.

  6. Use of supervisor and employee meetings, and what happens in these meetings.

  7. Existence of operational goals and objectives—do they exist at every level, are they understood, how are they set, are they viewed as fair and reasonable?

  8. Existence of measurements and feedback systems.

  9. Use of social reinforcement.

10. Use of performance appraisals—do they exist, how are they done, how helpful are they?

11. Decision-making/problem-solving styles and existence of/reaction to any employee involvement programs.

12. Existence of incentive plans (including group, individual, etc.).

13. Ideas for improvement—manager, supervisor, and employee evaluations of key areas for focus under gainsharing. Also, their assessment of the potential for gains through changes in employee behavior.

14. Job satisfaction—morale, trust, management/employee relations.

These interviews should be conducted one-on-one in private, and persons interviewed should be assured of the confidentiality of their answers to interview questions.

Once the feasibility study is completed, a formal report should be written outlining findings, conclusions, and recommendations. The report should cover both formula and involvement considerations.

There are three possible conclusions:

1. Gainsharing does not appear feasible and is not recommended.

2. Gainsharing is feasible and one of the standard plans might fit, possibly with some modification.

3. Gainsharing is feasible, but a customized plan will have to be developed.

If gainsharing is considered to be feasible, the feasibility report should outline preliminary recommendations about the formula. Which standard formula is most appropriate, if any, and why? If modifications are required, what type? If no standard formula will work, what should be included in a customized formula? Although no specific customized formula need be proposed at this time, the report should at least address the major factors that should be included in such a formula once it is developed.

In addition to discussing formula considerations, the feasibility report must address involvement issues. In this case, key findings should be presented for all the interview areas. This section of the report should be written whether or not gainsharing is found to be feasible. On occasion, we have found that we could not recommend gainsharing but have identified significant opportunities for improvement in management practices as a result of these interviews. Such findings should not be lost simply because gainsharing is not appropriate. In fact, it might be possible to correct some management problems identified during the feasibility study and, as a result, reconsider gainsharing at a later date.

If gainsharing is considered feasible, the involvement portion of the feasibility report must address how employees will be provided an opportunity to generate and implement ideas for performance improvement, and how information about the gainsharing program and performance will be shared with employees (what formal systems exist or can be developed). If changes are required, they should be identified, and a plan presented to the gainsharing task force for implementing them. This plan might call for training of managers and supervisors in MPM management techniques, the design and implementation of new reporting and feedback systems, and so on. Earlier chapters in this book outline the types of practices that should be in place prior to the start of gainsharing. In addition, a later chapter outlines an involvement system that will work for many gainsharing programs.

On the basis of the feasibility report, the gainsharing task force should now be able to make a recommendation either to proceed with the Design and Development step or to discontinue the effort. If a decision is made to proceed, the task force should draw up an implementation plan and cost estimates. These recommendations must then be submitted to senior management for approval.

Formula Design and Involvement System Implementation

Having obtained the feasibility study recommendations, the gainsharing task force can proceed with the third step—Formula Design and Involvement System Implementation. In effect, two activities occur simultaneously during this step—a formula is developed, and the implementation plan for enhancing management practices and opportunities for employee involvement is executed. The gainsharing task force has responsibility for both activities, although most of its time is spent on formula design. Its role in the involvement system is to oversee the activities of the consultant, human resources, information systems, and others who are responsible for carrying out steps in the involvement system plan. A key responsibility of the task force is to ensure that the development of the formula and implementation of the involvement system are coordinated so that the involvement part is in place and functioning by the time the formula is approved and gainsharing starts.

The work of the gainsharing task force should be organized around the preparation of a gainsharing design document, which will address all the major issues of implementation, operation, and on-going administration of the gainsharing program. The segments of the gainsharing design document are as follows:

1. Gainsharing task force membership

2. Implementation timeline

3. Objectives of the gainsharing program

4. Participant group

5. Eligibility

6. Allocation

7. Holdback provision

8. Gainsharing calculation (formula)

9. Bonus ceiling

10. Sharing ratio

11. Administrative provisions

The task force must make critical decisions about the gainsharing program in each of these segments. Here is a summary of the critical issues that must be addressed for each of the eleven segments.

1. Gainsharing Task Force Membership

Up to this point, the gainsharing task force has been composed of seven members:

- The president or a senior manager

- The plant or location manager

- The comptroller

- The personnel or human resources manager

- Three other key managers

Prior to the start of formula design, additional members should be added to the task force. These additional members should include:

- Functional area managers

- The union president or a union steward (if there is a union)

- Employee representatives.

After adding these members, the task force should ideally consist of between twelve and eighteen members.

Some argue that employee representatives should be selected by employees themselves, with perhaps each key functional area designating a representative. In our opinion, employee selection is not required as long as there is an honest effort to select members who can truly reflect employee views. When selecting members of the task force—employees or otherwise—remember that they must have the time to devote to task force duties.

2. Implementation Timeline

Once assembled, the first activity of the gainsharing task force should be to draw up an implementation timeline. This timeline is a project schedule or plan showing all the activities that must be completed prior to the introduction of gainsharing, including target dates for completion of these activities. The timeline should cover activities both related to formula development and approval as well as to implementation of the involvement system. A key to the timeline and success of gainsharing itself is the task force's decision about the targeted start date for gainsharing. Every effort should be made to pick a start date when the volume of work activity will allow gains to be made, provided employees work harder or smarter. For example, if the work load is seasonal, the low volume periods should be avoided. The worst thing that can happen is to start gainsharing and then experience months during which employees are unable to earn gains in spite of their efforts. Though selection of an appropriate start date requires a certain amount of forecasting on the part of task force members, it is a very important decision.

When discussing various possible start dates, the task force should ensure that it is allowing sufficient time for completion of all required activities and approvals leading up to gainsharing. For example, corporate attorneys or other officials will most likely have to review any proposed formula prior to its acceptance. Time must be built into the schedule for this review process. Don't be surprised if the timeline that is finally developed stretches over six months or even a year.

Obviously, one benefit of developing a detailed timeline at this point is that task force members will have to be taken through a description of the entire development and implementation process, thus they will understand the sequence of events and their responsibilities.

3. Developing a Statement of Gainsharing Objectives

After establishing a timeline, the task force should turn its attention to drafting a statement outlining the objectives of the gainsharing program. Although the objectives of the gainsharing program might seem obvious—to improve productivity, pay bonuses, etc.—they are actually more complicated than they first appear. Ideally, gainsharing should satisfy multiple, and sometimes competing, interests—those of employees, managers, stockholders, and customers. One of these interests is to share the financial and other gains from increased work performance with employees. However, sharing gains is not the only (and perhaps not even the most important) objective of gainsharing. Other and perhaps more important objectives might include the following:

- To provide more job security as a result of increased productivity

- To increase recognition for performance

- To improve communication

- To increase employee involvement

- To improve productivity

- To improve quality

- To increase problem identification and problem solving

- To improve teamwork and cooperation

- To increase organizational flexibility

- To improve competitiveness

- To improve sales and profits

- To reduce costs

- To provide an opportunity for increased earnings based upon performance

- To reduce resistance to change

- To promote a "continuous improvement" attitude

- To meet strategic goals and objectives

- To eliminate individual incentives

Obviously, there are many possible objectives of which these are only examples.

To assist gainsharing task forces in developing objectives, we ask them to consider all the relevant interests—managers, employees, stockholders, customers—and to develop objectives that could be supported by all these groups. Additionally, the objective should provide some direction concerning how it can be achieved. For example, instead of the objective "to reduce costs," we prefer something like the following:

To reduce unit costs with particular emphasis on the cost of labor, raw materials, and machine parts so that we can be the low cost producer and can ensure our competitive position and job security for the maximum number of employees.

4. Deciding upon the Participant Group

After preparing a statement of objectives, the task force must next decide upon who will be included in the gainsharing program. Again, this decision at first appears simple, but rarely is. For example, possibilities include

- only direct, or direct and indirect;

- only full time, or full time and part time;

- only permanent employees, or permanent and temporary;

- only hourly employees, or employees plus managers, supervisors, and nonexempts.

Key to these decisions, in our opinion, are the interdependence of the various groups and who can contribute to possible gains. For example, if the work of some or all of the indirect employees will significantly impact the potential for gains, then indirects should most likely be included. If large numbers of temporaries are used and their commitment will be required for gains, then consideration should be given to how they might be included.

A related issue is the size of the participating group. Experience with gainsharing generally suggests that the ideal size is five hundred or fewer employees. Larger groups, particularly those of more than two thousand employees, are generally considered poor candidates for a single gainsharing program, since the larger the group the less likely employees will see how their individual effort contributes significantly to group performance. If it is determined that the participant group will be very large, we normally suggest that consideration be given to subdividing the large group and creating separate gainsharing programs.

5. Eligibility

Eligibility refers to the requirements (if any) that must be met by members of the participant group before they can receive bonus payments. For example, normally there is a provision that new hires must complete a specified number of days of employment before being eligible for gainsharing bonuses. Additionally, decisions have to be made concerning the effect (if any) unexcused absences, personal leave, sick leave, and so on might have on the eligibility for or on the basis for calculating bonus payments. As a general rule, employees should be eligible when they can *contribute* to gains.

6. Allocation

Allocation decisions involve the method, "payout period," and, most importantly, how each person's share of the employee bonus pool will be determined. In respect to method of payment, bonuses can be paid as part of regular paychecks or in the form of a separate check. We prefer separate checks to maintain the distinction between the gainsharing bonus and base pay. Also, we feel separate checks have greater motivational impact.

The "payout period" involves both the time period over which gains are calculated and the amount of time allowed for calculating payments due and for issuing checks. Most gainsharing plans calculate gains and make payments monthly. Some companies base gains on quarterly or even semiannual performance. We prefer monthly plans since we feel longer periods are less motivating. In a few cases, we have seen plans that calculate gains based upon a four-week rolling average of performance or by some other more complicated method. Generally we don't prefer such plans since they are more difficult for employees to understand.

With the actual issuance of checks, the elapsed time required depends greatly upon the efficiency of your accounting and payroll functions. Generally we like to see checks issued as close as possible to the period of performance they cover; however, the task force needs to ensure that adequate time is allowed so that checks will be issued on time.

Perhaps the most controversial of allocation decisions concerns how individual bonus amounts will be calculated, since this decision effects the actual dollar amount of bonuses each employee will receive. Generally there are three methods:

1. *Equal shares*—The absolute amount in the bonus pool is divided by the number of employees so that each employee receives the same amount.

2. *Hours worked*—In this case, the absolute amount in the bonus pool is divided by the total hours worked to arrive at an amount of bonus due per hour worked. Each employee's payment is equal to the amount per hour times the hours that employee worked.

3. *Percent of total income*—Here, the amount in the bonus pool is divided by total wages (regular plus overtime) to arrive at a bonus percentage. Thus, if the bonus pool amount is 10 percent of total wages, each employee receives a 10 percent bonus (their individual wages for the period times .10).

In most cases, employees prefer that payments be based upon equal shares or hours worked, however the most frequently used method is percent of income. The reason for this choice is that the latter is the only sure way for a company to remain in compliance with the Fair Labor Standards Act.

Under the Fair Labor Standards Act (FLSA), bonuses and commissions paid to employees must be included as part of regular pay when calculating the rate for overtime (one and one half times the regular rate for hours over forty in one week). Only seven types of payments are excluded from this requirement: gifts, Christmas bonuses, special occasion bonuses, payments to profit-sharing, thrift plans, savings plans, and irrevocable contributions to a bona fide trust. Gainsharing payments are not among these exclusions. The only sure way to avoid problems under the Fair Labor Standards Act is to make bonus payments a percentage of total wages (regular plus overtime). In short, if you choose a different method, you should have the provisions reviewed carefully by your attorney to ensure you are not in violation of the FLSA or obtain permission in advance from the Department of Labor.

7. Holdback Provision

Many gainsharing companies include a provision to hold back a portion of employee bonuses to protect against short-term peaks in performance and to encourage employee concern about productivity gains over the long term. The danger from the company's viewpoint is that unusual conditions might result in very large bonuses for a few months of the year while productivity over the entire year doesn't improve or even worsens.

The gainsharing task force should consider the advisability of a holdback and the percentage of the bonus pool that should be held in reserve. When there is a holdback provision, the percentage placed in reserve in gainsharing plans typically ranges from as low as 10 percent to as much as 70 percent. Generally we prefer a holdback of 20 percent, since that level does not appear excessive but places enough of the bonus at risk to encourage employees to adopt a long-term view. Higher holdback percentages might be appropriate if the company experiences seasonal fluctuations, has a history of erratic performance, or spikes in performance are of concern to corporate management.

If there is a holdback provision, the task force needs to decide a number of other issues:

1. What will happen to the funds held back? Usually they are placed in a special account and paid out at the year's end provided performance for the total year is positive. Payments, if any, are usually made in the form of a separate check.

2. Can the reserve become negative, and if so, what happens? If a loss occurs during a period against the gainsharing target (that

is, performance falls below the Base for gainsharing), should the holdback be charged for the loss? If there are insufficient funds in the holdback to cover the loss, should the holdback be allowed to go negative? Also, should the holdback be the same for positive and negative periods, or should it increase for negative periods so that the funds in holdback absorb some or all of the loss? If the holdback is negative at the end of the year, should the company absorb the loss and "zero out" the account for the start of the new year, or should the loss carry over?

3. Finally, who is eligible to receive holdback payments at year's end? Are just those on the payroll at that time eligible, and if so, what about retirees, laid-off workers, or employees on extended leave?

8. Deciding upon the Gainsharing Calculation (Formula)

A critical decision for the task force will be to decide on the formula to be used for calculating gains. The feasibility study will have suggested some considerations in designing the formula, and these should be reviewed at this point. The task force should also review all the standard formulas (discussed earlier in this chapter) for their possible application.

Generally, possible formulas are of two types: performance based and financial based. Improshare and Objectives Matrix formulas tend to be performance based, while Scanlon and Rucker formulas are financial based. As might be expected, there are considerable arguments for and against each type, however, in our opinion, there is no right formula or type of formula. The task force should consider all types in light of the criteria for a good formula (see our earlier discussion) and the objectives for the gainsharing plan they developed earlier.

Part of the development of a formula is the establishment of a baseline from which gains will be calculated. Here there are two possible methods of calculation:

1. *Historical baseline*—Average performance is calculated over a period ranging from six months to as much as five years. Obviously, the length of time examined depends upon a number of factors, including the availability of data, the length needed to smooth out seasonal or cyclical fluctuations, and so on.

2. *Target baseline*—This approach is frequently used when past performance is considered to be poor. The argument is that gains should not be paid until a certain target level is reached, regardless of past performance.

The task force must additionally determine whether the baseline, once established, will remain "fixed" (all future gains will be measured from the same base performance level) or will change over time. If the Base is allowed to change, will it be "stepped up" by some predetermined level each year, or will the change be determined according to some recalculation of average performance (for example, be based upon a rolling average of the last X number of periods)?

Regardless of whether the Base is "fixed" or will "step up," the task force should consider management's option to change the Base should, for example, unit costs increase rather than decrease (perhaps as a result of a poor baseline), the company experience increased competitive pressure from a lower cost producer, or a significant price deterioration occur in the marketplace. In such situations, we prefer that the company be allowed to "buy back" a change in the Base by making a one-time payment to employees equal to some percentage of the difference between the "old" and the "new" baseline. For example, in return for being allowed to reset the Base from which gains are earned to the previous year's performance level, the company makes a one-time payment to employees equal to 50 percent of the difference between the old gainsharing Base and the new Base.

Finally the gainsharing document usually excludes gains that occur because of company action from payment to employees. For example, if the company changes the product mix substantially, makes significant capital investments, changes methods of operation, and so on, any gains directly associated with such changes are not shared with employees, since such changes are a result of company and not employee action. An exception might be the introduction of new technology or other changes initiated by the company but requiring employee cooperation. The company might then agree to share a percentage of any resulting gains with employees as an incentive to employees to help facilitate the change.

Having resolved the above issues, the task force should now run a number of test calculations with the gainsharing formula. These tests should illustrate the actual operation of the formula over several years of historical data, if possible, and for various hypothetical situations. Now is the time to ensure that the formula is operating as intended and meeting the gainsharing objectives outlined earlier.

9. Deciding on a Bonus Ceiling

In this step, the task force must decide whether there will be a cap on bonuses that can be earned during any single period. For example, the maximum bonus might be 10 percent, 20 percent, or 30 percent, with any gains in excess of the cap being lost or credited to the reserve (holdback) fund. Generally we prefer no cap, provided the formula is constructed so that gains are not too easy to make. In general, we do not believe that high wages translate into high operating costs, provided the wages result from true productivity improvements.

10. Deciding upon the Sharing Ratio

The sharing ratio specifies how the company and the employees will share in the savings achieved through gainsharing. This ratio must be fair to the company and to employees. We generally prefer a 50/50 split (company receives half and employees receive half) because such sharing seems equitable to both parties; however, other ratios (60/40, 75/25) have been used and are possible, provided there is some justification.

11. Deciding upon Administrative Details

In this final step, the task force will make a number of decisions concerning how the program will be administered during the first year. For example:

1. If the program starts in mid-accounting year, will the "first year" under gainsharing be shortened so that the holdback is paid out at the end of the current accounting year, thus bringing the gainsharing year into sync with the accounting year?

2. What about any training or start-up costs associated with gainsharing? Must they be absorbed by employees (costs must be overcome before gains are paid), or will the company absorb these costs?

3. Is there a need for and, if so, what will be the transition plan from individual incentive to gainsharing?

Implementation

After the task force has completed the gainsharing document and approval is obtained from company management, implementation should begin. Two steps are critical to implementation: (1) securing employee acceptance and approval, and (2) initiating employee involvement efforts.

To secure employee approval, the task force should initiate information programs to familiarize managers, supervisors, and employees with the specifics of the plan. The plan should be discussed in employee meetings, and employees should be provided with a summary of key features of the plan plus examples of test calculations. In particular, efforts should be made to explain the productivity-sharing emphasis in the plan (how everyone can win) and to dispel any fears employees might have that the formula will be manipulated by management to benefit the company unfairly. In some cases, it might be advisable to allow employees to vote on whether to adopt the plan. Though we do not feel that a vote is absolutely necessary, it can be helpful in securing employee commitment. We also use an employee survey to tell us how well the communication effort has worked.

Equally important to the introduction of the plan is the initiation of employee involvement projects. Ideally, the involvement program will have progressed to a point that employee problem-solving meetings are already being conducted on a regular basis and some projects are already underway. It is particularly important that these improvement efforts be tied into gainsharing. How will successful completion of these projects contribute to gains and bonuses?

Evaluation

Particularly throughout the first year, the gainsharing program must be monitored closely. The gainsharing task force should continue to meet on a regular basis to review these issues:

1. Do managers, supervisors, and employees understand the plan?

2. Are improvement projects being initiated?

3. Are improvements resulting from the implementation of employee ideas?

4. Are bonuses being paid?

5. Has company performance improved?

6. Are changes required in the gainsharing plan?

The result of this year-long evaluation should be a recommendation from the task force concerning whether or not the program should be retained and, if retained, whether modifications are necessary. We feel a formal, year-end review and another employee survey is appropriate to ensure that the program continues to meet the needs and objectives of both employees and the company. In fact, we often suggest that a "Sunset Provision" be included in the gainsharing plan. Such as provision requires a formal review of the plan after the first year and provides that the plan lapse unless a specific decision is made to continue.

Summary

In this chapter, we have examined gainsharing as a pay-for-performance system that will work well in many organizations. We showed how you can determine if gainsharing is appropriate for your company and discussed the steps to follow in implementing a gainsharing plan if it is appropriate.

As we noted previously, gainsharing programs have been extremely successful. For example, one review of thirty-three gainsharing programs, *Gainsharing—A Successful Track Record*, conducted by R. J. Bullock at the University of Houston, found the following:

- Performance improved in 80 percent of the programs.

- Quality of work life improved in 72 percent.

- Cost-saving ideas were generated in 89 percent.

- Labor-management relations improved in 67 percent.

- Gainsharing bonuses were paid in 91 percent.

Another study conducted by the U.S. General Accounting Office (GAO) in 1981 examined the experiences of thirty-six firms (U.S. General Accounting Office, *Can Productivity Sharing Programs Contribute to Increased Productivity?* U.S. GAO, 1981). The GAO concluded that gainsharing led to improvements in a number of areas including productivity, quality, equipment utilization, labor relations, and competitive position. It is these types of results that are generating the renewed interest in gainsharing in the 1980s and that have brought us to recommend gainsharing as a pay-for-performance system you should consider. But gainsharing is not without a significant weakness.

As we have noted, gainsharing is a group-based incentive program. As a result, gainsharing bonuses are distributed without regard to the performance of individuals within the group, and high performers frequently complain that under gainsharing they carry a disproportionate share of the work load. In the next chapter, we will examine how a properly implemented pay-for-knowledge system can be used to overcome this weakness.

Chapter 12

Pay-for-Knowledge: How to Increase Employee Flexibility

In the preceding chapter, we discussed a group-based pay-for-performance system called gainsharing that offers significant benefits to many organizations because it ties employee pay to performance while simultaneously encouraging teamwork, cooperation, employee involvement, and employee commitment to organization-wide objectives. We proposed gainsharing because of its benefits over other pay-for-performance systems and because we feel gainsharing has wide application, particularly for companies adopting the kind of participative and performance-oriented team approach to management suggested by MPM.

Although we obviously favor gainsharing as the performance-based compensation system of choice, we noted in the last chapter a significant weakness with gainsharing. As typically designed, gainsharing does not make individual performance distinctions in the distribution of bonus payments. As a result, exemplary performers often complain that under gainsharing they carry a disproportionate share of the work load without a corresponding increase in their share of bonus payments. Since we can always expect some differences in

235

performance between individual employees, the failure of gainsharing to distinguish between individual performance does represent a built-in inequity. Fortunately, in our opinion, there is a way to remove (or at least minimize) that inequity by using a second type of pay-for-performance system as an adjunct to gainsharing. This system is called pay-for-knowledge.

In this chapter, we will examine pay-for-knowledge systems—what they are, where they have been applied, their advantages, their disadvantages, how they can be implemented, and how they might work in conjunction with gainsharing.

What Is Pay-for-Knowledge?

Most simply, pay-for-knowledge systems are nontraditional compensation practices that tie base wages and salaries to knowledge and skill rather than to position or to the job actually performed. In addition to pay-for-knowledge, these systems are sometimes called "Skill-Based Compensation," "Knowledge-Based Pay," "Multi-Skill Compensation," "Pay-for-Skill," "Job Enrichment Progression," and so on. Regardless of the name, these systems are distinguished by the fact that employees who can perform a wider repertoire of jobs than other employees receive a higher base compensation.

In fact, there are two basic forms of pay-for-knowledge systems— "increased knowledge-based" systems and "multi-skilled based" systems. Increased knowledge-based systems base pay upon the range of skills employees possess in a single speciality or job classification. These systems are probably the most common pay-for-knowledge plans and, at their simplest, are nothing more than "technical ladders." For example, skilled trades often have a pay scale that increases as employees acquire additional skills and move from an entry to a journeyman level. Similar pay progressions based upon skill level can be found in universities, law offices, and R&D labs. Increased knowledge-based systems are sometimes called "vertical" systems because pay is tied to the depth of knowledge or skill in a defined job.

Multiskilled-based systems are a newer, less common, and more "revolutionary" form of pay-for-knowledge. In this case, pay progression is tied to the number of different jobs an employee can perform throughout the entire organization. For example, in a manufacturing environment employees might be paid higher rates based upon their ability to perform jobs "upstream" and "downstream" from their normal assignment in the production process. Maximum pay rates are paid to employees who can perform most or all jobs within the plant. Because they tie pay to the number of different jobs a person can perform, multiskilled-based systems are sometimes called "horizontal" systems.

In this chapter, we will be discussing both multiskilled and increased knowledge-based systems; however, our comments will focus primarily upon multiskilled systems since they are newer and provide by far the *most* potential for productivity improvement (30 to 40 percent more proactive, once they get going, than traditional plans and classifications).

Who Uses Pay-for-Knowledge?

Pay-for-knowledge systems can be found in some form in approximately 5 percent of American corporations. Most of these firms are in manufacturing, however pay-for-knowledge systems are expected to grow rapidly over the next few years and are expected to become much more common in the service sector. For example, the American Productivity Center survey we referred to in previous chapters projected that such systems will increase 75 percent overall—63 percent in manufacturing and 122 percent in the service sector. Also, pay-for-knowledge systems have so far usually covered just production workers.

Pay-for-knowledge systems—particularly multiskill-based systems—have been thought to be most successful and have been implemented with the greatest ease in new plants with a participative/team management style. In a new participative plant environment, such systems fit the management style, reinforce employees for learning new skills, and are more easily implemented because traditional attitudes about "job ownership" and "lines of demarcation" don't have to be overcome. In established plants, these systems are more difficult to implement precisely because of traditional views about "job ownership," yet they offer the possibility of breaking down such views and providing an incentive for veteran employees to learn new skills.

The Advantages of Pay-for-Knowledge

A number of specific benefits are normally cited by those who advocate pay-for-knowledge systems. These include the following:

1. *Greater flexibility*. By their very nature, pay-for-knowledge systems (particularly multiskilled-based systems) encourage employees to become more flexible in the types of jobs they are willing and able to perform. As a result, the company benefits because more people are available to substitute in the case of absenteeism or turnover or when employees are on leave or in training. When production bottlenecks occur, skilled employees who normally work further down the production line and are perhaps idle can be brought in to relieve the work load. Also, when production requirements change, employees can be moved to different product lines as needed. In effect, under pay-for-knowledge systems all employees are encouraged to become "utility" people, capable of performing work when and where they are needed.

2. *Leaner staff*. Since employees are more flexible, pay-for-knowledge systems frequently result in a leaner staff. Because of their increased flexibility, fewer employees stand idle waiting for work. Staffing for peak periods is avoided and employees are more fully utilized.

3. *Improved problem solving*. Expanded job knowledge leads to wider and more in-depth knowledge about the entire production process or service delivery system, and, as a result, employees are likely to be more effective problem solvers. In short, multiskilled employees have a broader perspective, are more innovative, and are more likely to propose solutions that will be effective systemwide.

4. *Improved horizontal communication*. Communication problems between functional units or job specialties are frequently aggravated by parochial interests, the use of jargon, and the inability of each area to understand the problems and needs of the other. In contrast, multiskilled employees are much more likely to overcome these barriers as a result of their wider experience and training.

5. *Improved vertical communication*. The failure of employees to understand and to support organization-wide goals and objectives often stems from their inability to view these objectives in an organization-wide context. In short, what makes sense to managers and supervisors who have a broader perspective might make no sense to an employee

who is restricted to a narrowly defined job speciality. Under pay-for-knowledge systems, employees are encouraged to develop a better understanding of the entire business, its needs and priorities. Not only are such employees in a better position to understand and accept upper level decisions, but they are in a better position to make suggestions that might improve these decisions.

6. *Supports employment security.* In an earlier chapter we discussed the movement away from "job security" and toward "employment security." We noted that the performance organization of the future will make every effort to secure continued employment, but not necessarily in a specific job or job specialty. Long-term employment requires company commitment to employee development (preparing the employee to assume more than one role) and employee willingness to be flexible in job assignments. Multiskilled-based pay-for-knowledge systems are fully consistent with this trend. Additionally, such systems demonstrate management's commitment to invest in the development of employees and to reward employees for developing expanded skills.

7. *Improved job satisfaction.* There is considerable support in the research on job design for creating jobs that allow employees to use a variety of skills and talents, to work on a "whole" process that has significance to the larger organization, and to exercise more control over their work environment (scheduling, procedures, etc.). For many people, such jobs result in higher intrinsic motivation, better quality, better productivity, reduced absenteeism, and so forth. Multiskilled-based pay-for-knowledge systems particularly encourage this type of job design.

The Disadvantages of Pay-for-Knowledge

Pay-for-knowledge systems tend to increase costs in three areas—labor, training, and administration. Labor costs increase because base pay rates under mature pay-for-knowledge systems are usually higher. Most such systems provide a range of pay levels from the entry level to mastery of all identified skills. At the entry level, rates are usually lower than in comparable companies with traditional pay systems; however, as employees acquire additional skills, their pay rates increase and they soon exceed the "average hourly wage" for personnel in companies with traditional compensation systems. Obviously, a strong attraction of pay-for-knowledge systems for employees is the opportunity to increase their base compensation. By adopting pay-for-knowledge, a company embraces the philosophy that employees with multiple skills have greater value, but that value does have to be produced. Increased labor costs do not present a problem if they are more than offset by increases in productivity, at least in the long term. However, such gains in productivity are not likely to occur overnight, and a company adopting pay-for-knowledge must be prepared to absorb the additional cost until productivity does improve. It must be remembered that the key factor in competitiveness is unit labor costs, *not* wages. High wages do not necessarily mean high costs.

In addition to an increase in labor costs, companies adopting pay-for-knowledge systems are also likely to experience an increase in the cost of training—both direct training costs and indirect costs due to loss of production while employees are being trained. Although some companies with pay-for-knowledge attempt to minimize training cost per employee by requiring that employees stay in a job for three to six months before learning additional skills, training costs are still high compared to traditional systems where employees stay for years in one job. As in the case of higher base wages, increases in training costs must be offset eventually by greater productivity if the pay-for-knowledge system is to work.

Finally, administrative costs are likely to increase under pay-for-knowledge. More elaborate record-keeping systems are required to keep track of the skill levels of individual employees, payroll systems have to handle perhaps a larger number of differing pay rates, and records have to be updated continuously to reflect skills acquired. All of this adds up to the necessity of having more sophisticated (and more expensive) administrative systems and perhaps additional administrative staff to support these systems.

How to Use Pay-for-Knowledge as an Adjunct to Gainsharing

On the surface, the cost disadvantages of pay-for-knowledge systems appear to make it a poor combination for a company with gainsharing. Many gainsharing formulas—particularly financial formulas—are negatively effected by any increased costs. Even if costs do not impact the formula, productivity does, and in the short term, pay-for-knowledge systems are likely to impact productivity negatively since experienced employees will be constantly rotated out of old jobs and into training or new jobs. Although we recognize these problems, we still believe for several reasons that pay-for-knowledge can be a useful addition once gainsharing is in place and has had time to mature.

First, as we said previously, we believe a pay-for-knowledge system can help correct any inequity that might exist with the gainsharing plan. We see the problem this way. Under most gainsharing plans, bonuses are distributed based upon a percentage of base pay (regular plus overtime) or, less frequently, by some other method that does not include an evaluation of individual contribution. A frequent objection of high performers to gainsharing plans is that their individual contribution is not recognized. If the gainsharing plan replaces an individual incentive system, high performers might actually receive, in some cases, smaller bonuses than they did under the former system. We believe a pay-for-knowledge system will correct this inequity, since it ties base rate compensation to the variety of skills an employee brings to the group. Though skills are not a direct measure of contribution, in the long term we believe that the most valuable individual to the company and to the team is not the person who can do one thing *exceptionally* well, but the person who can do a variety of things important to group goals *very well*. It is the latter person who is rewarded under pay-for-knowledge.

A second reason we are in favor of pay-for-knowledge is that it tends to correct any inequities in the distribution of bonus payments that can occur under gainsharing. As we noted, most gainsharing plans distribute bonuses as a percentage of pay (regular plus overtime); thus, employees with a higher base compensation receive a larger bonus (in dollars). Traditionally, base compensation is a function of seniority, position, and status. It does not necessarily correspond to skill level. Over time, a multiskill-based pay-for-knowledge system brings base compensation and skills more in line. As a result, larger dollar amounts of gainsharing bonuses go to employees with a wider variety of skills, and that is the key to the future—flexibility!

A third reason we favor a pay-for-knowledge system is because we feel it encourages the flexibility and the development of systemwide knowledge that is necessary for long-term gains. When gainsharing is first introduced, there are usually many opportunities for making relatively simple performance improvements that will lead to gains.

Over time, however, problem solving becomes more difficult, for the simple problems have already been solved. Additional gains, particularly when there is a moving Base for gainsharing, require greater sophistication, flexibility, and the ability to tackle systemwide problems. Pay-for-knowledge systems encourage the development of this flexibility and broaden the focus.

Finally, we see pay-for-knowledge as a natural companion to gainsharing because it extends the same management philosophy. As we said in the previous chapter, gainsharing is more than a system for awarding employee bonuses. When properly and successfully implemented, gainsharing is a complete approach to management that encourages teamwork, cooperation, employee involvement, and employee commitment to organization-wide goals. Pay-for-knowledge extends this philosophy by encouraging employees to learn more about the business and to develop a wider range of skills that can be used to support organizational objectives.

Obviously, the adoption of a pay-for-knowledge system has significant implications for gainsharing bonuses. Over the short term, the cost of installing and operating pay-for-knowledge can make gains difficult, if not impossible. It is in the long term that pay-for-knowledge can help. For this reason, we don't suggest that pay-for-knowledge systems be adopted until the gainsharing program has been installed and employees have become accustomed to nontraditional compensation. Initially under gainsharing, there typically is a short-term focus on next month's or next quarter's gains. This occurs in spite of the provisions in gainsharing—such as holdback—that attempt to instill a long-term view. Over time, however, employees begin to see the value of consistent, long-term improvement. It is at that point that a pay-for-knowledge system becomes feasible, in spite of its short-term costs.

A Guide to Designing and Installing Pay-for-Knowledge Systems

The design and installation of a pay-for-knowledge system requires just as much time and attention—if not more—than gainsharing does. Our first problem is that we do not have the years of experience with pay-for-knowledge (in particular, multiskill-based systems) that we do with gainsharing. For that reason, we cannot give you a model to follow based upon years of experience as we did with gainsharing. What we can do is to suggest some basic steps you should follow and some of the critical decisions at each stage. Although the activities at each step are different, the basic steps we suggest are the same as for gainsharing:

- Awareness raising

- Feasibility assessment

- Design

- Implementation

- Evaluation

Below we examine each of these steps.

Step #1: Awareness Raising

As with gainsharing, we recommend that you begin your consideration of a pay-for-knowledge system with awareness raising. Gather the books, articles, and other resources describing existing pay-for knowledge systems. Your disadvantage in this case is that there are not as many publications on pay-for-knowledge as there are on gainsharing. Here are three articles we can suggest: (1) G. Douglas Jenkins, Jr. and Nina Gupta, "The Payoffs of Paying for Knowledge," *National Productivity Review* (Spring 1985), pp. 121-30; (2) Nina Gupta, G. Douglas Jenkins, and William P. Curington, "Paying for Knowledge: Myths and Realities," *National Productivity Review* (Spring 1986), pp. 107-23; and (3) Edward E. Lawler and Gerald E. Ledford, "Skill Based Pay: A Concept that's Catching On," *Management Review* (February 1987), pp. 46-51.

Your objective during this step is to determine if sufficient interest exists to move forward to a formal feasibility assessment.

Step #2: Feasibility Assessment

We recommend that you now conduct a formal feasibility assessment before undertaking the design of any pay-for-knowledge system. Pay-for-knowledge systems are more complex than gainsharing, more difficult to design, and more difficult to administer. You need some up-front assessment of the appropriateness of pay-for-knowledge before you proceed to the design phase.

To conduct the feasibility assessment, we suggest you assemble a pay-for-knowledge task force similar in composition to the one you used for gainsharing. Members should include:

- A senior manager

- The company comptroller

- The personnel manager or human resources manager

- Three other key managers

In addition to the above, you should consider hiring an outside consultant experienced in the design of pay-for-knowledge systems to assist the task force.

The objectives of the feasibility study are:

- To determine the cost/benefit trade-offs of a pay-for-knowledge system. You will recall that the primary advantages of such a system are increased employee flexibility, leaner staffing, improved problem solving, improved communication, increased employment security, and improved job satisfaction. Disadvantages include increased costs for labor, training, and administration. The feasibility study should examine these advantages and disadvantages.

- To determine the extent to which existing jobs can be broken down into identifiable and learnable skills or skill levels. As we noted, not all jobs have clearly identified skills that can be tied to a pay rate. The feasibility study should determine which jobs, because of clearly identifiable skills, are appropriate/feasible for a pay-for-knowledge system. The study should also examine the impact on people in jobs that will *not* be part of pay-for-knowledge.

- To assess the ability of existing administrative systems to support a pay-for-knowledge system. As we have suggested, pay-for-knowledge systems place additional burdens on payroll and other personnel systems because they must keep track of employee skills, skill pay rates, and training needs. The feasibility study should examine existing systems in light of general requirements for a pay-for-knowledge system.

- To assess the ability of training functions to support the increased demands for training that pay-for-knowledge systems entail. Are training resources adequate to meet this demand? How much of the demand can be handled through informal, on-the-job training, if any?

- To assess the probable impact of a pay-for-knowledge system on gainsharing or other incentive systems. As we noted, pay-for-knowledge can result in a short-term loss in productivity and increased costs in several areas. The feasibility study should evaluate the probable impact of these changes.

- To assess the level of knowledge and support for a pay-for-knowledge system among managers, supervisors, and employees.

Based upon the results of the feasibility study, the task force should make a recommendation to either proceed or to discontinue consideration of a pay-for-knowledge system.

Step #3: Design of the Pay-for-Knowledge System

The design phase proceeds very much like the design phase for gainsharing, with the task force holding meetings and making a number of decisions about the operation of the system. As with gainsharing, we recommend that the original task force be expanded to include union representatives (if there is a union) and employees. Here are examples of the issues that should be discussed and the action that should be taken by the task force:

1. Which employees will be covered by the pay-for-knowledge system? Traditionally, these systems have been applied most often just

to direct employees or to production workers. However, if indirect employees are covered by gainsharing, should they be included in the pay-for-knowledge system also?

2. How will skills and skill levels be determined, and how many should there be? Usually tasks are identified for existing jobs, and then each task is broken down into the skills required to perform it. Depending upon the number of different tasks performed and the distinctiveness of the tasks, the number of identifiable skills can vary greatly. For example, in their "Myths and Realities" article, Gupta, Jenkins, and Curington found that plants using pay-for-knowledge identified as few as four or as many as ninety different skills. If a detailed analysis has not been conducted for all existing jobs in the areas to be covered by the new system, such an analysis might have to be directed by the task force.

3. Once skills are identified, the task force must determine whether individual employees will be allowed to learn all skills or just some. If there are a large number of skills, it is likely employees could not learn and remain proficient in all of them; thus, there probably should be some restrictions. If the restrictions are too severe, however (a person is allowed to learn only a few skills), there will be limited room for employee growth and employees will tend to "max out" (learn all available skills) too early. Gupta, Jenkins, and Curington found that most companies they surveyed did restrict employees to a maximum number of skills—usually seven or fewer. In our opinion, there should be some restrictions, dependent upon the complexity of the skills to be learned and how easily an employee can remain proficient in the skills once they are learned. Most companies end up with skills that can be mastered in six months or less and with a total block of skills such that, with steady progression, an employee could master all available skills and reach the top of the pay-for-knowledge scale within approximately five years.

4. Related to the question of skills is how proficiency in a skill will be determined. Most companies provide for some type of formal test and evaluation—usually when the person comes out of training. Some also use peer evaluations or supervisor ratings. There is usually some requirement for periodic retesting, refresher training, rotation through

a job requiring use of the skill, or some other method for ensuring that the skill is retained. If it is determined that the skill was not retained, employees might lose the incremental pay for that skill immediately or be placed in a type of probationary status and given a limited period to relearn the skill.

5. An important decision of the task force is how the training will be provided for and funded. In most cases, training is held during regular hours, and employees are paid for the training time. This cost can be absorbed by the company or charged back to the employee's unit. Usually training is scheduled as part of an employee development plan, and the company exercises some discretion over how many employees may receive training in a particular skill. For example, the company might not need all employees to be fully trained in all skills or at all skill levels. If restrictions are imposed on the skills that can be learned, the task force should discuss how to handle employees who are "held up" because of restrictions at any particular level (that is, the employee is ready to learn a new skill or skill level, but no vacancy exists). Some companies with pay-for-knowledge provide for a "Hold Up Rate"—a slight adjustment in compensation for employees who are ready to progress to a higher skill level but who cannot because no vacancy exists.

6. "Maxing out" occurs when an employee learns all available skills and reaches the top of the pay scale. Under most pay-for-knowledge systems, this does not happen for a few years since there are many skills employees can learn when a pay for knowledge system is first installed. However, eventually these skills are learned, and employees reach the top of the pay scale. The task force should discuss what, if anything, should be done once an employee "maxes out." Some companies provide only merit or cost-of-living increases at this point, others are concerned that, if employees are allowed to "max out," the pay-for-knowledge system will have a short-term life expectancy. An alternative to allowing employees to "max out" is to provide an increased knowledge-based skill progression as a supplement to the multiskill-based system. This addition would at least extend the program for a few years. Also, when a multiskill-based system is used with gainsharing, employees who are at the top of the pay scale receive higher dollar amounts in gainsharing bonuses, since their base rate is higher.

7. The task force should discuss the connection between skills and pay progression. If there is a relatively small number of skills (eight to ten), then pay progression may be tied directly to the acquisition of each skill, with a pay progression similar to the following:

Skill Level	Hourly Base Rate
Entry	$ 5.50
1	6.00
2	6.50
3	7.00
4	7.50
5	8.00
6	9.00
7	9.50
8	10.00
9	11.00
Top Level	$12.00

If a large number of skills are identified, the connection to pay might be through the accumulation of "skill units" or points. In this case, employees must accumulate a specified number of points or "units" to move from one pay level to the next. The increase in pay from one level to the next can be in equal increments or can vary depending upon the complexity of the skills acquired. However the progression occurs, the task force should establish the formula or pay chart showing the skill to pay level linkage.

8. Since under a pay-for-knowledge system base pay is tied to skill, the task force needs to consider what should happen if a skill becomes obsolete due to the introduction of new technology, work methods, or procedures. Three alternatives exist. Do nothing—base pay stays the same—reduce base pay by the amount of the obsolete skill, or freeze base pay for a period while an alternative needed skill is learned. Of these choices, the latter appears to be the best. In our opinion, base pay adjustments should be provided only for skills the company needs and can use. At the same time, we feel employees should have some protection from the immediate loss of pay should a skill become

obsolete through no fault of their own. The best option is to provide a grace period during which the pay level is protected and the employee is given the opportunity to learn a replacement skill.

9. Finally, the task force should discuss the probable impact of the pay-for-knowledge system on productivity and the gainsharing program. As we said previously, because of increased training and job rotation with pay-for-knowledge, it is likely that the pay-for-knowledge system, at least over the short term, will have a negative impact on productivity, will increase costs, and will consequently impact gainsharing bonuses. The task force should discuss how any negative impact on productivity and on gainsharing should be handled. One possibility is to make no adjustments on the assumption that any short-term losses will be more than made up for in the long term as a result of increased employee flexibility and business knowledge. In this case, any productivity losses are borne partially by employees, who might lose gainsharing bonuses. An alternative approach is for the company to absorb some or all of the increased training and administrative costs, thus reducing the negative effect on gainsharing. The latter might be reasonable, at least as an interim measure, to encourage employees to accept the pay-for-knowledge system.

Step #4: Implementation

The task force should now prepare a document summarizing its decisions about how the pay-for-knowledge system will operate. Once approvals are obtained, a communication program should be conducted to familiarize employees with the concept and with how the system works. We suggest that the plan be discussed with employees in employee meetings, and that summaries be prepared illustrating how the acquisition of skills will affect base pay rates. In particular, there should be an honest discussion of the probable impact of the system on gainsharing and of how that impact will be handled (will the company absorb some of the losses?). If appropriate, employees could be allowed to vote on adoption of the plan, or a survey can be taken to gauge employee acceptance.

Step #5: Evaluation

As with gainsharing, there should be ongoing evaluation of the impact of the pay-for-knowledge system. In particular, the task force should examine the following issues:

1. Have skills been identified properly?

2. Are any skills becoming obsolete?

3. Do new skills need to be added?

4. How rapidly are employees acquiring new skills?

5. What impact is the system having on gainsharing?

6. What impact is the system having on average pay rates?

It is very important that continuous evaluation be conducted throughout the first year. Additionally, a "Sunset Provision" should be included in the plan calling for a formal review and a decision on whether or not to continue after the first year.

Summary

In this chapter, we examined a second type of pay-for-performance system called pay-for-knowledge. We discussed how pay-for-knowledge can be used as an adjunct to gainsharing to reward exemplary individual performance, to encourage employee flexibility, and to promote increased communication and problem solving.

With this chapter, we conclude our discussion of financial incentives. Together with the social consequences discussed earlier, plus directive and confirming information, we believe a strong framework has been built for maximum performance. The remaining need is for a vehicle for employee involvement. How will employees use the information at their disposal? How will performance gains be made so that employees can receive social reinforcement and incentive bonuses? How will employees be involved in generating ideas and implementing solutions? Answers to these questions are addressed in the next chapter.

PART 4:
Employee Involvement

Chapter 13

How to Design and Install an Employee Involvement System

In previous chapters, we described methods for providing employees with directive and confirming information. We outlined systems for creating financial and social consequences that are conducive to high performance from all employees. But information and consequences are not enough. We need a structured process for involving employees in decision making and problem solving. Providing opportunities for employee involvement is the third primary task of MPM managers, and it is the most important task of all.

In this chapter, we examine employee involvement systems. We describe what has been tried, what doesn't work, and what we learned from our experience. Most importantly, we outline an involvement system that will work and a process for implementing that system. But let's start with the basics—why involve employees in the first place?

Why Employee Involvement Is Important

You will recall from our opening chapter that, in addition to differences in knowledge and motivation, another basic difference between excellent and typical employees is their mental and physical capacity. Excellent employees are often excellent simply because they bring to the workplace unique mental and/or physical talents that give them a decided advantage in performing the work that needs to be performed. Even if these individuals have no greater knowledge, skills, or information than their counterparts, they still perform at a higher level. Their internal motivation or external inducements for performance might be no greater than those of typical employees, yet they still perform better. Why? Because the work is simply easier for these people. If the work requires excellent hand and eye coordination, these people have that coordination. As we noted in our opening chapters, it is not the particular mental or physical ability that is important, but the unique match between the ability required for performance of the job and the natural ability of the excellent performer.

If jobs were static, if selection procedures were sufficiently precise, and if the pool of available talent was sufficiently large, we might be able to approach a perfect match between an employee's innate abilities and the requirements of the job. But jobs are not static—our needs change over time. Selection is as much an art as a science—even with the best procedures, we can never be completely sure of matching ability to requirements. Finally, our pool of available talent is always limited—even if the best person for each particular job could be identified, chances are he or she is not available when needed. With few exceptions, then, we are left with an imperfect match between man or woman and job. How do we compensate for the difference? How do we enable the average employee to perform more like the naturally gifted? We do so by providing average employees with methods, tools, procedures, techniques and technology. In fact, the only reason for such tools, techniques, and procedures is to allow average employees to maximize their contributions. But if these tools, techniques, and procedures are to work for us, employees must be involved in selecting them.

Why involve employees? Gradually, most of us have come to the realization that employees must be involved in arranging their own work environment. Not only do the people performing the work have the best ideas about how it should be performed, but, as trite as it sounds, we now realize that people don't resist their own ideas. A solution to a problem is much more likely to be developed and successfully implemented when we get employee input. As a result, we have tried throughout the years to involve employees. Too often, our efforts failed. We didn't get the kind of ideas and gains in performance we envisioned, and we didn't get the level of participation from employees we would have liked. In some cases, the involvement programs we installed didn't last over time.

Involvement Techniques—What Doesn't Work

American businesses have tried a wide variety of techniques to involve employees. Involvement techniques range from structured efforts by management to share information about company performance, competition, and the like to elaborate programs designed to encourage employees to develop and implement performance improvement ideas. Of all the techniques that have been used, three stand out, but only for the frequency with which they have been tried rather than for their effectiveness. These techniques are Employee Surveys, Suggestion Systems, and Quality Circles. Each of these techniques has its advocates, and each can work. But each has failed more often than it has worked. These, then, are our examples of involvement techniques that "don't work." We pick them not because they can't work, but because each has significant weaknesses that frequently doom them to failure over the long term. If you are using one or more of these techniques and they are working for you, keep them. The technique we suggest later as a better alternative will work along with a successful survey, suggestion system, or quality circle program. You don't have to abandon what is working to install what we will suggest. If you are not using an involvement technique, we encourage you to consider the following comments about the strengths and weaknesses of these more traditional involvement techniques before adopting one for your company.

Employee Surveys

One of the most popular techniques for involving employees is the annual or biannual employee survey. Usually the survey consists of a written questionnaire, distributed to all employees or to a representative sample of employees. Sometimes the written questionnaire is supplemented with employee interviews conducted by members of the survey team. These surveys collect data concerning employee opinions, attitudes, job satisfaction, reaction to company policy or management decisions, relationships with supervisors, and so on. Employees might be asked to indicate their opinions by marking rating scales and possibly to provide comments to elaborate on their ratings.

Surveys are popular for a number of reasons. They are relatively easy and inexpensive to implement, they collect a large amount of data on the opinions of everyone in the organization, and, when administered over a period of years, they allow management to assess trends in employee attitudes over time. Based upon this data, judgments can be made about whether employees perceive a particular issue or problem as improving or deteriorating.

Though employee surveys represent a step in the direction of involvement, they have severe limitations. First, they are relatively infrequent. Surveys usually are conducted only once per year. Second, although they solicit input from all or a large sample of employees, that input is "one way" and limited. Employees answer questions and provide ratings on prepared scales, and comments, if any, tend to be short and cryptic. Third, the validity of the survey depends greatly on its design. All too often, written surveys are poorly worded with questions that are biased or vague. The validity of the resulting data suffers accordingly. Even if the surveys are properly constructed, however, no action results in most cases, as various levels of management try to interpret or even disregard findings inconsistent with their interests. Too often, employees become disenchanted with surveys when they receive very little feedback on the results and see no action to remedy problems. The surveys eventually become a joke, or perhaps worse, no more than an opportunity for employees to vent their frustrations.

Suggestion Systems

One of the oldest involvement techniques, dating back to the 1800s in some companies, is the suggestion system. With this technique, employees are encouraged to submit suggestions to their supervisor and/or a suggestion review committee. If an employee's suggestion is accepted and implemented, the company might share some of the savings reaped from the idea with the employee.

As with surveys, employee suggestion systems have the advantage of being relatively easy to install. They are a low cost method of involving employees, and everyone has the opportunity to become involved since anyone can submit a suggestion. Unlike surveys, suggestion systems are ongoing. An employee can submit a suggestion at any time; there is no need to wait a year or longer to voice an idea. Additionally, employees can benefit personally—and occasionally substantially—by submitting a suggestion that saves the company money.

Even with all their potential, suggestion systems typically have not worked. There are just too few suggestions submitted under most systems. When suggestions are submitted, they tend to be vague and undeveloped, and they usually cannot be implemented as submitted. If the basic idea is good and management or others develop the idea to a level that can be implemented, to what extent should the employee who originally submitted the vague suggestion receive credit? Often there is a lengthy delay between the submission of the idea and its consideration and eventual adoption. Feedback to the employee submitting the suggestion is delayed, and other similar suggestions might have been made. Perhaps the idea was already under consideration by management and thus does not qualify for a suggestion award. Eventually, with the delay and confusion about who deserves credit for the idea, employees become frustrated with the whole system. Why submit ideas? They will only be ignored, or worse, "stolen" by management. Like surveys, suggestion systems frequently become nothing more than a joke.

Quality Circles

Developed in Japan, quality circles have been popular in the United States since the late 1970s. As typically implemented in the United States, circles are voluntary small groups of employees who meet on a regular basis to discuss problems in the workplace. Members review data, identify problem areas, analyze the possible causes of problems, and recommend solutions. Usually the groups work under the guidance of a trained leader or facilitator, and usually the circle members have a formal opportunity to submit their proposals as a group to senior managers.

Quality circles have the reputation of being very successful in Japan. In fact, Japan's ability to change the meaning of the phrase "Made in Japan" from one signifying junk merchandise to one signifying quality has been attributed, at least in part, to that country's use of quality circles. By 1980, it was estimated that over 10 million Japanese workers were involved in circles. In 1974, quality circles were started in the United States, and they gained popularity quickly.

On the surface, quality circles have much to offer. Employees in these circles have the opportunity to participate on an ongoing basis in the identification and resolution of problems. Perhaps most importantly, circle members receive training and guidance in the use of often very sophisticated problem-solving techniques and have a structured opportunity to apply these techniques. As a result, circles are much more likely than suggestion systems to produce ideas that are fully developed and workable. In some instances, circles have been able to generate solutions that improved quality, reduced costs, increased safety, or improved the work environment. However, for the most part, quality circles have not produced these kinds of results.

In our travels, we have encountered many quality circles. Most were succeeding in the "soft" measures and failing in the "hard." Employees who participated in circles invariably felt more involved in the business, had learned new problem-solving skills, and had better morale. At the same time, managers frequently complained that they were spending more and more time on the operation of their quality circle program but not seeing the kind of improvement in quality, cost reduction, or customer service they had expected. All too often, quality circles were solving problems such as "where to place the water cooler," but were not addressing task-oriented problems such as "how to reduce rework." Circles operated out of the mainstream of the business with little, if any, management focus or direction. In most cases, the program was administered by staff such as human resources, quality control, or engineering. Line managers did not see circles as a part of the day-to-day operations. Circle meetings took employees away from the job, and the ideas generated by circle members by-passed the normal chain of command. Some middle managers felt threatened by their lack of involvement and lack of control of circle activities. Feeling "left out of the process" and actually competing with the staff functionaries who administered the quality circle program, some line managers sought to sabotage the program. To counter this resistance, quality circle facilitators often spent more of their time as advocates trying to sell the program than they did actually administering the program. Additionally, for most employees nothing changed in their own work environment. Since quality circles were voluntary programs with limited participation, the vast majority of employees were not involved. Not only did these employees receive no benefit from the "quality of work life" improvements experienced by circle participants, but nonparticipants often resented employees who were circle members. For many companies, quality circles became "just another program." These companies routinely bragged about the number of circles they had in operation, but no one talked about results. For too many companies, circles became a technique or gimmick—just the latest management "fad."

Involvement Systems—What We Should Have Learned

The problems and poor experience with quality circles and other employee involvement techniques does not mean that we should abandon employee involvement. However, it does mean that we should learn from our mistakes. What should we have learned?

1. Voluntary programs don't work. First, we should have learned that voluntary employee involvement programs just don't work. Too few employees participate, and those who aren't involved have no "buy-in" to the decisions and might sabotage, or at least resist, the proposed changes. We need every employee's ideas, not just those of a chosen few, even if those chosen few are self-selected.

2. Management direction and participation is mandatory. We should have learned that involvement systems require management direction and participation. Providing more information to employees will help, but we still need to guide and direct employees in their problem-solving efforts. We must shift the focus away from "where to place the water cooler" to "how to improve quality, on-time delivery, or customer service." We must move from purely "comfort or trivial pursuits" to meaningful business concerns.

3. Involvement systems can't be peripheral to running the business. We need to make employee involvement a structured part of the way we run the business. It shouldn't be some "off line" program administered by a corporate or staff functionary. Involving employees should be the responsibility of line managers and supervisors. Involvement should not be a program or technique, but a day-to-day way of managing. Problem solving should be a regular part of management and supervisory activity at every level, with all employees participating.

4. Every employee must be trained in problem solving-skills, not just a few. Identifying and solving problems should be the responsibility of everyone in the organization, not just a few. It should be an ongoing activity, not something special. For this to happen, every employee needs training and coaching in problem solving. Although employees have much to offer in the way of creative solutions, they are often frustrated in their efforts simply because they lack skills in problem identification, causal analysis, and how to develop creative solutions. Our experience with quality circles should have taught us that all employees are capable of developing these skills, but that they can't do it by themselves. They need our help.

5. Cross-functional teams and special task forces should address cross-shift, cross-departmental problems. We should not create special problem-solving teams to address interdepartmental or interfunctional problems. Those problems should be solved by employees within the department or function. Special teams are appropriate, however, for dealing with plantwide, departmentwide, or divisionwide problems. Since such task forces will operate in a matrix type environment, task force leaders and members should be provided with training and coaching in areas such as negotiation, consensus decision making, and conflict resolution so they can avoid the typical problems of cross-functional teams.

An Involvement System that Does Work

The involvement system we recommend for MPM addresses the problems associated with traditional approaches such as surveys, suggestion systems, or quality circles. This MPM system is nonvoluntary, directed by line management, is an integral part of running the business, involves every employee in problem-solving activities, and provides for the creation of short-term task forces to address cross-functional problems as needed. The approach calls for the creation of work group teams that follow the traditional organizational hierarchy. Here is how the system works.

Employees in each division, department, shift, and so on are members of a work group team. There are teams at the senior management level, middle management level, supervisory level, and hourly/worker level. The leader of each team is the supervisor or manager of that particular work group. Team members are the employees who report directly to that leader. There is thus a hierarchy of teams as illustrated in figure 9.

Membership in MPM teams is not voluntary. Everyone in the organization, regardless of title or level, is a member of a team and receives training in problem-solving skills. All team leaders (all managers and supervisors) receive training in team building and leadership skills. Supervisors and middle managers are involved in two teams. They lead the team consisting of the people reporting directly to them, and are also members of their boss's team. Any new employee automatically becomes a member of his/her boss's team.

Since the leader of each team is a manager or supervisor, every team receives direction from management. Also, since teams follow the traditional organizational pyramid, team activity is always "on line" and an integral part of running the business. The MPM involvement system is not a special program.

MPM teams look much like the traditional organization. In fact, because they follow traditional organizational lines, they can be installed with little, if any, disruption to the existing structure. But MPM teams differ from the traditional organization in three ways: (1) their activities center around a regular team meeting that is significantly different from normal staff meetings, (2) the supervisor's or manager's role is changed drastically, and (3) employees assume responsibilities that were traditionally reserved for managers and supervisors. Let's look at each of these differences.

Team Meetings—The Centerpiece of MPM Involvement

In the traditional organization, it is not unusual for employees to meet as a group with their supervisor on a regular or special basis. Many supervisors hold weekly or monthly staff meetings. In such

NATURAL WORK UNIT TEAMS

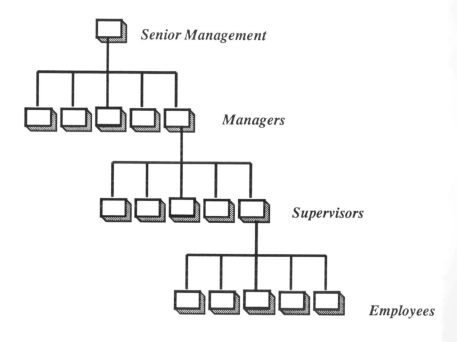

- *An Organized Grapevine*
- *Natural Work Group Teams*
- *Management Directed*
- *100% Employee Participation*
- *Supports Cross-Functional Problem Solving*

Figure 9

meetings, usually the manager or supervisor talks, and employees listen. Upper level decisions are announced, plant or company news is reported, orders are issued, mistakes are criticized, poor performance is berated. If employees participate at all in the meeting, it is to answer questions, to report on the status of projects/activities, and occasionally to defend themselves from attack. In some instances, employees use these meetings to gripe, complain, socialize, point fingers, or frequently dump problems on their boss. If problems are discussed, they are *just* discussed. There is usually little, if any, problem solving. A typical conclusion to a discussion of problems is, "I guess we have to do something about that . . ." Of course, nothing is done. The same problem will surface at several consecutive meetings, will remain unresolved, and eventually is forgotten as new and more currently pressing problems emerge.

MPM team meetings differ from traditional staff meetings in that they have both specific objectives and a specific structure. The objectives of the MPM team meetings are:

1. To share information and ideas. The MPM team leaders link everyone in the company in an organized grapevine. The leader collects ideas, questions, and concerns from team members and passes these upward to higher level teams. In addition, the leader passes down information about the goals, objectives, concerns, and priorities of higher levels.

2. To monitor performance and provide feedback. Each team has a clearly defined mission and measures of performance in critical areas. The team meeting is a major focal point for reviewing group performance in critical areas on a regular basis.

3. To recognize and reinforce good performance. The team leader and team members use the meeting to recognize and reinforce team members who are performing well and/or have contributed in some special way toward the achievement of group goals.

4. To get everyone's input and ideas for improving performance. A portion of each team meeting is set aside for problem identification, analysis, and the development of action plans to solve problems.

5. To establish accountability for action. Team meetings are used to review the status of action plans and task assignments from previous meetings. Individual team members are required to report back to the team on completion of their own task assignments.

To meet these objectives, each team meeting follows a standard agenda of five parts. The following shows the order in which they generally occur in the meeting:

1. Follow-up items. The leader opens each meeting by responding to questions, ideas, concerns, and/or recommendations from the previous team meeting. Usually there are one or more items that the leader had agreed to discuss with higher levels. In this segment, the team leader reports back to the team members on the status of those items. After the leader is finished, individual team members who had task assignments from the previous team meeting are called upon to report on the status of those assignments.

2. Performance feedback. The second agenda item for a team meeting is a review of group performance on key indicators for the current period. This review usually involves display of the graphs on performance that are maintained by members of the team. The focus of discussion is on positive and negative trends in performance over time.

3. Recognition and reinforcement. During this segment, individual team members and/or the entire team is recognized and reinforced for performance improvement or goal attainment. Reinforcement is initiated by the team leader, who has identified in advance of the meeting one or more individuals to reinforce. Reinforcement is contingent on performance and follows the other rules for reinforcing performance that we discussed in previous chapters. A very important part of this segment is the reinforcement that individuals receive from their peers on the team.

4. Problem solving and development of action plans. Based upon its review of performance trends and of follow-up on action plans or task assignments from previous meetings, the team identifies one or more problems that deserve attention. These problems usually relate to performance on the key indicators being tracked by the group, those reviewed during the feedback segment of the meeting. Problem-solving efforts are facilitated by the team leader and involve the use of problem-solving techniques such as brainstorming, nominal group technique (NGT), cause and effect diagrams, or Pareto diagrams. At least the team leader has had formal training in the use of these problem-solving tools. The leader also has had formal training in leading problem-solving groups. The result of the problem-solving activity is the development of written action plans that specify what is to be done, who on the team is responsible for taking the action, and the target date for completion of the action. These action plans are developed by the team members based upon group consensus. They are not dictated by the team leader. Problems of a cross-functional, cross-departmental, or cross-shift nature are referred by the team to higher level teams for resolution or assignment to a special, cross-functional task force.

5. News/announcements and meeting conclusion. The final segment of the team meeting is devoted to announcements and general news of interest to team members. The team leader closes the meeting with a brief recap of the decisions that were made by the team concerning action plans and task assignments.

How Managerial, Supervisory, and Employee Roles Change

As you reviewed the objectives of team meetings and the team meeting agenda we just presented, you probably noticed that managers, supervisors, and employees are assuming new roles. Consider, for example, the following differences between traditional management systems and MPM teams:

Traditional systems—Managers and supervisors tell, direct, order. Employees listen, take direction, and follow orders.

MPM teams—Managers and supervisors provide structure and information, facilitate meetings, teach, coach, and guide. Employees inquire, learn, and participate actively in problem solving and decision making.

Traditional systems—Managers and supervisors are responsible for the performance of their functional area.

MPM teams—Responsibility for performance rests with the team as a whole.

Traditional systems—Problems are either solved by managers and supervisors who make their decisions with limited employee input, or they are not solved at all. Managers and supervisors are responsible for monitoring and follow-up.

MPM teams—Problems are routinely discussed, debated, and prioritized by the entire team. Action plans to solve problems are developed through group consensus. The team monitors results of action steps and takes follow-up action as decided by the group.

Traditional systems—Managers and supervisors are responsible for monitoring and controlling both internal and external group relationships. Everything that happens is his/her responsibility.

MPM teams—Employees assume increased responsibility for monitoring and controlling their own behavior. Managers and supervisors spend more time managing relationships with external groups to ensure that the team has the external resources to support the achievement of its objectives.

A Guide to Designing and Installing the MPM Involvement System

Throughout the last eighteen years, our company has installed hundreds of employee involvement systems consistent with the MPM model. We have helped hundreds of companies change from traditional management systems to MPM teams. That experience has taught us three keys to a successful transition:

1. Top management must support and participate in the change. Involving employees requires a change to a new style of management. You cannot make that change unless senior management is willing personally to support the change in private and in public. As with any major change, various individuals in your organiza-

tion will fear, resent, and resist the change. You are not likely to overcome that resistance unless top managers are willing to exert their influence to prod, pressure, and persuade lower level managers.

2. Managers and supervisors at every level must learn new skills in interpersonal communication, team building, conducting meetings, and so forth. Most managers and supervisors do not have these skills to the extent necessary for an MPM involvement system to be successful. You must provide these managers with training and follow-up coaching. Just sending managers and supervisors to training classes is not enough. You must invest the time and resources to provide each manager with one-on-one, follow-up assistance in applying the newly acquired skills.

3. The MPM involvement system must be implemented top down for an entire organization, or at least for a vertical slice of the entire organization. You cannot implement the system for isolated pockets in the organization since MPM involvement practices cannot work if they are inconsistent with upper level practices.

In respect to the design and implementation of MPM teams, we suggest that you approach the task in four phases: Assessment, Start-Up, Implementation, and Maintenance. Here is a breakdown of activities during each of these steps.

Assessment

As with gainsharing and pay-for-knowledge, we suggest that you begin your implementation of MPM teams with a formal assessment. Implementation of MPM teams will take time (up to perhaps a year or longer) and considerable resources (training, consulting, etc.). You will need the information from an up-front assessment to guide your implementation efforts.

The objectives of your assessment are as follows:

1. To determine the extent to which existing management polices and practices are consistent with the MPM model.

2. To determine the reaction of managers and supervisors to the MPM team concept. How much resistance or support is there among managers and supervisors for involving employees in decision making and problem solving?

3. To determine what internal resources exist to support the MPM team implementation effort. In particular, you need to assess whether management/supervisory training is available internally for providing the skills needed to lead MPM teams. Later in this chapter, we describe specific training that must be available.

To oversee this assessment, you should appoint a task force consisting of:

- A senior manager

- Your personnel or human resources manager

- Three other key managers

Additionally, we recommend that you hire an external consultant familiar with installing employee teams to assist you with the assessment and, later, the implementation.

In conducting the assessment, we suggest you interview all managers and at least a representative sample of supervisors and employees at the site where you plan to install the MPM teams. Assessment interviews should be confidential and should cover the following areas:

1. Reaction to changes that have occurred in management practices, strategies, procedures, technology, capital investments, standards at this location over the last few years. How receptive is this group to change in general? Recent bad experiences with change, particularly attempts to install employee involvement systems that failed, can make it more difficult for you to install MPM teams.

2. Employee knowledge of values, business strategies, and critical success factors as they affect this location.

3. Existing communication patterns, both vertical and horizontal.

4. Meetings (type, frequency, purpose, content, results, etc.).

5. Performance goals and objectives (Do they exist? How are they set? Are they perceived to be fair and reasonable?).

6. Measurements and feedback systems.

7. Reinforcement/balance of consequences.

8. Performance appraisals/evaluations and their impact on performance.

9. Decision-making/problem-solving styles and the current level of employee involvement, if any.

10. Ideas that employees and managers have on key areas for improvement.

11. Current level of job satisfaction and morale.

As you probably noticed, these are many of the same areas covered in the gainsharing feasibility study, since employee involvement is the most important driver for gainsharing. Obviously, if you have recently conducted such a study, you can use the gainsharing results and conduct assessment interviews only as necessary to supplement the gainsharing findings.

In addition to conducting assessment interviews, the task force should gather information on the type of management and supervisory training available within your company. You need to uncover the type of training that managers and supervisors receive. In particular, you must determine the type of training available on interpersonal skills (communication, conflict resolution), team building, and problem solving. Compare the training content of internal programs with the modules we describe later and with the concepts of MPM as described in this book. Any required training that you cannot support internally will have to be acquired from outside sources. In particular, you should determine if internal resources exist to provide one-on-one, follow-up assistance to managers and supervisors in applying the skills required of MPM.

The result of your assessment should be a report outlining findings in each of the areas covered by the interviews, plus a review of training resources. The report should include recommendations concerning the feasibility of MPM teams at the target location, the compatibility of existing management/supervisory practices with MPM, and any training requirements.

Start-up

Assuming the assessment results in a recommendation to proceed with installation of MPM teams, your next activities are to appoint a steering committee and to conduct introductory sessions for managers, supervisors, and employees. The steering committee is responsible for overseeing the implementation of the MPM team system. It provides guidance, support, and direction to ensure that the system is implemented in a timely manner. Additionally, it oversees the work of any external consultant and internal resources that will have specific responsibilities during the implementation. The steering committee meets on a regular basis throughout implementation to review progress. During implementation, the steering committee has responsibility for monitoring progress in training, for establishing teams, and for ensuring that problems are addressed and action plans are being developed by teams.

We recommend that the steering committee be composed of the following:

- The senior manager at the location where MPM teams will be installed

- Those who report directly to that manager

- An internal consultant

- An external consultant

- A union representative (if there is union representation at the site)

- Several supervisors

During a series of initial meetings, the steering committee should accomplish the following:

1. Decide upon objectives for the MPM team system. What does the company expect to achieve by installing the system? An obvious objective of the MPM team system is to increase employee involvement. Other objectives include: to improve communication, to encourage teamwork and cooperation, to improve the quality of work life, to reduce costs, to improve productivity, to improve quality.

2. Identify key performance areas to improve. What will be at least the initial focus of team problem-solving efforts (productivity, cost, quality, customer service)? This focus should be consistent with corporate values, business strategies, *and* objectives.

3. Determine how much flexibility teams will have in selecting problems to solve, and what authority teams will have to make decisions and implement solutions. Generally we believe MPM teams should be given wide discretion to make any internal changes they feel are necessary to solve problems and improve performance. An exception are solutions involving capital expenditures above a predetermined level, which should be submitted by the team leader to higher levels for approval.

4. Determine the sequence and content of training to be provided for managers and supervisors. The exact content of training will depend upon results from the assessment.

5. Establish a timeline for implementation.

6. Determine the team structure. How many teams? Who is on what team? Teams generally follow the existing organizational hierarchy, with each manager or supervisor serving as leader of a team composed of his or her direct reports. Ideally, the organization follows the structure of the performance organiza-

tion we discussed in chapter 4. If so, each team has a clearly defined mission and accomplishments that are tied to overall company strategies.

7. Arrange for and conduct (or have the internal or external consultant conduct) separate overview sessions for managers/supervisors and employees. These sessions should outline the goals and objectives of the implementation, explain the purpose of MPM teams and how they operate, provide an opportunity for participants to voice their concerns, and review the timeline for implementation (what will happen and when). Any reservations or concerns voiced by managers, supervisors, or employees during the assessment should be discussed during these overview sessions. We believe it is extremely important that senior management participate in these sessions to demonstrate their support and personal commitment to MPM as a way of managing.

Implementation

The implementation of MPM teams usually involves scheduling and conducting a series of training and follow-up coaching sessions for managers and supervisors, designed to provide them with the skills they require to begin conducting MPM team meetings. Our recommendation is that you arrange to conduct the training in half-day modules over a period of several weeks (approximately one module per week) so that you can provide individual follow-up coaching in applying the skills, module by module. Note that this follow-up is critical. Don't just deliver the training.

The exact content of the training you provide and the nature of the follow-up activity will depend upon the results of the assessment and the decisions of the steering committee. We use some or all of the modules shown on the following pages. As you review the content of these training modules, notice that they are designed to develop skills managers and supervisors will use in leading MPM team meetings. The last two modules involve applying these skills in actual team meetings. Also, note that each module provides one or more individual, follow-up coaching sessions, during which the trainer reviews skills taught in the training and helps the manager or supervisor apply these skills to a real life situation. As we have said previously, the follow-up coaching is actually more important than the formal training session, since it is through this type of coaching that managers and supervisors begin to change their behavior.

Module #1

Introduction to Maximum Performance Management

Objectives

Upon completion of this module and follow-up coaching, you will:

1. Understand what you can do to motivate people;

2. Apply the Antecedent-Behavior-Consequences Model (ABC Model) to analyze performance problems; and

3. Use antecedents and consequences to achieve maximum performance.

Training Content

1. Overview of Maximum Performance Management

2. What motivates excellent performance

3. Explanation of the ABC Model

4. How to apply the ABC Model to analyze and improve performance

5. Practice in application of the ABC Model

Individual Follow-Up Coaching Session

1. Review training content

2. Apply the ABC Model to an existing performance problem

Module #2

Pinpointing and Performance Feedback

Preparation

Prior to conducting this training module, the trainer will review key performance reports with management to identify critical measures and to collect current data for use in the training session.

Objectives

At the conclusion of this training session and the individual follow-up coaching, you will:

1. Identify key performance measures;

2. Pinpoint behaviors needed to improve key performance measures;

3. Know how to improve current methods of giving performance feedback; and

4. Use performance feedback to motivate people.

Training Content

1. How to pinpoint performance measures.

2. How to pinpoint desired behaviors and outcomes to improve performance.

3. Practice in pinpointing.

4. What is performance feedback?

5. Benefits of feedback.

6. Criteria for effective feedback.

7. Assessment of current feedback systems.

8. Explanation of the performance area selected by the management team.

Individual Follow-Up Coaching Session

1. Review training content

2. Pinpoint key performance measures

3. Pinpoint behaviors to improve performance measures

4. Collect data on key performance measures

Module #3

Graphing and Data Analysis

Objectives

Upon completion of this module and the individual follow-up coaching, you will:

1. Design and create performance feedback graphs;

2. Post feedback graphs in the work areas;

3. Explain feedback graphs to employees; and

4. Analyze and explain current performance trends.

Training Content

1. Graphing as a tool for providing feedback

2. Benefits of graphs over other feedback systems

3. How to design a performance feedback graph

4. How to analyze trends in performance data

5. Analysis of current performance on key measures

6. Group consensus on performance measures for employee feedback

Individual Follow-Up Coaching Session—One or More Sessions

1. Review training content on graphing and data analysis

2. Design performance feedback graphs

3. Post performance feedback graphs

4. Explain graphs to employees

Module #4

Reflective Listening

Objectives

Upon completion of this training and the individual follow-up coaching, you will:

1. Ask employees for ideas on how to improve performance;

2. Rephrase employee concerns to make sure they are fully understood; and

3. Use empathy to encourage employees to express their ideas and concerns.

Training Content

1. How to improve communication through the use of reflective listening skills: asking open-ended questions to draw out ideas from others; rephrasing to increase understanding; prompting

for more information; and using empathy to acknowledge emotions.

Individual Follow-Up Coaching Sessions

1. Review training content

2. Use listening skills to solicit ideas for improving performance

3. Receive feedback on application of listening skills from consultant

Module #5

Reinforcement

Objectives

Upon completion of this training and the individual follow-up coaching, you will:

1. Pinpoint behaviors to reinforce;

2. Identify possible reinforcers; and

3. Reinforce employees for good performance related to posted feedback graphs, following guidelines for effective reinforcement.

Training Content

1. What reinforcement is

2. Different types of reinforcers

3. How to identify behaviors to reinforce

4. How to select appropriate reinforcers

5. Guidelines for effective reinforcement

6. Practice in reinforcing good performance

Individual Follow-Up Coaching Session

1. Review training content

2. Identify behaviors to reinforce related to improving performance on feedback graphs

3. Select possible reinforcers for identified behaviors

4. Practice reinforcing, with observation and feedback by consultant

Module #6

Correcting Undesirable Performance

Objectives

Upon completion of this training module and the individual follow-up coaching, you will:

1. Select an appropriate model for use in correcting undesirable performance; and

2. Use the selected model effectively to correct undesirable performance.

Training Content

1. The difference between punishment and correcting

2. Benefits of correcting

3. Models for effective correcting: Empathy Model, Shaping Model, Negative Feedback Model

4. When and how to use each model

5. Practice in selecting and using correcting models

Individual Follow-Up Coaching Session

1. Review training content

2. Identify undesirable performance or behavior

3. Select appropriate correcting model

4. Apply model and discuss results with consultant

Module #7

Creative Problem Solving

Objectives

Upon completion of the training and the follow-up coaching, you will:

1. Apply the group problem solving skills of brainstorming, consensus decision making, and action planning to improve performance; and

2. Lead groups in problem solving using these skills.

Training Content

1. Discussion of current methods for employee involvement in problem identification and problem solving

2. Explanation of creative problem-solving skills: brainstorming, consensus decision making, and action planning

3. Application of creative problem-solving skills

4. Introduction of Creative Problem Solving Model

Individual Follow-Up Coaching Session

1. Review training content

2. Apply creative problem-solving skills in management team meeting

3. Receive feedback on application of creative problem-solving skills from consultant

Module #8

Effective Meetings

Objectives

Upon completion of this training and the follow-up coaching session, you will:

1. Conduct management team meetings;

2. Encourage participation in a team meeting;

3. Effectively handle disruptive behavior in a team meeting; and

4. Use skills acquired in the previous training to conduct these meetings.

Training Content

1. What makes a good meeting?

2. How to prepare a team meeting agenda.

3. How to prepare for a team meeting.

4. How to lead a team meeting.

5. How to encourage participation.

6. How to handle disruptive behavior.

Individual Follow-Up Coaching Session

1. Review training content

2. Prepare for a team meeting

Module #9

Team Meetings

Objectives

Upon completion of this training and the follow-up coaching, you will:

1. Conduct a team meeting that includes performance feedback, reinforcement, problem solving, and communication.

Training Content

Mock team meetings are used to illustrate the process and development of team meetings over time. Participants refine their skills in conducting team meetings in a variety of situations.

Individual Follow-Up Coaching Session

1. Prepare to lead a team meeting

2. Conduct a team meeting and receive feedback on team leadership skills from consultant

Module #10

Advanced Creative Problem Solving

Objectives

Upon completion of this training and the follow-up coaching, you will apply creative problem-solving skills to define a problem, analyze potential causes of the problem, develop alternative solutions, select among alternative solutions, and implement solutions.

Training Content

1. Review steps involved in the Creative Problem-Solving Model: problem identification and definition; problem analysis using cause and effect diagrams, check sheets, and Pareto diagrams; development of solutions; and implementation and follow up

Individual Follow-Up Coaching

1. Review training content.

2. Use Creative Problem-Solving Model and skills in team meetings.

3. Receive feedback on application of Creative Problem-Solving Model and skills from consultant.

Maintenance

Like any other employee involvement system, MPM teams require some ongoing maintenance. One advantage of MPM teams is that a certain amount of maintenance will be accomplished as a result of the operation of teams themselves. Upper level teams should be checking on reinforcement, action planning, and problem solving at lower levels. However, the steering committee should assign responsibility for at least the following maintenance tasks:

1. Training of new managers and supervisors in MPM team skills and periodic refresher training as needed

2. Regular reporting to upper management on the operation of the MPM team system (that is, frequency of team meetings, number of teams, status of action planning, number of action plans showing improvement, dollar savings from implementation of action plans, etc.)

Summary

In this chapter, we described an employee involvement system that overcomes the weaknesses of traditional involvement efforts such as surveys, suggestion systems, and quality circles. If you successfully implement the MPM team involvement system we described in this chapter, everyone in your organization will be participating on a regular basis in generating ideas to improve performance. The focus of their efforts will be on solving problems that directly impact your ability to compete. Involving every employee will not be peripheral to running your business, but will actually be the *way* you run your business day-to-day. Managers and supervisors will meet with their employees on a regular basis to share information and ideas, to monitor and provide feedback on performance, to recognize and reinforce good performance, and to get everyone's ideas for improvement. Everyone is accountable for performance, and everyone is involved in making performance happen. Most importantly, with MPM teams you have taken a major step toward a new style of management where the organizational structure is flat, where employees assume even more responsibility for performance, and where managers/supervisors assume totally new roles. In the next chapter, we look ahead to the future of American management practices and this new management style.

PART 5:

The Future

Chapter 14

Beyond MPM—The Future of American Management Practices

Picture a 130 employee Kansas plant where worker output has increased 80 percent in just six years. Absenteeism is a mere 2 percent. Employee turnover is one percent.

There are no time clocks. No supervisors. No job classifications. No definite work assignments.

If something has to be moved with a fork-lift truck, no one yells to the fork-lift truck driver—because there isn't such a driver. Instead, anyone at hand hops onto the truck and gets the job done.

There are no hourly workers. Everyone is salaried. In six years, the plant work force has grown by only 12 percent. Yet the workers produce as much as a plant with 33% more people.

Everyone is involved in major decisions affecting the plant.

The workers also participate in such matters as production scheduling, solving quality problems, evaluating performance and recommending new equipment. They undertake disciplinary actions. They even hire and train other workers.

In fact, the plant's entire operation, top to bottom, is in the hands of "worker teams." What there is of old style management, in the form of a

287

general manager and his staff, now exists merely in a support role. They are there to assist the workers, who, quite literally, run the plant.

Profits are piling up. (*Productivity*, September 1982)

The above is not a futuristic scenario or a dream. It is not a trip to the "Land of Oz." It is reality. The plant is TRW's Oil Well Division at Lawrence, Kansas. This description was written in 1982, and the results continue today—after over eleven years. But Lawrence, Kansas is not the only story to be told.

Picture an automotive assembly plant that is 20 to 40 percent more efficient than traditional American automotive plants. Workers in this plant are divided into teams of as few as five people and as many as twenty. Each worker does not just one job, but many. There are only a few basic job classifications. Workers control their own jobs, make their own decisions, and solve their own quality problems. Executives, managers, group leaders, and workers all wear the same uniform and eat together in the same cafeteria. Executives wait in line and dispose of their own trays. There are no assigned parking spaces and no time clocks. Any worker can stop production at any time by simply pulling a cord. Employees rotate from job to job as often as every two hours. Teams of employees meet regularly to discuss problems and take action to solve problems on their own. There are no industrial engineers. Instead, team members, team leaders, and group leaders do the industrial engineering work themselves. Management has told employees in this plant, "You are responsible for the quality of the cars you make. You are responsible for the effectiveness of the plant. You are accountable for your own success and the company's." Picture this plant—not in Japan—but in the United States. It is General Motors NUMMI plant in Fremont, California.

TRW's Lawrence, Kansas, plant and General Motor's Fremont plant are examples of a radically different style of management. Delco-Remy, Best Foods, Shell Oil Canada, M & M Mars, Continental Can, and a number of other companies have experimented with this management style. It works. It goes beyond MPM to change the fundamental nature of management/employee relations. Called "self-managed" or "semi-autonomous" work teams, this way of organizing and managing will be the future American management practice for many, if not most, companies.

What exactly are self-managed work teams? What is it like to work in a self-managed work team? What will happen to supervisors and middle managers? Why is this style of management appropriate now and for the future? How do you determine if this new style of management is right for your company? Most importantly, how do you move to this new style of management if it is right? We examine these questions in this chapter.

The Future American Management Practice—"Self-Managed Work Teams"

Under the MPM team system of employee involvement, managers, supervisors, and employees assumed new roles. Many of these changes centered around team meetings—a special form of regular meetings where, among other activities, the manager or supervisor facilitates group efforts to identify and solve problems. The logical extension of these meetings (particularly when coupled with MPM organization and compensation strategies) is for employees to become even more self-directed and self-controlling. The ultimate is an evolution to self-managed or semi-autonomous work teams.

Self-managed or semi-autonomous work teams are natural work units composed of five to fifteen people. These teams are organized in such a way that there are natural boundaries between teams (each team produces a whole product, completes an entire process, or provides a complete service). In short, each team is a small business unit unto itself. Typically, the output of one team becomes the input of another. Beyond the team, there are no managers or supervisors in the traditional sense, rather there is a support team and coordinators. In a plant, the support team might consist of a plant manager, a human resources manager, a quality assurance manager, an accountant, and a chief engineer. Coordinators are similar to line supervisors, with technical, behavioral, and operational responsibilities; however, they act in an advisory rather than in a directive capacity. The coordinator is available to help the team with technical or social issues when requested to do so by the team. Otherwise, the team is self-running and self-managed. Team members, as a group, make job assignments and production decisions, hold their own team meetings, problem solve and implement solutions, order their own parts and supplies, plan and schedule their own work, select team members, evaluate team members' performance, and so on. Practically all functions traditionally performed by managers or supervisors are performed by the team.

Within teams, there are usually no job descriptions and few, if any, job classifications. Team members are cross-trained and capable of performing most, if not all, the jobs required for team performance, and there is often a pay-for-knowledge system to encourage this flexibility. The team itself has wide discretion to decide how tasks will be performed and who on the team will be responsible for specific tasks.

How the Workplace Changes with Self-Managed Teams

In addition to the improvements in performance reported by companies that have experimented with self-managed teams, significant changes have occurred in team cohesion, cooperation between employees, and morale. For example, Henry Sims and Charles Manz, professors at Pennsylvania State University and the University of Minnesota respectively, described the group interaction they observed as a result of several weeks of research at a plant with a self-managed team (see Henry P. Sims, Jr. and Charles C. Manz, "Conversations within Self-Managed Work Groups," *National Productivity Review* [Spring 1982], pp. 261-69). They reported:

1. Frequent exchanges of verbal rewards (compliments, thank you's, praise) among and between team members for useful or helpful action.

2. Group members disciplined each other. There was strong peer pressure for everyone to contribute to the performance of the group.

3. Employees agreed to rotate jobs so that the "dog" jobs and "gravy" jobs were shared equally on a weekly, daily, and sometimes even hourly basis.

4. When problems arose or disagreements occurred, those involved were required by the team to sit down and work the problem out among themselves.

5. Employees regularly discussed production scheduling, produc-

tion goals, performance levels, and so on. They also frequently referred to their own team's activities as "our business."

6. Numerous graphs and charts were maintained by the team to track performance. Additionally, team members kept their own informal charts and graphs and posted these near machines and work stations.

7. When special problems arose, employees took action to correct the problems without being prompted to do so. In addition, employees voluntarily sought out and acquired new knowledge or skills needed to solve the problems, and would acquire this new knowledge on their own time if necessary.

8. Team members sought out evaluations of their own work performance. Regular reviews were normally conducted by the coordinator and other team members. Additionally, team members aggressively managed entry and exit from the team. No specific set of rules governed assignment of employees to teams, it was just "worked out" among the various teams.

What Happens to Supervisors and Middle Managers?

Do self-managed teams mean the end to supervision and management? As employees take over more and more of the traditional functions of management, what happens to those who used to supervise and manage? And, with employees running the shop, does anarchy prevail? Commenting on the reaction to the unconventional management style at TRW's Lawrence, Kansas, plant, Gino Strippoli, the former vice president and general manager of TRW's Oil Well Cable Division, has said:

They often think we are running a country club; we've relinquished responsibility for managing; employees can make sweeping organizational changes at whim; and anarchy prevails. Most emphatically, that's not the case. Our division does have managers. But they are managers with a difference—people who don't automatically embrace the old, counterproductive ways of doing things, who are willing to strike out in new directions to gain the cooperation of employees. Perhaps most importantly, our managers treat employees as problem solvers, as first-echelon managers. That frees our managers from putting out fires; instead they can perform bona fide management tasks (Gino T. Strippoli, "Is This Any Way to Run a Cable Business," *The TRW Manager* 1, no. 1 [October 1982], p. 7).

As Strippoli says, self-managed work teams do have managers— fewer in number, but still present. The role of these remaining managers, however, changes dramatically. Carl Bramlette, a professor of management at Georgia State University in Atlanta, has described the change in management roles in this way:

As the group members demonstrate acceptance of group norms, as they develop skills in maintaining production and troubleshooting problems, and as they begin to assume some of the group leadership functions, the group leader (supervisor or manager) experiences a subtle change to team coordinator. As a team coordinator, the supervisor shares a great many group leadership functions with other team members. . . The team coordinator manages the group primarily through coordination of their skills and activities, and uses their resources as fully as possible (Carl Bramlette, "Free to Change," *Training and Development Journal* [March 1984], p. 36).

As the supervisor becomes a team coordinator, he or she assumes what has been called the "enabling role," with two primary responsibilities: (1) to build team competence and skills, and (2) to manage links with other components of the business (see Audrey E. Bean, Carolyn Ordowich, and William A. Westley, "Including the Supervisor in Employee Involvement Efforts," *National Productivity Review* [Winter 1985-86], pp. 66-68). In performing both functions, the former supervisor—now team coordinator—educates and coaches the team to encourage team members to be even more self-directed and self-controlling. "He or she makes sure that the goals are clear and shared, that feedback flows and that people have the necessary skills. The supervisor helps the team devise strategies for winning and helps them learn from setbacks. As the team matures, the supervisor delegates more and more to them, coaching them until he or she feels confident that they will make effective decisions" (Bean, Ordowich, and Westley, p. 66). Simultaneously, the team coordinator manages external relationships, making sure that the team gets the resources it needs to function and is integrated into the overall business strategy. He or she becomes a link to the rest of the organization, passing communication back and forth, creating and maintaining positive relationships with others in the organization, and securing financial, material, and other resources the team requires but is unable to obtain on its own. Obviously, the team coordinator role requires exceptional interpersonal skills and the ability to acquire authority as a result of trust and respect rather than of position.

Some current supervisors and middle managers will make the transition to the team coordinator role with ease, relieved that they no longer have to play the role of "policeman" or "order giver." Others will find this transition difficult, if not impossible. Fortunately, another role is available for those who cannot make the transition. That alternative role is to provide technical support. As we noted earlier, in a self-managed work team team members are cross-trained and capable of performing most, if not all, the jobs required for team performance. This cross-training and the pay-for-knowledge incentive means that team members can be expected to develop an exceptional breadth and depth of technical knowledge and skills, at least as compared to the typical work group. Yet they cannot be expected to acquire sufficient technical skills to resolve highly unusual or difficult technical problems. When such problems arise, the team needs a resource or support person who has a much higher level of technical knowledge. Therein lies the technical support role.

Like the team coordinator, the supervisor or middle manager who moves into a technical support role serves multiple teams. He or she is available when needed and when called upon by the team. The technical role is an advisory role—the team seeks the advice of the technical expert but is free either to take that advice or not to take it. The self-managed team still makes the decision—at least to the extent that the decision falls within their defined range of authority.

The "enabling role" and technical support role represent two alternative avenues for the supervisor or middle manager replaced by the new organization. However, these two new roles will be insufficient to absorb all current supervisors and managers in the new organization. What will happen to managers and supervisors who cannot or will not make the transition to an enabling or technical support role? The fact is that for many of these managers and supervisors, their positions will simply disappear, not to be replaced. Some of the displaced will retire, some will return to membership in the self-managed teams. Necessity and choice will impel a few toward an entrepreneurial role either within the larger organization or outside it.

The business climate of the 1990s and beyond will create enormous opportunities for entrepreneurship. In response to increased competitiveness, practically every company will be forced to become more innovative and to seek out ever narrowing market niches. Such a climate is ripe with opportunity for the entrepreneur. With advancement closed within the normal hierarchy, and with being unwilling or unable to move into the alternative roles, some of the displaced managers and supervisors will be forced to create their own small business either within or outside the company umbrella. In fact, we are already seeing this happen. The "lean and mean" downsizing of the 1980s has resulted in an enormous growth in new business start-ups.

How to Determine if Self-Managed Teams Are Right for You

Self-managed work teams represent the most radical departure from traditional management styles we have described in this book. Not only do they significantly change management and supervisory roles— as we have just seen—but they drastically alter the very functioning of the business. Because they constitute such a radical departure, self-managed teams are not right for every company. How do you determine if they are right for you? Ask yourself the following questions:

1. *Will self-managed teams help you obtain your strategic business objectives?* Self-managed work teams place almost total responsibility on groups of employees for a product/service or for entire subsets of tasks leading to a product or service. Such an arrangement usually results in the following benefits (see "Work Cells and Work Teams: Are They Right for You?" *Productivity Improvement Bulletin* [September 10, 1984], pp. 1-4):

1. Increased flexibility

2. Reduction in response time

3. Reduction in work-in-process (WIP) inventory

4. Early detection of defects and improved quality

5. Increased pride in workmanship

2. Do the advantages of self-managed teams outweigh the costs? In spite of their advantages, self-managed teams usually result in increased costs, particularly in the following areas:

1. *Machine/equipment costs*—Each work cell requires its own complement of equipment.

2. *Training costs*—Typically, implementation of self-managed teams requires a significant and ongoing investment in additional technical training, as well as in training for cell members in traditional management/supervisory skills such as planning, scheduling, communication, group dynamics, selection.

3. *Floor space*—The physical layout of work cells is usually less efficient. Although there are some savings in space requirements due to reductions in work-in-process inventory, they might not be sufficient to offset additional space demands for duplicate equipment.

3. Can you break the work to be performed into logical business units? Self-managed work teams represent the ultimate extension of the performance organization we described in chapter 4. Since teams normally consist of five to fifteen people, you must be able to extend the product/service or market/customer organizational structure to this size work group. Additionally, you must be able to define and track specific performance goals at this level.

4. Can you handle the displacement of middle managers and supervisors in a manner that is consistent with your values? By their very nature, self-managed work teams result in a significant reduction in management and supervisory positions. If you install these teams in a start-up location (as many companies have done), create new teams around the introduction of new technology, or install these teams after the completion of downsizing, you might be able to avoid such displacement. Otherwise, you must be prepared to deal with this issue.

5. *Are employees prepared to assume new roles in a self-managed team?* Self-managed teams require that employees assume responsibility for performing functions normally performed by managers and supervisors. Are your employees prepared to do so? Typically, we do not recommend that our clients move to self-managed teams without first gaining experience with involvement systems such as MPM teams. Employees who have worked in such teams will have acquired experience with information sharing, group dynamics, problem solving, and decision making that is invaluable for their expanded role in the self-managed team. With this experience, the transition to self-managed teams is smoother, quicker, and less traumatic.

6. *Can your existing administrative procedures and practices support self-managed teams?* First, measurement and information systems must exist or be created to support feedback on performance at the smaller business unit level. If you can move the measurement, reporting, and goal setting procedures we described in chapters 5, 6, and 7 to the level of the self-managed team, you will meet this requirement. Second, your compensation practices must be consistent and supportive of the self-managed team concept. For example, you need to ensure that your gainsharing program, which might be based on a macro, plantwide measure, is consistent with the operation of relatively independent work cells. The skills and skill levels of your pay-for-knowledge system must include and support the skills necessary in the self-managed work teams. Finally, you must have the training resources to support the additional training requirements of self-managed teams. Team members will require additional technical skills training—much like that required in pay-for-knowledge systems. Additionally, team members will require social/group skills training similar to the type of training we described for managers and supervisors in the previous chapter.

A Guide to Designing and Installing Self-Managed Work Teams

Unlike other initiatives we have discussed in this book (such as gainsharing), accumulated experience with self-managed work teams

...ıs to give you an ideal implementation strategy. ...
...ıre just too new. However, our experience and th...
...sts the following:

Step One: Awareness Raising

To an even greater extent than other techniques we described in this book, the concept of self-managed teams will be new to most people. Additionally, since self-managed teams are such a radical departure from traditional management styles, the potential for opposition, disbelief and outright rejection is much greater. For these reasons, it is even more important that you secure the support of key stakeholders before attempting to install such teams. Senior management, middle managers, supervisors, employees and the union all have the potential for significant gains and losses as a result of the installation of self-managed teams.

Awareness raising is an education process. As in the case of gainsharing, we suggest that you start by assembling books and articles on self-managed teams. Look for works on "Self-Managed Teams," "Semi-Autonomous Teams" or "Work Redesign." Your selection will be more limited than for gainsharing, but numerous articles do exist, particularly since 1980. Many of these articles will be case studies describing experiments in various companies. From these you should be able to identify sites for a visit. We encourage you to contact these companies and to visit their self-managed locations. You can learn much from the managers and employees at these locations who have already been through the process.

Step Two: Feasibility Study

Assuming your reading and on-site visits have convinced you and your key stakeholders that the concept of self-managed teams is worth pursuing, we suggest that you then conduct a feasibility study. To do this, assemble a Task Force composed of twelve to fifteen members including:

- a representative of senior management

- the company comptroller

the personnel or human resources manager

- the industrial engineering manager

- the production manager

- other key managers

- a union representative

- an internal or external consultant familiar with the design of self-managed teams

This Task Force should conduct or have conducted a formal feasibility study to answer the following questions:

1. In what way would self-managed teams help the company to implement its business strategy?

2. What are the potential costs/risks from installing self-managed teams?

3. What logical breakdown of work processes into business units is possible?

4. What impact will self-managed teams have on machine usage, process flow, plant layout, etc.? What will it cost to make any necessary adjustments?

5. Will managers or supervisors be displaced? How can such displacement be handled?

6. What level of support/opposition exists among managers, supervisors and employees for an experiment in self-managed teams?

7. Are employees prepared/wiling to assume the additional roles/responsibilities that they must assume within a self-managed team?

8. Can administrative policies/practices (information systems, training, compensation, etc.) support self-managed teams? If not, what changes will be required?

Step Three: Site Selection

Assuming that the results of the Feasibility Study are positive and that key stakeholders still support the effort, your next step should be to select a pilot site. A new plant/office or start-up site is perhaps the easiest location for an experiment with self-managed teams because there are no managers or supervisors to be displaced and no existing management culture to change. If a new location is not available, an alternative is a location undergoing a major change in technology of work processes. The self-managed team experiment could be a logical extension of other major changes. Finally, you could select a pilot site within an existing facility. If you do, your challenge is to somehow insulate the pilot—physically and otherwise—from the rest of the facility, manage the redistribution of equipment, and minimize any negative impact of self-managed teams on process flow with the rest of the facility.

Step #4: Identification Of Business Units

Your selection of a pilot site will partially dictate your identification of business units. You must be able to divide the work force into teams of five to fifteen people around the production of a complete product or relatively independent sub-set of tasks leading to a complete product. Lyman Ketchum, a consultant in work redesign, describes your task this way: "The essential requirement is the logical division of the technical process into operating subunits of reasonable size that can become partially independent." ("How Redesigned Plants Really Work," *National Productivity Review* [Summer, 1984], p. 247)

The business units you define must be sufficiently independent that you can develop "an explicit and comprehensive mission statement for each team and its logical segment of the production process" (Ketchum, p. 247). You must be able to identify several measurable areas of performance for each team that link back to the overall team mission statement. In short, self-managed teams operate as if they were small, independent businesses. Therefore, you must be able to clearly identify and measure the performance of each team much as you would measure the performance of a small business. There must be no doubt about the yardstick by which the success of team performance will be measured.

Step #5: Definition Of Roles And Responsibilities

You must redefine and clarify the roles and responsibilities of managers, supervisors and employees in order to create self-managed work teams. Earlier, we defined new roles for managers and supervisors—enabling and technical support. These should be formalized with titles, position descriptions, selection criteria, and clear definitions of limits of authority.

Likewise, you must clarify the role of team members. How much independence will team members be allowed? How much responsibility and discretion will they have for performing such functions as planning, scheduling, hiring, task assignment, quality control, purchasing, etc.? Just how far should operating and decision making authority of the group extend? Additionally, consider how the following day-to-day situations might be handled (See Thomas O. Taylor, Donald J. Friedman, and Dennis Couture, "Operating Without Supervisors: An Experiment," *Organizational Dynamics* [Winter 1987], p. 30):

1. What if the employees demand management pay?

2. What if an employee comes in drunk or on drugs?

3. What if someone gets hurt on the job?

4. What if employees are excessively late?

5. What if a fight breaks out?

6. What if a customer demands to speak to a supervisor?

7. What if results are bad—performance declines?

8. What if an employee files a complaint or grievance?

9. What if there is a strike?

10. What if a team member steals company property?

Step Six: Layout/Process Flow

Inevitably, the creation of self-managed teams results in the need to redesign office/plant layout and process flow. In order for teams to function they must have access to equipment/machinery needed for completion of the entire production process or their segment of the process. Additionally, the layout and flow of materials into and from the group will change. New design work will be required from space planners and process flow engineers.

Step #7: Selection

By there very nature, self-managed work teams are not right for all employees. Some just do not want the increased responsibility. Others do not want the peer pressure and personal demands of group membership and group accountability that are common to self-managed teams. Consequently, the task force must give serious consideration the selection criteria. What types of skills will be needed? How will the selection process ensure compatibility of team members? Will team members select other team members? If so, what type of training in selection must team members be provided to ensure that legal and/or regulatory requirements (EEO, etc.) are not violated?

Step #8: Training

As we have noted, the creation of self-managed teams requires a significant investment in training. The team members will require training in technical skills and a skill development plan similar to that required for pay-for-knowledge systems. Additionally, all team members will require training and follow up coaching in many of the same skill areas provided to managers and supervisors with MPM teams—communication, group dynamics, conflict management, negotiation, etc. The task force must identify the content of this training and arrange for it to be delivered.

Step #9: On-Going Maintenance

Like any other initiative, self-managed teams require follow up maintenance. We recommend that the Task Force meet on a regular basis during and after implementation to assess progress. Three issues should be addressed at each meeting:

1. Are performance goals being met?

2. Are training and other implementation steps proceeding on schedule?

3. What adjustments/revisions are necessary?

Summary

In this chapter, we have outlined an involvement system that is revolutionary in scope. For most practical purposes, managers and supervisors are eliminated. Employees become self-managed, self-directing and self-controlling. This revolutionary form of business management is not right for every company or every employee. We have tried in this chapter to suggest how you can determine if self-managed teams are right for your company. Additionally, we have suggested a process to follow to implement such teams if they seem right.

Self-managed teams are a radical vision of the future. In our concluding note in the next chapter, we provide some further comments on that future.

Chapter 15

A Brief Concluding Note

Each age defines its own management style. Right or wrong, good or bad, the style that survives is the style that works, that creates value, that enables the impersonal corporation to survive. In a sense, in spite of all of the problems we face, we are lucky. This age demands a style of management that not only creates value but enables dignity.

In 1972—over 15 years ago—Studs Terkel wrote this about the American working condition:

This book, being about work, is by its very nature about violence—to the spirit as well as to the body . . . It is above all (or beneath all), about daily humiliations. To survive the day is triumph enough for the walking wounded among the great many of us.

It is about a search, too, for daily meaning as well as daily bread, for recognition as well as cash, for astonishment rather than torpor, in short, for a sort of life rather than a Monday through Friday sort of dying. Perhaps immortality, too, is part of the quest (*Working*, New York: Pantheon Books, 1972, p. xi.).

Until recently, the life at work that Terkel described had barely changed. But it is beginning to change—slowly. It is changing not just because it should change (what right have we to condemn anyone to a Monday through Friday sort of dying?), but because it must change. We are compelled to change to survive. We are compelled to change because it is the only way that we can continue to create value and feed the monster corporation we have created.

Ted Levitt, editor of the *Harvard Business Review,* has said, "Organizations exist to enable ordinary people to do extraordinary things" (*Harvard Business Review* [January-February 1988], p. 7). So they do. But they also exist—or should exist—to enable ordinary people to do ordinary things well and to take pride in doing so.

In 1984, we sat across from a young French Canadian woman. We spoke only English. She spoke English poorly. We were there to interview employees about work life and management practices in a large Canadian utility. She was trying to explain her frustrations with what was and what wasn't but could be. Finally, in desperation, she reached across the table, held her hands in front of her and said: "Can't you understand? I just want to feel passionate about what I do."

Don't we all, Michele? And why shouldn't we be allowed to feel that way?

In South Carolina, we conducted interviews with distribution center employees about their jobs. John, a young black man, told us of his work operating a crane, storing boxes in a cavernous warehouse. He spoke of "building walls," of "using every available space," and of having everything in order and completed by the end of his shift. He spoke with pride and dignity of an ordinary job done well. He felt passionate about what he did.

In North Carolina, Ted told us about his work on a loading dock. He told us about his plant manager who took the time to listen to Ted's idea and helped Ted develop it and make it work. Ted spoke with pride about the difference his idea had made in the work on the loading dock and the value of his idea to the company. He also told us he had another idea—an even better idea.

Michele, John and Ted point the way to the future of American management practice. And yes, we are finally listening. Our friend Joe Gorman at TRW has put it this way:

U.S. industry is in a crisis situation brought on by the advent of worldwide competion. We are steadily losing ground. Our living standard is being eroded.

We need an ongoing minor labor/management miracle, not just for this year, but for next and the year after, knowing our competitors will be trying equally hard.

It cannot and will not be done without changes in much of what we in business do.

"Business as usual" must be totally unacceptable. The changes must be fundamental and pervasive.

We must end up with a work force that cares more, knows more, and does more. In other words, a work force that is more "involved" with the success or failure of the enerprise.

A work force that cares about and takes pride in the product shipped to the customer. One that feels some sense of power and influence over the result. One with enough meaningful information to make informed, intelligent decisions. One that feels it is appropriately appreciated and rewarded for its contribution (Joseph T. Gorman, "We Can't Survive 'Business As Usual,' " *Commitment Plus* [July 1987], p. 5).

Right, Joe—oh, so right! Let's begin . . .

Bibliography

American Productivity Center. *Nucor Corporation—Gainsharing Program Boosts Productivity for Steel Producer.* Case Study 28. Houston, Texas: American Productivity Center, 1983.

American Productivity Center. *White Collar Productivity: Results of the American Productivity Center's Two-Year Action Research Project.* Houston, Texas: American Productivity Center, 1986.

American Productivity Center. *Reward Systems and Productivity: A Final Report for the White House Conference on Productivity.* Houston, Texas: American Productivity Center, 1983.

"An American Miracle That Works," *Productivity* (November 1982), pp. 1-5.

Ashkenas, Ronald N. and Todd D. Jick, "Productivity and QWL Success without Ideal Conditions," *National Productivity Review* (Autumn 1982), pp. 381-388.

Bean, Audrey E., Carolyn Ordowich, and William A. Westley, "Including the Supervisor in Employee Involvement Efforts," *National Productivity Review* (Winter 1985-86), pp. 66-68.

Bennis, Warren and Burt Nanus. *Leaders: The Strategies for Taking Charge.* New York: Harper & Row, 1985.

Boyett, Joseph H., "Gainsharing: How to Pay for Performance," *The Tarkenton Productivity Update* (Winter 1987), p. 1-7.

Bramlette, Carl, "Free to Change," *Training and Development Journal* (March 1984), p. 36.

Brown, Arnold and Edith Weiner. *Super-Managing: How to Harness Change for Personal and Organizational Success.* New York: New American Library, 1984.

Burns, James MacGregor. *Leadership.* New York: Harper & Row, 1978.

Christopher, William F. *Management for the 1980's.* New York: American Management Association, 1980.

Cole, Robert E. and Dennis S. Tachiki, "Forging Institutional Links: Making Quality Circles Work in the U.S.," *National Productivity Review* (Autumn 1984), pp. 417-429.

Cook, Frederic W. "Rethinking Compensation Practices in Light of Economic Conditions," *Personnel* (January 1987), pp. 46-51.

Crosby, Philip B. *Quality is Free: The Art of Making Quality Certain.* New York: New American Library, 1979.

Cummings, L. L. and Donald P. Schwab. *Performance in Organizations: determinants & appraisals.* Glenview, Illinois: Scott, Foresman and Company, 1973.

Daniels, Aubrey C., "Performance Management: The Behavioral Approach to Productivity Improvement," *National Productivity Review* (Summer 1985), pp. 225-236.

Doyel, Hoyt and Thomas Riley, "Considerations in Development Incentive Plans," *Management Review* (March 1987) pp. 34-37.

Drucker, Peter F. *Managing in Turbulent Times.* New York: Harper & Row, 1980.

Drucker, Peter, "The Coming of the New Organization," *Harvard Business Review* (January-February 1988), pp. 45-53.

Drucker, Peter. *Management: Tasks, Responsibilities, Practices.* New York: Harper & Row, 1974.

Fasman, Zachary, D., "Legal Considerations in Work-Force Redesign," *National Productivity Review* (Spring 1982), pp. 164-172.

Fast, Norman. *The Lincoln Electric Company.* Harvard Business School Case 376-028. Boston: Harvard Business School, 1975.

Fedor, Donald B. and Gerald R. Ferris, "Integrating OB Mod with Cognitive Approaches to Motivation," *Academy of Management Review* 6, No. 1 (1981), pp. 115-25.

Geis, A. Arthur, "Making Merit Pay Work," *Personnel* (January 1987), pp. 52-60.

Gilbert, Thomas F. *Human Competence: Engineering Worthy Performance.* New York: McGraw-Hill, 1978.

Ginnodo, Bill, "Teaching an Old Plant New Tricks," *Commitment Plus* (July 1987), pp. 2-4.

Goodman, Paul S., "Why Productivity Programs Fail: Reasons and Solutions," *National Productivity Review* (Autumn 1982), pp. 369-380.

Gorman, Joseph T., "We Can't Survive 'Business As Usual'," *Commitment Plus* (July 1987), p. 5.

Grayson, C. Jackson, Jr. and Carl O'Dell. *American Business A Two Minute Warning: Ten Changes Managers Must Make to Survive into the 21st Century.* New York: Free Press, 1988.

Greater Cleveland Roundtable. "Retaining and Developing Jobs in Cleveland: The Need for Labor & Management Cooperation." *Report on the Third Labor Management Conference,* Sponsored by the Labor Management Forum of the Greater Cleveland Roundtable, March 14, 1987.

Gregerman, Ira B., "Introduction to Quality Circles: An Approach to Participative Problem-Solving," *Industrial Management* (September-October, 1979), pp. 43-48.

Gupta, Nina, G. Douglas Jenkins, and William P. Curington, "Paying for Knowledge: Myths and Realities," *National Productivity Review* (Spring 1986), pp. 107-23.

Hamner, W. Clay and Dennis W. Organ. *Organizational Behavior: An Applied Psychological Approach.* Dallas, Texas: Business Publications, Inc., 1978.

Harmon, Frederick G. and Garry Jacobs. *The Vital Difference: Unleashing the Powers of Sustained Corporate Success.* New York: American Management Association, 1985.

Harvey, Eric, "Discipline VS. Punishment," *Management Review* (March 1987), pp. 25-29.

Hauck, Warren C. and Timothy L. Ross, "Sweden's Experiments in Productivity Gainsharing: A Second Look," *Personnel* (January 1987), pp. 61-68.

Hickman, Craig R. and Michael A. Silva. *The Future 500: Creating Tomorrow's Organizations Today.* New York: New American Library, 1987.

Howard, Robert, "High Technology and the Reenchantment of the Work Place," *National Productivity Review* (Summer 1984), pp. 255-264.

Jenkins, G. Douglas, Jr. and Nina Gupta, "The Payoffs of Paying for Knowledge," *National Productivity Review* (Spring 1985), pp. 121-30.

Kanter, Rosabeth Moss, "From Status to Contribution: Some Organizational Implications of the Changing Basis of Pay," *Personnel* (January 1987), pp. 12-37.

Kanter, Rosabeth Moss, "The Attack on Pay," *Harvard Business Review* (March-April 1987), pp. 60-67.

Kanter, Rosabeth Moss, "The Middle Manager as Innovator," *Harvard Business Review* (July-August 1982), pp. 95-105.

Kazdin, Alan E. *Behavior Modification in Applied Settings.* Homewood, IL: The Dorsey Press, 1975.

Ketchum, Lyman, "How Redesigned Plants Really Work," *National Productivity Review* (Summer 1984), pp. 246-254.

Kirp, David L. and Douglas S. Rice, "Fast Forward-Styles of California Management," *Harvard Business Review* (January-February 1988), pp. 74-83.

Kochanski, James, "Hiring in Self-Regulating Work Teams," *National Productivity Review* (Spring 1987), pp. 153-159.

Kopelman, Richard E., "Improving Productivity through Objective Feedback: A Review of the Evidence," *National Productivity Review* (Winter 1982-83) pp. 43-55.

Kopelman, Richard E., "Job Redesign and Productivity: A Review of the Evidence," *National Productivity Review* (Summer 1985), pp. 237-255.

Kotkin, Joel, "The Great American Revival," *Inc* (February 1988) pp. 52-63.

Kyd, Charles W., "Waste Not, Want Not," *Inc* (December 1987), pp. 177-178.

Latham, Gary P. and Gary A. Yukl, "A Review of Research on the Application of Goal Setting in Organizations," *Academy of Management Journal* (December 1975), pp. 824-45.

Lawler, Edward E. and Gerald E. Ledford, Jr., "Skill-Based Pay: A Concept That's Catching On," *Management Review* (February 1987), pp. 46-51.

Lawler, Edward E. and Susan A. Mohrman, "Quality Circles after the Fad," *Harvard Business Review* (January-February 1985), pp. 65-71.

Lawler, Edward E., "What's Wrong with Point Factor Job Evaluation," *Personnel* (January 1987), pp. 38-44.

LeBoeuf, Michael. *The Productivity Challenge: How to Make It Work for America and You.* New York: McGraw Hill, 1982.

Levering, Robert. *A Great Place To Work: What Makes Some Employers So Good (and Most So Bad).* New York: Random House, 1988.

Luthans, Fred and Robert Kreitner. *Organizational Behavior Modification.* Glenview, Illinois: Scott, Foresman and Company, 1975.

Mager, Robert F. and Peter Pipe. *Analyzing Performance Problems: or You Really Oughta Wanna.* Second Edition. Belmont, CA: Pitman Learning, 1984.

Mager, Robert F. *Good Analysis.* Belmont, CA: Fearon-Pitman Publishers, Inc., 1972.

McAdams, Jerry, "Rewarding Sales and Marketing Performance," *Management Review* (April 1987), pp. 33-38.

Moore, Brian E. and Timothy L. Ross. *The Scanlon Way to Improved Productivity.* New York: John Wiley & Sons, 1978.

Naisbitt, John and Patricia Aburdene. *Re-Inventing the Corporation.* New York: Warner Books, 1985.

National Productivity Report, "City Boosts Productivity as Alternative to Tax Hikes, Service Cuts," *National Productivity Report* 14, no. 19 (October 15, 1985).

O'Dell, Carla and Jerry McAdams, "The Revolution in Employee Rewards," *Management Review* (March 1987), pp. 30-33.

O'Dell, Carla with Jerry McAdams. *Major Findings from People, Performance, and Pay: The American Productivity Center/American Compensation Association National Survey on Non-Traditional Reward and Human Resource Practices.* Houston, Texas: American Productivity Center, 1986.

O'Dell, Carla. *The American Work Place: Issues and Innovations.* Productivity Brief No. 32. Houston, Texas: American Productivity Center 1984.

O'Toole, James. *Vanguard Management.* Golden City, NJ: Doubleday, 1985.

Peters, Thomas J. and Robert H. Waterman, Jr. *In Search of Excellence.* New York: Harper & Row, 1982.

Peters, Tom and Nancy Austin. *A Passion for Excellence.* New York: Warner Books, 1986.

Peters, Tom. *Thriving On Chaos*. New York: Alfred A. Knopf, 1987.

Proctor, Barcy, H., "A Sociotechnical Work-Design System at Digital Enfield: Utilizing Untapped Resources," *National Productivity Review* (Summer 1986), pp. 262-270.

Productivity Improvement Bulletin, "Work Cells and Work Teams: Are They Right for You?," *Productivity Improvement Bulletin* (September 10, 1984), pp. 1-4.

Ringham, Arthur J., "Designing a Gainsharing Program to Fit a Company's Operations," *National Productivity Review* (Spring 1984), pp. 131-144.

Robertson, James M., "Downsizing to Meet Strategic Objectives," *National Productivity Review* (Autumn 1987), pp. 325-330.

Rosen, Corey, "Making Employee Ownership Work," *National Productivity Review* (Winter 1982-83), pp. 13-21.

Ross, Timothy L. and Ruth Ann Ross, "Productivity Gainsharing: Resolving Some of the Measurement Issues," *National Productivity Review* (Autumn 1984), pp. 382-394.

Ross, Timothy L. and Warren C. Hauck. *Gainsharing in the United States.* Bowling Green, Ohio: Bowling Green State University, BG Productivity and Gainsharing Institute, 1983.

Ruch, Frank J., Jr., "Inverting the Hierachical Pyramid at ETC," *National Productivity Review* (Autumn 1982), pp. 389-395.

Ruch, William A., "The Measurement of White-Collar Productivity," *National Productivity Review* (Autumn 1982), pp. 416-425.

Schilling, Donald J. and Thomas F. Bremer, "Implementing Productivity Strategies: A Program Case Study at TRW Ramsey," *National Productivity Review* (Autumn 1985) pp. 370-384.

Schuster, Michael, "Gainsharing: Do It Right the First Time," *Sloan Management Review* (Winter 1987), pp. 17-25.

Shonk, James H. *Working in Teams; A Practical Manual for Improving Work Groups.* New York: American Management Association, 1982.

Sims, Henry P., Jr. and Charles C. Manz, "Conversations within Self-Managed Work Groups," *National Productivity Review* (Spring 1982), pp. 261-69.

Skeats, Arthur E., "Employment Security: Is it Free?," *National Productivity Review* (Autumn 1987), pp. 307-313.

Strippoli, Gino T., "Is This Any Way to Run a Cable Business?," *The TRW Manager* 1, no. 1 (October 1982), p. 7.

Taylor, Thomas O., Donald J. Friedman, and Dennis Couture, "Operating Without Supervisors: An Experiment," *Organizational Dynamics* (Winter 1987), pp. 26-38.

"Teamwork Works for Higher Productivity at TRW," *Productivity* (September 1982), pp. 1-4.

Terkel, Studs. *Working.* New York: Pantheon Books, 1972.

Thor, Carl, "Knowledge Worker Gainsharing," *APC Productivity Brief* (August 1987).

Tomasko, Robert M. *Downsizing: Reshaping the Corporation for the Future.* New York: American Management Association, 1987.

Tregoe, Benjamin B. & John W. Zimmerman. *Top Management Strategy: What It Is & How To Make It Work.* New York: Simon and Schuster, 1980.

U.S. Department of Labor. *Participative Approaches to White-Collar Productivity Improvement.* Washington, D.C.: Bureau of Labor Management Relations, 116. Government Printing Office, 1987.

U.S. General Accounting Office. *Can Productivity Sharing Programs Contribute to Increased Productivity?* Washington, D.C.: Government Printing Office, 1981.

Walton, Richard E., "From Control to Commitment in the Workplace," *Harvard Business Review* (March-April 1985), pp. 77-84.

Walton, Richard E., "Work Innovations in the United States," *Harvard Business Review* (July-August 1979), pp. 88-98.

Werther, William B., Jr. and William A. Ruch. "Productivity Strategies at TRW," *National Productivity Review* (Spring, 1983), pp. 109-125.

Werther, William B., Jr., William R. Ruch, and Lynn McClure. *Productivity Through People.* St. Paul, MN: West Publishing Company, 1986.

Winpisinger, William, "Labor Looks at 'New Management'," *Management Review* (July 1987), pp. 52-53.

Zander, Alvin. *Making Groups Effective.* San Francisco: Jossey-Bass, 1982.

Index